God's Covenant
of Blessing

God's Covenant
of Blessing

By
John P. Milton

STRAUS PUBLISHING CO.
MADISON, WISCONSIN

Other books by John P. Milton:

Psalms

Prophecy Interpreted

Preaching from Isaiah

Holy Garments

People are Asking

More People are Asking

God's Word to Men

The Way

Our Hebrew-Christian Heritage

Library of Congress Card Number 61-17513

Printed in United States of America by
STRAUS PRINTING AND PUBLISHING COMPANY
Madison, Wisconsin.

To

the people of God under the New Covenant,

on whom has come the Blessing of Abraham

in Christ Jesus our Lord.

Galatians 3:14.

ACKNOWLEDGMENTS

Grateful acknowledgment is herewith given to the following publishers and authors for permission to quote from previous publications:

Abingdon Press: from *The Theology of the Old Testament* by Otto Baab, 1949; from The Interpreter's Bible, art. "Jeremiah" by James Philip Hyatt, Vol. 5, 1956; and from "The Bible After Twenty Years of Archaeology" by W. F. Albright, in *Religion in Life*, 1952.

Cambridge University Press: from *The Bible Today* by C. H. Dodd, 1952, and from *The Book of Genesis* by Herbert E. Ryle, in the *Cambridge Bible for Schools and Colleges*, 1921.

The John Day Company, Inc.: from *Tears and Laughter* by Lin Yutang, 1943.

Doubleday & Company, Inc.: from *The Book of the Acts of God* by G. Ernest Wright and Reginald H. Fuller. Copyright 1957 by G. Ernest Wright. Reprinted by permission of Doubleday & Company, Inc.

Wm. B. Eerdmans Publishing Co.: from *Biblical Theology* by Geerhardus Vos, 1948, and from *The New Bible Commentary*, edited by Davidson, Stibbs, and Kevan, 1953.

Faber & Faber, Limited: from *The Throne of David* by A. G. Hebert, 1941, and from *Abraham* by Leonard Woolley, 1936.

Fleming H. Revell Company: from *The Archaeology of Palestine and the Bible* by W. F. Albright, 1932

Harper & Brothers: from *Everyman's Adventure* by Merle William Boyer, 1947; from *Light from the Ancient East* by Adolf Deissmann, 1927; from *Theology of the Old Testament* by Edmond Jacob, 1958; from *The History of Israel* by Martin Noth, 1958; from *Introduction to the Old Testament* by Robert H. Pfeiffer, 1941; and from *The Bible: a New Translation* by James Moffatt (Copyright 1922, 1935 and 1950 by Harper & Brothers. Used by permission.)

The Jewish Publication Society of America: from The Holy Scriptures, 1917.

The Liturgical Press: from *Theology of the Old Testament* by Paul Heinisch, translated by Rev. William Heidt. Copyright 1950 by The Order of St. Benedict, Inc., Collegeville, Minn.

Lutterworth Press: from *The Witness of the Old Testament to Christ* by Wilhelm Vischer, 1949.

The Macmillan Company: from *A Commentary on the Holy Bible* by J. R. Dummelow, reprint 1944, and from *A Theological Word Book of the Bible*, ed. by Alan Richardson, 1952 (art. "Law" by W. A. Whitehouse).

J. C. B. Mohr (Paul Siebeck): from *Die Genesis der Genesis* by Otto Eissfeldt, 1958.

Muhlenberg Press: from *Old Testament Commentary*, ed. by Herbert C. Alleman and Elmer E. Flack, 1948.

Nordiska Uppslagsböcker: from *Svenskt Bibliskt Uppslagsverk*, art. "Abraham" by H. S. Nyberg, 1948.

Oxford University Press: from *Pentateuch and Haftorahs*, ed. by J. H. Hertz, 1929.

G. P. Putnam's Sons: from *The Prophet* by Sholem Asch. Copyright 1955 by Sholem Asch.

Charles Scribner's Sons: from *The Goodly Fellowship of the Prophets* by John Paterson, 1953; from *Dictionary of Christ and the Gospels*, art. "Covenant" by Geerhardus Vos, 1911; and from *Dictionary of the Apostolic Church*, art. "Covenant" by Wilfred J. Moulton, 1916.

St. Anthony Guild Press: from *The Old Testament and the Critics* by J. Coppens, 1942.

Sheed & Ward, Inc.: from the *Old Testament*, Vol. I, in the translation of Monsignor Ronald Knox. Copyright 1948, Sheed & Ward, Inc., New York.

Student Christian Movement Press Limited: from *Genesis I-XI* by Alan Richardson in Torch Bible Commentaries, 1953.

The University of Chicago Press: from *The Bible: an American Translation* by J. M. Powis Smith and Edgar J. Goodspeed. Copyright 1923, 1927, 1948 by the University of Chicago.

Vandenhoeck & Ruprecht: from *Evangelisches Kirchenlexicon*, art. "Abraham" by H. Kremers, 1956.

The Westminster Press:

From *A History of Israel* by John Bright. Copyright 1959, W. L. Jenkins.

From *An Outline of Biblical Theology* by Millar R. Burrows. Copyright 1946, W. L. Jenkins.

From *The Distinctive Ideas of the Old Testament* by Norman Snaith. Copyright 1946, W. L. Jenkins.

From *The Westminster Historical Atlas to the Bible*, rev. ed. by Wright and Filson. Copyright 1956, W. L. Jenkins.

From *Biblical Archaeology* by G. Ernest Wright, 1957.

From *The Westminster Dictionary of the Bible*, (rev.) by John D. Davis. Revised and rewritten by Henry S. Gehman. Copyright 1944, The Westminster Press.

From *The Westminster Study Edition of the Holy Bible*. Copyright 1948, W. L. Jenkins. The Westminster Press. Used by permission.

The Weston College Press: from *Foreword to the Old Testament* by Frederick L. Moriarty, 1954.

J. P. M.

TABLE OF CONTENTS

INTRODUCTION

ONE OF THE MAJOR RELIGIOUS CONCEPTS in the Old Testament is that of God's covenant, or covenants, with men.

The concept of covenant stems from the Hebrew word *berith*. The very fact that this word is found no less than 278 times in the Old Testament bears witness to its importance. So does the fact that the instances of its use are widely and rather evenly distributed through the Old Testament: 80 times in the Pentateuch, 97 times in the historical books (Joshua to Esther), 76 times in the prophets (Isaiah to Malachi), and 25 times in the poetical books (Job, Psalms, and Proverbs). The Greek word employed as its equivalent in the Septuagint is *diatheke*. This word is found 33 times in the New Testament, making a total of more than 300 Scriptural references to the concept expressed in the Hebrew *berith*. It is obviously an important Biblical word.

In a few instances the word *berith* is used in the Old Testament to denote a relationship between men, but in most cases it refers to a relationship between God and men. It is, therefore, essentially a religious concept. This fact also bears witness to its importance; and so does the fact that in actual Biblical usage the word may refer to one of several divine covenants: with Noah, with Abraham, with Israel (at Sinai), with Israel (in the land of Moab), with the Levites, with David, with Israel again (the new covenant of Jeremiah 31:31-34), the new covenant mediated by Jesus Christ. The word is also used in several significant combinations, such as "the book of the covenant" (Ex. 24:7), "the blood of the covenant" (Ex. 24:8), "the words of the covenant, the ten commandments" (Ex. 34:28), "the two tables of the covenant" (Deut. 9:15), "the ark of the covenant" (Num. 10:33, etc.), "the salt of the covenant" (Lev. 2:13), "the messenger of the covenant" (Mal. 3:1), "the prince of the covenant" (Dan. 11:22), "the covenant of God" (2 Chron. 34:32), "the covenant of our fathers" (Mal. 2:10), "the covenant of brotherhood" (Amos 1:9), "my covenant of peace" (Num. 25:12; Is. 54:10), "my covenant with day and night" (Jer. 33:20, 25). In addition to such direct references to *berith* some of the most significant terms in the religious vocabulary of the Old Testament are covenant related in usage and meaning: words for sin such as *pesha,* rebellion, and *chate'ah,* missing the mark or failing to attain the goal of God's calling for His people; words that indicate the character and that describe the acts of God, such as *hesed,* steadfast love, *emeth,* truth, *tsedeq,* righteousness, and *yesha,* salvation; and above all, *Torah,* or the law. If we were to follow up all the words associated with the word *berith* we would find that the concept of covenant is like a tree with wide-spreading and deep-reaching roots, and with equally far-flung and fruitful branches; for it is not something superimposed upon the Biblical material as a literary framework only, but it permeates all of that material and unifies it, so as to make of the Biblical message a living whole. The *berith* of God is the most important single integrating factor in the Old Testament revelation. That is true whether we look at the Old Testament from the literary, or from the theological, or from the historical, point of view.

It is the author's firm conviction of this primary importance of the divine covenant or *berith* in the Old Testament history and message that motivates this book on *God's Covenant of Blessing.* The title is not meant to suggest that this is a study of one covenant among many: rather, the covenant with Abraham is the key to the interpretation of what is essentially a single covenant or of one unified covenant purpose of God within the Holy Scriptures of the Old and the New Testaments. Beginning with the Covenant of Blessing, we shall press on in our study of the Biblical concept of covenant until we reach the new covenant in the blood of Christ; and when we do so, we shall discover that there is a strange but wonderful relatedness between the beginning and the end, and of both of these to all that lies in-between in the history of Israel and in the covenant faith of the Old Testament people of God. Such, at least, is the conviction of the writer; and it is his hope that the reader may see with him something of the deep significance of the divine *berith,* and especially of the covenant of blessing with Abraham, for a true understanding of the Holy Scriptures and of the saving acts of God.

Chapter One

THE MEANING OF THE WORD BERITH

ALL BIBLE STUDY that is worthy of the name drives us sooner or later to a study of significant words. Back of the words are the religious concepts which they represent and with which we are chiefly concerned in reading the Bible; but we cannot grasp the full clear meaning of Biblical truth unless we first understand the meaning of the words that are used to express it.

There are many such significant words in the Bible. One of the more significant is the Hebrew word *berith*. The English versions usually translate it as *covenant*. In the Septuagint, the Greek version of the Old Testament, it is rendered as *diatheke* in all except two passages. The Hebrew word is used 278 times, which gives some indication of its significance in the religious vocabulary of the Old Testament. The significance carries over into the vocabulary of the New Testament through the Greek *diatheke*. It can readily be seen from a study of the Biblical usage of the word *berith* that the "covenant" is an important concept, a key to the correct understanding of both the Old Testament and the New.

1

What Is a Covenant?

Before we try to interpret the covenant, or the covenants, between God and men of which the Bible speaks we must first define terms. What is a covenant? What is the meaning of the English word? What is the meaning of the Hebrew word *berith* which it translates? What is the meaning of the Greek word for berith, which is *diatheke*? The answers are important, as we shall see, not merely for philological reasons but for theological reasons as well. How adequately do the Greek and English words convey to us the religious significance of the divine *berith*?

The simplest and most natural definition of a covenant is as "an agreement between two or more persons or parties."[1] The word *contract* is given as a synonym. A contract, however, suggests a mutual agreement between equals. That does not seem to fit the situation between God and man. A mutual agreement there might well be between them, but not on the basis of equality or in the sense of a negotiated contract. If a covenant implies such a contractual relation, the use of the word to translate the Hebrew *berith* is inadequate and may be misleading.

2

What Is a Berith?

We shall not delve into the disputed problem of the etymology of *berith*. We must note, however, three significant definitions: or perhaps we should say *three viewpoints* as to the basic significance of the Hebrew word.

The first is the familiar definition by Johs. Pedersen: Berith is said to denote "the mutual relationship of belonging together (Zusammengehörigkeit), with all the rights and duties that this relationship entails for the participants."[2] Here the emphasis is on the aspect of mutuality: the relationship is a reciprocal one that seems to imply a certain equality of status. If the Biblical usage seems to imply that the berith at times has a unilateral character, this is due to the fact that the content of the particular berith in question, especially the divine-human berith, has acted transformingly upon the form of the berith.

The viewpoint of Pedersen is shared by many Old Testament scholars today. A dissenting voice is that of J. Begrich who contends that berith originally always denoted a relation between two unequal partners. "A mightier one offers the berith-relationship to one who is not mighty": it is therefore completely one-sided, so that only the one who makes the covenant is bound thereby.[3] The maker of the berith alone acts; the recipient is completely passive, except as he may express the wish or the request that the berith be made. This does not exclude a certain response by the recipient of the berith, but the emphasis is on the guarantee of the one who makes it.

According to George E. Mendenhall there is a marked resemblance in form between the Mosaic covenant in the Old Testament and the suzerainty treaty of western Asia in the second millennium B.C.[4] This was a political covenant between a suzerain and a vassal. It was offered by the suzerain to the vassal, who could only receive it as it was offered; but in making the treaty the suzerain does not base it on his possession of power alone: he reminds also of his own acts of benevolence towards the vassal. We shall examine this political treaty more closely later when we analyze the Mosaic covenant. We note now that the emphasis in this political covenant is not on the mutual but on the unilateral character of the treaty. In this it resembles the definition given by Begrich for the Hebrew *berith*.

Our concern at the moment, however, is not so much with the original meaning of the word *berith* as with its actual usage in the Old Testament. What is the Biblical viewpoint itself with respect to the meaning of *berith*?

The colloquial use of berith, where it refers to human relationships, can readily be seen to approximate that of covenant in the sense of a mutual agreement. We read of Abraham and Abimelech in Gen. 21:27, that "the two men (ASV, they two) made a covenant." A similar statement is found in 1 Sam. 23:18 with reference to Jonathan and David, "And the two of them made a covenant before the Lord." In both of these instances the Hebrew has a plural verb with a plural subject, which seems to indicate a mutual agreement between equals. It should be noted, however, that in the case of David and Jonathan the priority of position belonged to Jonathan and that it was he who took the initiative in making the covenant. The context will show that RSV has rightly interpreted the force of the singular verb in 1 Sam. 18:3, "Then Jonathan made a covenant with David, because he loved him as his own soul." The reference in 1 Kings 20:34 to the covenant between Ahab and Ben-hadad is similarly worded, as befits a covenant between victor and vanquished: "So he made a covenant with him, and let him go." Even the berith between men is not necessarily an agreement negotiated by and between equals.

It is, however, a mutual agreement of the most sacred and binding kind. The ceremony of making a covenant is usually called *karath berith*, or cutting a covenant. That might suggest a covenant by sacrifice (Ps. 50:5). The covenant at Sinai was enacted and ratified by the offering of sacrifices (Ex. 24:1-8); but this was a religious covenant between God and Israel rather than a secular covenant between two individuals. The covenant with Abraham in Gen. 15, though also a religious covenant, perhaps reflects more accurately the nature of the ceremony by which covenants were originally made. The slain animals were cut in two and each half laid over against the other, and then a flaming torch, symbolizing the Lord as one party to the covenant, passed between the pieces. It is probable that the religious ceremony here incorporates significant elements from a traditional pattern in the making of covenants. "There can be no doubt," says E. Kautzsch, "that berith belonged at first to secular speech and meant 'dissection' (Zerschneidung); that is, the dissection of one or more sacrificial animals, so that the parties concluding the agreement passed between the pieces and invoked upon themselves the fate of these animals in case of a breach of covenant (or oath). For every *berith* consisted partly of an oath, indicating the obligation which one took upon himself, and partly in a curse invoked upon oneself in case of a breach of that oath."[5] Whether or not this was actually the original *form* of making a berith, H. Clay Trumbull has presented convincing evidence that there was a widespread primitive rite of blood-covenanting, "a form of mutual covenanting, by which two persons enter into the closest, the most enduring, and the most sacred of compacts, as friends and brothers, or as more than brothers."[6]

In the Old Testament the manner of making the covenant varies greatly, and only occasional vestiges of the primitive ceremony remain; but the binding nature of the berith as an agreement between men is clearly evident. The covenant of Abraham with Abimelech at Beersheba was witnessed to by the giving of presents and confirmed by a mutual oath (Gen. 21). When the covenant was renewed with Isaac, the oath between the two men became the basis of peace between them and between their herdsmen (Gen. 26). When Jonathan entered into covenant with David, it meant for him taking David's part even against his own father (1 Sam. 20). When fortunes were reversed, and David became king, it seems to have been a matter of honor with him to keep the covenant by befriending Jonathan's lame son Mephibosheth (2 Sam. 9). The prophet Amos utters a stinging indictment of Tyre for its transgression in not remembering the covenant of brotherhood (Amos 1:9), and the prophet Malachi records God's stern disapproval of faithlessness to the covenant of marriage (Mal. 2:13-16). It is clear that a berith between men was an agreement to be honored at any cost. As used in the Old Testament, the word may refer to a covenant of friendship between individuals (1

Sam. 18:3), or to a covenant between a king and his people (2 Sam. 5:3), or to the marriage covenant (Mal. 2:14), or to a military alliance (1 Kings 15: 19), or to a treaty of peace (1 Kings 20:34), or to a league between nations (1 Kings 5:12); but in every use of the word the binding nature of the berith as a mutual agreement is implied. Though the mutuality may sometimes be a forced one, as when the victor imposes terms on the vanquished, the words, "They two (the two of them) made a covenant," seem to fit the berith between men.

3

The Religious Berith

But do they fit also the relationship between God and man? It is of this relationship that *berith* is used in the overwhelming majority of cases in the Old Testament. It may be a berith with individuals, such as with Noah, with Abraham, or with David; it may be a berith with Israel as a nation, at Sinai, in the plains of Moab, or in the new covenant of Jeremiah (Jer. 31:31-34). The relationship between these several "covenants" awaits further study; but they have this one thing in common, that God is represented as being a party to the covenant: the berith is a religious one.

This much can be said with finality, that nowhere in Scripture is it written of the divine berith, "And they two (the two of them) made a covenant." The religious berith is in one sense unilateral: it is God alone who initiates the covenant always. It is intended to become a mutual agreement, and does so become, by the response of man to it; but in its origin the berith is unilateral: it is God's covenant with man.

What we have just said might be assumed from the very nature of God and of man: Creator and creature, sovereign Lord and servant, Savior and helpless sinner. But we may also illustrate it from the oft-repeated phraseology of the Bible narrative, where the *direction* of the covenant is always from God to man.

In Genesis 6:18, the word berith is used for the first time in the Old Testament. God says, "I [not we] will establish my [not our] covenant with you [not "between us"]." It is God who makes the covenant and calls it His own. The same terminology marks the expanded covenant with Noah in Gen. 9: the pronoun "I" is emphatic throughout the section, and doubly so in v. 9; the covenant (berith) is called "my covenant," not "our covenant"; it is a covenant "between me and you," or from me to you (v. 12). The direction of the covenant is evident; and yet, it is a covenant with man, or between God and Noah, and seems to call for some sort of response on the part of man, whose heart ought to be filled with grateful trust in God on the basis of His covenant.

This manner of speaking is not limited to the covenant with Noah. The covenant with Abraham follows the same speech pattern, "The Lord made a covenant with Abram" (Gen. 15:18). "And I will make my covenant between me and you" (Gen. 17:2). "As for you, you shall keep my covenant" (Gen. 17:9). "And I will establish my covenant between me and you and your descendants after you throughout their generations for an everlasting covenant, to be God to you and to your descendants after you" (Gen. 17:7). Of this covenant we read in Ex. 2:24, that "God remembered his covenant with Abraham, with Isaac, and with Jacob," and again, in Ex. 6:5, "I have remembered my covenant."

The covenant with Israel at Sinai also follows the same familiar pattern. It is referred to in Ex. 19:5 as "my covenant," which Israel is to keep. When the book of the covenant was read to the people, they replied, "All that the Lord has spoken we will do, and we will be obedient" (Ex. 24:7). When Moses took the blood and threw it upon the people he said, "Behold the blood of the covenant which the Lord has made with you in accordance with all these words" (Ex. 24:8). When Moses met the Lord for the second time in the holy mount, the Lord said to him, "Write these words; in accordance with these words I have made a covenant with you and with Israel" (Ex. 34:27). The direction of the covenant is from God to man. The covenant originates with Him; He speaks the words; He lays down the conditions; it is His covenant, which takes on the aspect of mutuality when the people respond by accepting the terms and by promising to be obedient.

The pattern continues the same in the Book of Deuteronomy, with its backward reference to the covenant at Sinai from the viewpoint of its renewal in the plains of Moab. See Deut. 4:13, 23, 31; 5:2, 3; 7:9, 10; 29:1; 29:10-14. The covenant is from God; it is His covenant with His people Israel. It continues the same in the prophets. Again and again the Lord, speaking by Isaiah and by Jeremiah and by Ezekiel, calls the covenant "my covenant" (Is. 56:4, 6; 59:21; Jer. 11:

10; Ezek. 16:60, 62; 17:19; cf. Hos. 8:1; Zech. 9:11); "my steadfast love" and "my covenant of peace" (Is. 54:10; cf. Ezek. 37:26); "my covenant with day and night" (Jer. 33:20, 25); "my covenant with David" (Jer. 33:21); "the covenant of the Lord their God" (Jer. 22:9). The most significant passage of all is the one where Jeremiah as the spokesman for the Lord proclaims the making of a new covenant (Jer. 31:31-34). The direction of the covenant is unmistakable. The personal pronoun "I" dominates the whole prophecy. "I will make a new covenant" with Israel, even as "I made" the covenant with their fathers which they broke (vv. 31, 32). The covenant (berith) is "my covenant" (v. 32), the law (Torah) is "my law" (v. 33). It is God who makes promises (vv. 33, 34), and it is God who gives commands (v. 33); it is He who acts under the covenant to forgive sin (v. 34) and to put His law within them as a spiritual rule of life (v. 33).

We shall return to these passages when we consider the content of the divine berith; but even from this cursory examination the direction of the berith should be evident. A berith in the religious sense is not a two-sided contract. In so far as the English word "covenant" suggests such a contract, it is an inadequate translation of the Hebrew "berith," and may leave an altogether false impression; for "the idea of contract is not of the essence of a 'berith' but a purely accidental accompaniment when found in the context."[7]

How then shall we define a berith? What constitutes a berith, a religious berith, the religious concept so frequent in the Old Testament?

It might be defined as "a sovereign disposition of God" or as "the absolute sanction by God of an arrangement." According to Vos, the characteristic mark of a berith is not that it relates to an agreement, but that the agreement is concluded by some special religious sanction. "A purely one-sided promise or ordinance or law becomes a berith, not by reason of its inherent conceptual or etymological meaning, but by reason of the religious sanction added."[8] The berith has also been said to be "a divine arrangement or disposition, which comes into existence without the co-operation of man," but which is "absolutely binding" on man.[9] John D. Davis has described it as "a free promise on his [God's] part, generally based upon the fulfillment of certain conditions by man."[10] According to one Hebrew-English lexicon, it is "a divine constitution or ordinance with signs and pledges."[11]

Whether these definitions are completely adequate we need not determine now. We shall return to them later after we have examined all the evidence. But in one thing they clearly agree with one another and with the witness of the Old Testament as already outlined: the religious berith is unilateral in origin. God lays down the terms of the berith. Those terms may consist of commandments or of promises. When confronted by these terms man may accept or reject them, but he may not help to determine their content. The berith between God and man is never negotiated by mutual agreement: it is in no sense a contract between equals. Every covenant of God is an expression of His sovereign will, the terms of the covenant being of divine origin, and the response of man being only a matter of Yes or No, acceptance or rejection of those terms. That is not minimizing the importance of the acceptance of the terms by man as making the covenant mutual. When God makes a berith He expects a response from man. If the covenant is promissory in character, the expected response is faith; rejection takes the form of unbelief. If the basis of the covenant is a divine commandment or law, the expected response is obedience; rejection takes the form of disobedience, or of transgression (a stronger word is *rebellion*). Very often the nature of the covenant is such as to call for a combination of faith and obedience, or what Paul calls "obedience of faith" (Rom. 1:5). The divine berith does call for the human response which makes it a mutual agreement, but it is not a bilateral contract. If we use the word "covenant" to translate "berith," we must give it another meaning than the simple and natural one of "an agreement between two or more persons or parties."

We may ask: Would it not be better to use another word? The difficulty, however, is in finding that word. What word should we use? What word will give the exact meaning of berith when it refers to the relationship between God and man?

4

Berith and Diatheke

One suggestion comes from the Septuagint, where *berith* is rendered as *diatheke* in all passages except two. The two exceptions are Deut. 9:15, where the Greek word is *martyrion*, meaning testimony, and 1 Kings 11:11, which has *entole*, or commandment.

The choice of *diatheke* in preference to *syntheke* as an equivalent for the Hebrew *berith* is interesting. R. F. Girdlestone comments,

"The translators of the Septuagint evidently felt the difficulty (i.e. of translation), and instead of using *syntheke,* which would be the natural word for a covenant, used *diatheke,* which means a legal Disposition, and hence a Testament."[12] The choice of "diatheke" might therefore suggest that the English word "testament" is better than "covenant" as a translation of "berith."

Two questions confront us at this point. The first is as to the primary meaning of the Greek word diatheke. Does it always and necessarily mean "testament?" The second concerns the adequacy of the English word testament as well as of the Greek diatheke to convey the essential meaning of the Hebrew berith.

There is an interesting history of fluctuating opinion as to how diatheke should be understood and translated in the New Testament, where the word is used 33 times. In the so-called Authorized Version (AV) it is rendered as "covenant" in 21 places and as "testament" in 12 places; the latter rendition mostly in the Epistle to the Hebrews and in connection with the Lord's Supper. In the American Standard Version (ASV) it is rendered as "testament" only twice, in Heb. 9: 16, 17, where the context clearly demands it. ASV quite evidently reflects a trend away from "testament" towards "covenant" as the best translation for "diatheke." A little later, however, there came a reversed theological trend, which was much more favorable to "testament" than to "covenant." It should perhaps be called a linguistic or a philological trend rather than a theological one; for it was based on the claim that "testament" was the only meaning for "diatheke" during the Hellenistic period. A much quoted statement is the one by Adolf Deissmann: "There is ample material to back me in the statement that no one in the Mediterranean world in the first century A.D. would have thought of finding in the word diatheke the idea of 'covenant.' St. Paul would not, and in fact did not. To St. Paul the word meant what it meant in his Greek Old Testament, 'a unilateral enactment,' in particular 'a will or testament.'"[13]

It is now generally conceded that Deissmann's definition of *diatheke* is essentially correct; but it does not necessarily follow that we should therefore translate the Hebrew *berith* as testament. As Wilfred J. Moulton says, "It does not, however, seem possible to grant that St. Paul, who read his Hebrew Bible as well as his Greek, always thought of a will when he read of the divine berith."[14] For a testament naturally suggests, as Heb. 9:16 also clearly says, the death of the testator; and that simply does not fit the situation in the case of the Old Testament berith. It does not fit every New Testament situation where diatheke is used. In Acts 7:8, for example, "the testament [diatheke] of circumcision" would be a misleading translation. The English word "testament" is just as inadequate as the word "covenant" as an equivalent for the Hebrew "berith." Since the New Testament diatheke often refers back to the Old Testament berith, testament is inadequate even as an equivalent for the Biblical diatheke, except in certain special cases where the context suggests the added element of a death which puts the instrument into effect.

5

Conclusion

We reach, then, these conclusions with respect to the Biblical use of the word berith:

1. The concept of a will or testament is not present in the Hebrew *berith* as used in the Old Testament.

2. The word *diatheke,* which does mean testament in Hellenistic Greek, was chosen by the translators of the Septuagint because it was the word that came closest to expressing the meaning of the Biblical berith.

3. When so used in the Greek version of the Old Testament, diatheke acquired a new shade of meaning which is determined by the Biblical berith rather than by Hellenistic usage.

4. We get little help, therefore, from the Greek diatheke in the translation of the Hebrew berith into English; for "testament" falls just as far short as "covenant" of being an adequate word with which to express the Biblical concept of a religious berith.

5. We must look for something that is a common denominator in the Hebrew berith and the Greek diatheke, recognizing that neither "contract" nor "testament" constitutes the essence of a berith, though a berith may sometimes be a contract and at other times a testament.

What is that common denominator, and how shall we translate it into English? Or what is a berith, a diatheke, a covenant, in the religious sense in which these terms are used in the Old Testament?

Three quotations may serve to illustrate the answer before we attempt a formal statement. The dictionary definition of a covenant in the religious or theological sense of the word is "the promise of

God as revealed in the Scriptures, conditioned on certain terms on the part of man, as obedience, repentance, faith, etc."[15] This agrees with the definition of John D. Davis that "his covenant with man is a free promise on his part, generally based upon the fulfillment of certain conditions by man."[16] The same basic thought is made more specific still by Herbert E. Ryle when he says, "In a covenant between God and man God makes the promise and lays down the conditions. Man accepts the terms unconditionally, while God 'establishes,' or ratifies, them. There is no equality of relationship as in a covenant agreement between men. Man is pledged to obedience on the strength of God's promise of blessing."[17]

The common denominator in the Hebrew berith and the Greek diatheke is the emphasis on *the divine initiative* in the covenant between God and man. Both berith and diatheke suggest "a unilateral enactment" which is intended to become "a mutual agreement." The berith is not limited to a divine promise to be received in faith: it includes also the divine commandment, to which man responds in obedience; and by the obedience of faith the divine berith becomes a mutual agreement. In its origin, however, the religious berith is always unilateral. For an adequate and clear-cut definition we return to the statement by Geerhardus Vos that it is "the absolute sanction by God of an arrangement instituted by him."[18] But since we cannot translate a word with a definition, we do just as the Greek translators did: we select an English word that comes close to the meaning of the original, and we give to it a new emphasis. That word seems to be "covenant," at least as an equivalent for "berith" in the Old Testament, and in most instances also for "diatheke" in the New.

But as we read "covenant" in the many places where the word occurs in our English Bible with reference to a relationship between God and man, we must remember to stress the Biblical content: the covenant is neither a contract nor a testament, but simply an arrangement initiated by God, and often solemnly ratified, which aims at becoming a mutual agreement when the divine commandment or promise is accepted by man in the obedience of faith. The initial direction of the covenant is from God to man; it is, first of all, *God's* covenant with man. When man responds to it as God wants him to do on God's own terms, it becomes a mutual agreement: a mutual commitment to be faithful to the terms of the covenant.

Of such a nature was also the covenant of God with Abraham.

NOTES

[1] Webster's New International Dictionary, 2nd edition, 1948. Vol. I, p. 612.

[2] Johs. Pedersen, *Der Eid bei den Semiten,* p. 34. Quotation taken from J. Begrich's article "Berit," Zatw.

[3] J. Begrich, art. "Berit," *Zeitschrift für die Alttestamentliche Wissenschaft.* Berlin: Alfred Töpelmann. 1944. pp. 1-11.

[4] George E. Mendenhall, "Law and Covenant in Israel and the Ancient Near East." Pittsburgh: The Biblical Colloquium. Reprinted from *The Biblical Archaeologist.* New Haven: The American Schools of Oriental Research. Vol. XVII, No. 2 (May, 1954), pp. 26-46, and No. 3 (September, 1954), pp. 49-76.

[5] E. Kautzsch, *Biblische Theologie des Alten Testaments.* Tübingen: J. C. B. Mohr (P. Siebeck), 1911. p. 59.

[6] H. Clay Trumbull, *The Blood Covenant.* Philadelphia: J. D. Wattles & Co. 1898. p. 4.

[7] Geerhardus Vos, Lecture notes on the Epistle to the Hebrews. Princeton, 1926-27.

[8] *Ibid.*

[9] E. Kautzsch, *op. cit.* p. 60.

[10] John D. Davis, *A Dictionary of the Bible.* Philadelphia: The Westminster Press. 4th rev. ed. 1925. p. 151.

[11] William Gesenius, *A Hebrew and English Lexicon of the O.T.* Edited by Francis Brown, S. R. Driver, and Charles A. Briggs. Boston and New York: Houghton Mifflin Co. 1907.

[12] R. F. Girdlestone, *Synonyms of the O.T.* Grand Rapids: Wm. B. Eerdmans Publishing Co. Reprint 1948, p. 214.

[13] Adolf Deissmann, *Light from the Ancient East.* New York: Harper & Brothers. 1927. p. 337.

[14] Wilfred J. Moulton, art. "Covenant," *Dictionary of the Apostolic Church.* New York: Charles Scribner's Sons. 1916. Vol. I, pp. 261-263.

[15] Webster's New International Dictionary, 2nd ed., 1948.

[16] John D. Davis, *op. cit.*

[17] Herbert E. Ryle, *The Book of Genesis,* Cambridge Bible for Schools and Colleges. Cambridge and New York: Cambridge University Press. 1921. p. 124.

[18] Geerhardus Vos, *op. cit.*

Chapter Two

THE RELIGIOUS SIGNIFICANCE OF THE CONCEPT OF COVENANT

THE BIBLICAL CONCEPT OF COVENANT, and especially of a God who enters into covenant with men, has significant religious and ethical implications. It may be well to note some of them now; we shall illustrate them more fully later, in connection with our analysis of the actual content of the divine covenant or covenants.

1

We must start with the concept of berith as it pertains to human relationships, or covenant in the sense of a mutual agreement between two or more persons or parties. Even such a covenant, as we have seen, was often associated with religious sanctions and was regarded as absolutely binding on the parties thereto. The covenant between Isaac and Abimelech put an end to strife and established peace between their herdsmen (Gen. 26). The covenant of Jacob with Laban brought to an end the misunderstanding and the strained relations between them, God being witness to the solemn agreement of which the heap of stones was a symbol and an abiding testimony (Gen. 31). Even when Joshua had been tricked by the Gibeonites into making a covenant or treaty of peace, the leaders of Israel felt obligated before God to let them live (Josh. 9). Throughout the Old Testament covenants made between men are regarded as inviolable. It is with good reason, therefore, that Dummelow says of the Hebrew concept of berith, "The idea lies at the root of the whole conception of law among the Jews. Covenants, as made between men, form the beginnings of civilized government."[1]

We need not claim that this concept of covenant was uniquely Hebrew in origin and practice in order to recognize how profound and far reaching has been its influence in its Hebraic or Biblical form upon Western civilization and in countries where the democratic ideal prevails. If we have lived to see the day when treaties between nations have all too often been treated as a mere scrap of paper, and when men have become clever in evading personally assumed obligations to one another, it is to our sorrow and shame; for without a sincere regard for the principle of personal obligation involved in the Hebrew berith, and in all law worthy of the name, there can be no peaceful society. The Biblical concept of berith in relation to law and government and human relations becomes even more significant when we see it illustrated in the Mosaic covenant. Here a religious berith, with religious sanctions, and with a divinely promulgated moral law, is seen to undergird all of Israel's social and legal relationships. The berith between men has a religious significance, in that it is a matter of divine concern that men keep their pledged word not only to God, but to one another. For as between Jacob and Laban of old, so God is still a witness between men in every mutual agreement that they may make; and it is when men perform as before God their pledged word to one another, that law and order prevail, and selfish strife gives way to mutual concord and peace.

2

The human berith, however, significant as it may be, is overshadowed by the divine berith, where God makes a covenant with men.

The concept of a covenant-making and covenant-keeping God is not an isolated occurrence in the Old Testament, but is a constant and characteristic factor in Biblical theology and in Biblical religion. The classic statement is in Deut. 7:9, 10: "Know therefore that the Lord your God is God, the faithful God who keeps covenant and steadfast love with those who love him and keep his commandments, to a thousand generations, and requites to their face those who hate him, by destroying them." This is not the viewpoint of the author of Deuteronomy alone. We do not cite the verse as a proof text but by way of illustration; for it gives clear expression to the theology of the whole Old Testament. The covenant concept reveals a God who is both capable and desirous of entering into a person-to-person relationship with men.

The Biblical concept of a God of covenant is essentially the same as that of Christian theism. It combines the belief in the transcendence and in the immanence of God. The words of the prophet, though not directly covenant related, nevertheless express the truth that is at the heart of the covenant with Abraham and with Israel:

> For thus says the high and lofty One
>   who inhabits eternity, whose name is Holy:
> "I dwell in the high and holy place,
>   and also with him who is of a contrite and humble spirit,
> to revive the spirit of the humble,
>   and to revive the heart of the contrite." (Is. 57:15)

As Geerhardus Vos rightly says, "Its covenant character marks off the religion of Israel as a religion of real, conscious, spiritual fellowship between God and His people, in distinction from the religions of paganism, in which either the Deity and the creature are pantheistically fused, or the Godhead after a deistic fashion is so far removed from the creature as to render true communion impossible, and where the relation between a national god and his worshippers is not a matter of choice but of necessity on both sides."[2] According to Wright and Filson, "The close relation of God and people, as symbolized in the covenant, was Israel's nomadic heritage, and the most important factor in saving her from idolatry."[3] God is! God lives! God acts! He who is man's Creator enters into personal covenant with him. In such a God Israel believed.

Such a God is in the very nature of the case a God of revelation. There can be no covenant without self-revelation on the part of him who makes it. So also the divine berith implies a revelation of the divine will and purpose, and these in turn reflect the divine character. Revelation does not consist in a list of divine attributes so much as in a series of divine actions. That God makes a covenant with men, whether it be with an individual or with a community of individuals, is the same as to say that he acts in relation to them with gracious purpose; that he seeks fellowship with them and offers fellowship to them; and not least, that he calls them into a holy partnership of service in relation to other men. The covenant is a way of interpreting history which recognizes the presence and activity of God in the historical process; which believes that God has set a goal for human history, and has given to men whom he has called a divine mission relevant to that goal. Election, covenant, and mission are, as Edmond Jacob has pointed out, inseparable; and all three are a part of the self-revelation of God in redemptive history.[4] It is true that we may see more of this divine self-revelation in some covenants than in others; it is very much to the fore in the covenant with Israel, less so in the Noachian covenant: but it is completely foreign to none of them. We must not overlook the fact that there is a unity and a continuity of purpose between the several covenants mentioned in the Old Testament which make them essentially *one* covenant, and this a covenant of revelation and redemption. God reveals himself in the making and keeping of covenant; the covenant which from the beginning had as its gracious purpose and goal the salvation of the world, a redeemed humanity, a people for God's own possession, a holy nation (Ex. 19:6; 1 Peter 2:9).

This divine goal of a redeemed people and a holy community is, of course, especially prominent in the covenant with Israel and with the New Testament church. It is also clearly implied in the covenant with Abraham, as we shall try to show later; for it is involved in the very principle of *separation unto God* which is at the heart of every divine berith. For the moment, we note that the relationship implied and illustrated by the divine covenant with Israel is not only an "I-thou" relationship, but a relationship of "your God—my people." These expressive Old Testament words are indicative of an ultimate spiritual fellowship, a relationship of belonging to one another, with mutual expectations and obligations. Under the covenant man is seen as the recipient and God as the giver of blessings; but man is also expected to be responsive to the requirements of God as Lord. The covenant goal is one of enjoyment of spiritual blessings by a people willing to respond to the will of God in the obedience of faith. The covenant implies mutual commitments, and mutual claims based upon those commitments. In so far as God's covenant with man is "a free promise on his part," man has a right to claim the promise, even as God is under a self-imposed obligation to keep it; but inasmuch as His promise is "generally based upon the fulfillment of certain conditions by man," man is under a voluntarily assumed obligation to meet those conditions.[5] Otto Baab has pointed out that the uniqueness of the Hebrew covenant lay in this that God is not regarded as "automatically obligated, upon request, to help his people: his proffer of help depended upon the merits of each case, which were determined by a standard of measurement derived from the objectively righteous will of God."[6] The goal sought is a holy community, which required Israel's response in the obedience of faith; but mark that *it was a re-*

sponse to what God had done, or to the saving acts and promises of God.

In speaking of the divine fellowship as the goal of the berith, we must not overlook the fact that the covenant was in its very nature prophetic. It was in itself a part of the saving acts of God. It contemplated more than a temporary present fellowship with some chosen individual or people; for God is "the God of the whole earth" (Is. 54:5; cf. Ex. 19:5, "for all the earth is mine"), and any covenant to which He is a party must ultimately envision a universal and permanent holy community. That is to say, if we concede any objective participation by God in the making of the covenant with Abraham and with Israel we must also conclude that it had a missionary purpose: that it belonged, as we have said, to the saving acts of the Lord in relation to all the nations of the earth. Of this we shall say more when we consider the covenant with Abraham; but Edmond Jacob is right in saying that "the election of Israel was to lead of necessity to a missionary duty."[7] In the case of the covenant of blessing with Abraham the missionary motif, as we shall see, is of fundamental significance; for Abraham is told in so many words, "and be a blessing" (Gen. 12:2, ASV). The Hebrew verb in the last clause is imperative. Though RSV makes it a purpose clause, indicating *the intended result* of God's blessing on Abraham, the sense remains the same: "so that you will be a blessing." For this Abraham was called. It is quite impossible to separate the covenant concept in the Old Testament from that prophetic missionary purpose for which the New Testament claims the fulfillment in Christ, and in the church, which is called His body.

A covenant once made was regarded as inviolable. Therefore it called for faithfulness on the part of each participant. The faithfulness of God is a major Biblical teaching, with its roots in the concept of the covenant. He is a God who keeps covenant (Deut. 7:9). It is significant that the Hebrew verb translated "keeps" is a participle, which is used to express *continuous action*. It is, as it were, His very character or His nature to keep covenant or to be faithful in what He has promised. Therefore He is called a God of *hesed,* the Hebrew word so aptly translated by RSV as "steadfast love." This is one of the most significant theological terms in the Old Testament. The original use of the word was to denote "that attitude of loyalty and faithfulness which both parties to a covenant should observe towards each other."[8] The liturgical refrain in Ps. 136, "for his steadfast love endures for ever," is but an echo of the Old Testament faith in a God who is faithful. He is faithful in His love for His covenanted people. Hesed, however, is only one of several words with the connotation of faithfulness which are frequently associated in the Old Testament with covenant or berith. One of the most significant of these is *emeth*, a word which can be translated either as *truth* or *faithfulness*. See the significant combination of hesed and emeth in Ex. 34: 6, "abounding in steadfast love and faithfulness," and of berith and hesed in Deut. 7: 9, "who keeps covenant and steadfast love." In Hosea, and again in Jeremiah, Yahwe is pictured as a faithful husband of His people, even though they have acted like a faithless wife. One of the most striking testimonies to this faithfulness of God is in Is. 65: 16, where He is literally called "the God of Amen" (RSV, "the God of truth"). We are reminded of Luther's explanation of the word *Amen* as used in prayer: "Amen, Amen, that is, yea, yea, it shall be so."[9] We can have such confidence because He who promised is faithful (Heb. 10: 23). God is faithful to His covenant of promise. Such is the witness of the Old Testament as well as of the New. It inheres in the very nature of the Biblical concept of a God of covenant. Though this does not mean, as Baab has pointed out,[10] that He is automatically obligated to bless where the conditions for receiving a blessing are absent, it does mean that the sincerely seeking will find that His covenant mercies are sure, and that in the ultimate missionary purpose of the covenant He will not fail. It is the God of covenant faithfulness who says to His people, even to the people that has turned away from Him "in perpetual backsliding" (Jer. 8: 5), "You will seek me and find me; when you seek me with all your heart, I will be found by you, says the Lord, and I will restore your fortunes and gather you from all the nations and all the places where I have driven you, says the Lord, and I will bring you back to the place from which I sent you into exile." (Jer. 29: 13, 14)

In contrast to the faithfulness of God is the frequent and persistent faithlessness of men, on whom the covenant also imposed the obligation to be faithful. When the book of the covenant was read in the hearing of the people at Sinai they said, "All that the Lord has spoken we will do, and we will be obedient" (Ex. 24: 7). This was the right thing to say; and by saying it, they signified their assent to the covenant and became parties to it. From this moment there rested on them the obligation to be obedient to the terms of the covenant as given them. That it was a faith-motivated obedience is clear, for it was a response to the gracious act of God in initiating the covenant; but just because the initiative was God's, "the covenant between God and Israel necessitated a specific statement of what God promised and also of what He required of Israel. . . . Thus the idea of the covenant carries with it as a corollary the revelation of the law."[11] Merle William Boyer, in speaking of "the ethical dynamic of the Word of God," says that the Biblical tradition in which Protestantism is rooted "is impregnated from beginning to end with the profoundest ethical principle that man has ever known, namely the principle that God is a covenant-making God and man a morally responsible being called by God to live in a covenant relationship with him now and throughout eternity."[12] We speak specifically now of the covenant with Israel, the covenant with a nation; but what we have said applies equally to the covenant with Abraham, the covenant with an individual, that anticipated the covenant with the nation. The characteristic thing about Abraham, according to the book of Genesis, is that he *was* faithful to the God of the covenant in the obedience of faith, and was signally commended for it. (Gen. 15: 6; 22: 15-18). In the case of Israel, on the other hand, the Biblical witness of both historian and prophet is that they were guilty of a great and frequently recurring unfaithfulness, which gave evidence both of a lack of faith and of a spirit of disobedience. The tension between the obligation to be faithful and the constant tendency to be unfaithful is the most pronounced human aspect of the actual covenant relationship as it existed in Israel. It was only because of the faithfulness of God that He did not reject His people nor swerve from His declared covenant purpose which, beginning with Israel, included the world.

3

Beginning with Israel!—Or did it begin there? The witness of the Bible is that it began when God made a covenant with a man named Abraham. Or even earlier! There is mention of covenant and of saving acts of the Lord before the time of Abraham. There are flashes of illumination on the ways of God with men to be found in Gen. 1-11. That is especially true of Gen. 3:15, which many believe to be a true Protevangelium in which is outlined or unfolded the entire history and order of salvation. Franz Delitzsch says of this verse: "Like a sphinx, it crouches at the entrance of sacred history.—It is only solved by him through whom and in whom that has been revealed towards which this primitive prophecy was aimed."[13] In similar fashion Alan Richardson, while denying that the writer had a clear-cut Messianic prophecy in mind, admits that "perhaps he is here hinting in his parable at the ultimate redemption of the human race, and Christians will rightly interpret his unformulated hope as having found its realization in Christ's victory over sin and death."[14]

But it is the covenant with Abraham which, according to the Biblical witness as it stands, marks the real beginning of those saving acts and promises of God that in a very special sense constitute sacred history. What precedes the story of Abraham is in the nature of *introduction*. Wilhelm Möller has summed up the significance of the book of Genesis in two fine sentences: "The first eleven chapters show that humanity can be saved, that it needs to be saved, and that God has begun to accomplish His work of salvation. At the point where the history of humanity passes over into the patriarchal family history, there stands as an introductory text, impossible to misunderstand, God's promise to Abraham in 12:3: 'In you all the families of the earth will be blessed.' "[15] In somewhat similar fashion C. H. Dodd has formulated the main theme of the Old Testament Scriptures as received by the church: "They record the inception of the covenant in the calling of Abraham, its establishment under Moses in the giving of the Law, and the vicissitudes, changes and developments in the relations of the covenanted people with their God, before the coming of Christ."[16] More explicit still is Willis J. Beecher's summary of the New Testament viewpoint "that Yahaweh, when he called Abraham, announced a promise given through him to the human race; that the history of Israel is the unfolding of this promise; that the promise was renewed with David and preached by all the prophets; that it began to be fulfilled directly after it was made, and has been fulfilling ever since; that its greatest fulfillment is in the person and work of Jesus Christ; that it will never cease being in process of fulfillment; and that this promise-doctrine is the sum of what the prophets teach in the scriptures."[17]

It is to this calling of, or promise to, or covenant with, Abraham that we now turn our attention.

NOTES

[1] J. R. Dummelow, *A Commentary on the Holy Bible.* New York: The Macmillan Company. Reprint 1944, p. 15. Used with the permission of The Macmillan Company.

[2] Geerhardus Vos, art. "Covenant," *Dictionary of Christ and the Gospels.* New York: Charles Scribner's Sons. 1911. Vol. I, pp. 373-380.

[3] From *The Westminster Historical Atlas to the Bible,* rev. ed. by Wright and Filson. Copyright 1956 by W. L. Jenkins. Philadelphia: The Westminster Press. p. 5.

[4] Edmond Jacob, *Theology of the Old Testament.* Translated by Arthur W. Heatcote and Philip J. Allcock. New York: Harper & Brothers. 1958. pp. 201-223.

[5] From *The Westminster Dictionary of the Bible,* (rev.) by John D. Davis. Revised and rewritten by Henry S. Gehman. Copyright 1944, The Westminster Press. p. 118.

[6] Otto Baab, *The Theology of the Old Testament.* New York and Nashville: Abingdon Press. 1949, p. 136.

[7] Edmond Jacob, *op. cit.,* p. 217.

[8] From *The Distinctive Ideas of the Old Testament* by Norman Snaith. Copyright 1946, W. L. Jenkins. Philadelphia: The Westminster Press. p. 124.

[9] Martin Luther, *The Small Catechism. The Book of Concord,* edited by Henry Eyster Jacobs. Philadelphia: General Council Publication Board. 1916. p. 370.

[10] Otto Baab, *op. cit.,* p. 136.

[11] From *An Outline of Biblical Theology* by Millar R. Burrows. Copyright 1946, W. L. Jenkins. Philadelphia: The Westminster Press. pp. 11, 12.

[12] Merle William Boyer, *Everyman's Adventure.* New York: Harper & Brothers. 1947. p. 105.

[13] Franz Delitzsch, *Messianic Prophecies.* Edinburgh: T. & T. Clark. 1891, p. 37.

[14] Alan Richardson, *Genesis I-XI,* Torch Bible Commentaries. London: Student Christian Movement Press Limited. 1953. Distributed by Macmillan. p. 75.

[15] Wilhelm Möller, *Inledning till Gamla Testamentet.* Tr. from German. Stockholm: Evangeliska Fosterlands-Stiftelsens Bokförlag. pp. 83-84.

[16] C. H. Dodd, *The Bible Today.* Cambridge and New York: Cambridge University Press. 1952. p. 9.

[17] Willis J. Beecher, *The Prophets and the Promise.* New York: Thomas Y. Crowell Co. 1905. p. 179.

Chapter Three

THE MAN NAMED ABRAHAM

1

There *was* a man named Abraham.

Such is certainly the impression that the Bible gives to one who reads with uncritical eye the story as it is written. The Abraham who confronts us in Genesis is seen as an individual, with a clearly defined personality and a sharply outlined personal experience. To him, together with Isaac and Jacob, the history of Israel looks back as to "the founding fathers"; Israel is regarded as "the offspring of Abraham" (Ps. 105:6; Is. 41:8). One prophet comforts and encourages his people, when they have been reduced in numbers to a small remnant, by reminding them of the rock from which they were hewn:

> "Look to Abraham your father
> and to Sarah who bore you;
> for when he was but one I called him,
> and I blessed him and made him many." (Is. 51:2)

What God has done once He can do again. He can begin with one, and by His blessing multiply the one into many. That is what He did with Abraham. Another prophet, in another kind of situation, uses the same starting point to warn his people against the false confidence which says, "Abraham was only one man, yet he got possession of the land; but we are many; the land is surely given us to possess" (Ezek. 33:24). From the Biblical point of view it is not only a matter of historical fact, but also of some real religious significance that God began with one man, Abraham, when He chose Israel to be a people for His own possession (Deut. 7:7-8).

The Jews in the time of Jesus certainly believed that there was a man named Abraham, whose children they were. "We are descendants of Abraham," they said to Jesus (Jn. 8:33); and Jesus acknowledged that so far they were right, "I know that you are descendants of Abraham" (Jn. 8:37). What they misunderstood were the spiritual qualifications that were necessary if they were to say in truth, "Abraham is our father" (Jn. 8:39). The physical descent from the one man Abraham is not at issue; but according to Jesus it is not enough. "If you were Abraham's children, you would do what Abraham did" (Jn. 8:39); you would have the faith and obedience of Abraham. The backward look both historically and spiritually is to the man Abraham.

It is to Abraham that the genealogy of Jesus is traced back by Matthew: "The book of the genealogy of Jesus Christ, the son of David, the son of Abraham. . . . So all the generations from Abraham to David were fourteen generations, and from David to the deportation to Babylon fourteen generations, and from the deportation to Babylon to the Christ fourteen generations" (Mt. 1:1,17).

It was not until the rise of literary-historical criticism in the eighteenth and nineteenth centuries A.D. that the existence of Abraham as an historical figure was seriously doubted or denied. The application of historical principles to the study of the Old Testament yielded new insights, which must be welcomed by every serious student of Scripture. There were at the beginning, however, many radical conjectures which masqueraded as historical truth; and some of these concerned the Genesis story of Abraham. Many Old Testament scholars denied any true historicity to the patriarchal stories. Bernard Stade expressed the prevalent opinion when he wrote, "The traditional way of thinking, according to which Abraham, Isaac, Jacob, etc., were historical persons and the actual ancestors of Israel, with whom Yahve entered into a relationship prefiguring his later relation to Israel, stands in contradiction of the course of history and of the conclusions of the history of religion (der Religionsurkunde), and is not fair to the religious, historical, and local significance of the patriarchal legend (der Vätersage)."[1]

There were several reasons for this opinion so widely prevalent at the turn of the century. We may mention two: the late dating of the sources of Genesis, which put a question mark over their historical credibility; and the interpretation of Old Testament religion as essentially a national religion (Volksreligion), which saw in the patriarchal narrative only a witness to the development of Israel's religion after the entrance into Palestine. Stade, for example, says of "Jahvereligion": "It was from the beginning never anything else than a nation-

23

al religion (Volksreligion)"; it was never the religion "of a few individuals chosen by God."[2] According to J. Coppens the first of three presuppositions on which "Classical Wellhausenism" rested was "an almost absolute scepticism toward documents relating the history of ancient Israel."[3] In the case of Genesis it was more than scepticism as to the accuracy of specific details; for the whole viewpoint from which the patriarchal narratives are written was regarded as historically false. It makes, of course, a radical difference in the way the text is understood and interpreted. If there never was a man named Abraham, then the whole story about him becomes fiction; religious fiction, perhaps, and if so not devoid of religious relevance, but fiction nevertheless. By some scholars the patriarchs were believed to be purely legendary figures. According to others they were personifications of the tribes from which the Hebrew nation derived its origin. Some scholars regarded them as former deities, downgraded to the human level but possessing still something of the character of mythical heroes or demigods. Many noted with Gunkel the resemblance of these stories of Abraham, and Isaac, and Jacob, to the "sagas" of other primitive people.[4] Wellhausen, who hesitated to apply the personification theory to Abraham as he did to Isaac and Lot, said of him: "We dare not, of course, on that account hold him in this connection as an historical personage; rather than that he might be a free creation of unconscious fiction."[5] "The stories about Abraham do not reflect, at least not exclusively, nor even primarily, the life-destiny of an individual," says H. S. Nyberg, "but tribal and cultic history, and a religious Ideal. . . . Abraham is Israel's great idealized religious and ethical personality."[6] And Kurt Galling, speaking from the premise that the Exodus tradition is the point of departure in the formation and illumination of Genesis, says that "the structure is determined in the strongest way, if we may use the formulation of Staerk, 'by a religious Ideology imposed on it from without.' "[7]

2

It is not our intention here to give a critical evaluation of these theories as to the patriarchal narratives in Genesis. It was necessary to survey them in order to understand the situation in the field of Old Testament studies during the last century. We would not deny that there may be elements of truth in some of them. It is obvious that they cannot all be fully true, for they tend to cancel out one another.

Without choosing between them so as to become the advocate of one against the other, and with awareness of the questions raised by all of them, we turn our attention now to the positive affirmation that there is something to be said for the assertion of faith that there was a man named Abraham, and for the essential objectivity of the Abraham story.

There is, of course, the impression given by the narrative itself. Even Gunkel admits that *according to its form* the patriarchal narrative is the history of a family, and of an individual whom God chose to become the ancestor of a people (Israel), and whom he guided, protected, and blessed throughout his life.[8] "The majority of the deeds recorded in it," says John D. Davis, "cannot be explained as tribal movements without violence and improbable interpretations."[9] That is, they *seem* to be the acts of an individual. Though there is a tribal element discernible, it is not of the kind to be explained by a theory of personification; it is rather that of a tribal group associated with a leader, and it is the person of the leader that is sharply delineated in the narrative. It would, indeed, be easier to think of Abraham as a fictitious character, "a free creation of unconscious fiction," as Wellhausen said, rather than as simply a tribal name. A writer of fiction can create a character that is surprisingly lifelike; but where is the evidence, not to say the proof, that Abraham was such a fictitious character? Who were these nameless fiction writers of Israel, who could invent an Abraham in order to explain the origins of Israel as a nation and to motivate Israel's faith and life as a religious community?

It is one thing to recognize with Franz Böhl and others "the great artist" who worked "original independent stories into a unity";[10] it is quite another to assert that this "great artist" also created the very stuff out of which the Genesis narrative, with Abraham as its main character, is made up. To explain this creative story-telling in terms of folklore and the growth of popular legends does less than justice to the clearly delineated personality and personal experience of Abraham as he appears in the Genesis story. If there are legendary accretions to it, the story is nevertheless more than legend. It gives the unmistakable impression that it is in essence the life story of a man named Abraham, as historically real as his contemporary, Hammurabi.

The archaeological discoveries of the twentieth century have done much to confirm the natural impression given by the Genesis narrative. It is true that we have no direct witness to Abraham outside of the Bible; the name is found elsewhere as a personal name, but there is no reference to the Biblical patriarch.[11] It is the historical background of the narratives about him, or the whole social and cultural milieu of the patriarchal period, that archaeology has illumined. Especially significant for our understanding of the Mesopotamian background which is reflected in Genesis have been the Mari and Nuzi tablets, extensive archives discovered in the excavated ruins of these ancient Mesopotamian cities. The Mari tablets alone number more than 20,000 and illustrate almost every phase of the city's life and culture, from the political to the commercial; and Mari was no isolated city, but representative of the culture of that part of the ancient world to which it belonged.

It is on the basis of this more accurate knowledge of the Biblical world of the second millennium before Christ that the story of Abraham and his family appears in a new light. As early as 1932 W. F. Albright wrote, "It is difficult to see anything very remarkable in the conclusion which has been forced upon us by recent archaeological discoveries, that the saga of the Patriarchs is essentially historical."[12] In 1954 the same author refers to his earlier book, which was written before the discovery of the Mari tablets, and says, "Now we can speak even more emphatically, and with a wealth of additional detail. . . . It is becoming increasingly clear that the accounts of the Patriarchs go back largely to early narrative poems transmitted orally into Israelite times and then written down in shortened prose paraphrases of the poetic originals. In no case are these Patriarchal stories mere reflections of the life of Israel in the Divided Monarchy, as used to be held by most literary critics; they actually do go back almost a thousand years to the Middle Bronze Age."[13]

An increasing number of voices have been raised in agreement with the position of Dr. Albright. Thus S. H. Hooke concludes that through the fresh light thrown by archaeology on the Patriarchal period "Genesis has been shown to reflect faithfully the life and customs of Canaan and the movements of peoples in the first half of the second millinnium B.C."[14] So also the *Westminster Historical Atlas to the Bible* asserts that the customs reflected in the Nuzi documents "demonstrate that Patriarchal life as described in Genesis is that of the second millennium, and not that of the first millennium, when Israelites were retelling the stories and putting them into writing."[15] "We shall probably never be able to prove that Abram really existed, that he did this or that, said thus and so," says G. Ernest Wright, "but what we can prove is that his life and times, as reflected in the stories about him, fit perfectly within the early second millennium, but imperfectly within any later period."[16] What is the natural inference with respect to Abraham? While we may not be able to *prove* that he existed ("prove" is a strong word in any area of human knowledge!), there is *a strong presumption* that if the Genesis narrative is generally accurate as to the historical milieu, it is equally reliable as to the historical existence of the chief character in the story. As H. Kremers has succinctly put it, "The historicity of the person of Abraham was formerly often questioned. On the other hand, newer or more recent investigations have shown that Abraham probably really once lived as a nomadic sheik in the wilderness on the border of the cultivated land of Palestine."[17] (The author's phrase, "am Rande des palästinensischen Kulturlandes," may denote the *settled* as well as the *civilized* status of Palestine at this time.)

We do not mean to infer that there are no dissenting voices. It is significant, however, that not even Martin Noth, whose critical and sometimes radical examination of the Biblical tradition seems to allow for very little of the truly historical in it, denies the strong presumption that the patriarchs once lived as "historical persons."[18] The so-called "tribal personification" and "mythological" and "fairytale" interpretations he dismisses, on the basis of A. Alt's *Der Gott der Väter*, as having been "exploded once for all." It is true that he does not believe that we have much evidence "for making any definite historical assertions about the time and place, presuppositions and circumstances of the lives of the patriarchs as human beings." In this respect the archaeological evidence of the last few decades does not seem as convincing to him as it does to others. Nevertheless the fact that "the figures of the patriarchs lived on among the Israelite tribes as the recipients of divine manifestations and the founders of systems of worship which continued to be practiced by their descendants and with which their names remained associated" is cited as an indication that "they were clearly men who had once lived as historical persons."[19] More significant still, he speaks of "the divine promises that had been made to them" as if they were a fact, and a central idea in the original tradition before it evolved into its present form. Noth has his own theory as to when and where and how this evolution took place, but of that we need not speak now; for we are concerned primarily with the starting point of the tradition, that there was a man named Abraham to whom God gave a promise with a unique significance in the history and religion of Israel. Though Noth is not as explicit as John Bright, who says, "We can assert with full confidence that Abraham, Isaac, and Jacob were actual historical individuals,"[20] there is no fundamental disagreement between them at this point. The patriarchs were "clan chiefs who actually lived between the twentieth and the seventeenth centuries."[21]

We must in all fairness note that none of these scholars would deny that the actual writing of the patriarchal stories probably took place much later than the events of which they speak, and that "the actual events were vastly more complex than the Bible indicates."[22] There may be a history of oral tradition back of their present form. There may have been a good deal of refraction and rearrangement of materials in the process, as Albright suggests.[23] There may be discernible a pedagogical use of the narratives within the family history of Abraham. There may be difference of opinion as to how definitely the essential historicity of the narrative in terms of its "local color" implies also a personal rather than a tribal "Abraham," or how much of the experience belongs to the individual and how much to the clan. Leonard Woolley is quite positive, on the basis of the excavations at Ur, that there was a person named Abraham who came originally from Ur, and who was the founder and head of the clan which later developed into the Hebrew nation. He believes, however, that there may have been two or even three by that name, three generations of Abraham ben-Abraham, whose life is reflected in the Genesis story.[24]

We shall not attempt to evaluate every shade of critical opinion; for far more important is the growing unity of conviction among Old Testament scholars that there is a strong presumption of "substantial historicity" for the Abraham stories when seen in the light of archaeology. Though in reading them we may feel that they have something of the quality of folk tales, we must go on to say with C. H. Dodd, "Yet there is history behind them."[25] They are too true to life, the life of the second millennium B.C., in the Fertile Crescent from the Euphrates to the Nile, of which according to their own witness they are a part, to be explained otherwise. And of this history, however literally or freely we understand it, the central figure is a man named Abraham.

3

We may with some confidence assert that there was a man named Abraham, a man who lived almost 4,000 years ago. For the moment we say nothing more about him than this, that he *was*. Before we consider *who* he was, or *what* he was, we confront the question, What difference does it make *for Christian faith* whether there really was an Abraham or not?

The wording of the question is deliberate, and definitive of the viewpoint from which we would pursue our further inquiry concerning him. Our primary concern is with the relation of the Abraham story to the content of our Christian faith. We are concerned with the place of Abraham in Biblical religion, and therefore in the preaching and teaching ministry of the Christian church today. Is Abraham fact or fiction? In either case, is he relevant for Christian faith? Is there a different relevance if he really existed than if he did not?

Let us admit at once that it is not strictly a queston of either-or. The religious relevance of the Abraham story is not wholly dependent on its historical objectivity.

If we believe that the Bible is primarily a religious book, we must also admit that the truth of it cannot be scientifically determined. Paul's dictum, "for we walk by faith, not by sight" (2 Cor. 5:7), applies far beyond the immediate context wherein it stands. The historian may help to correct or to confirm the human data with which faith deals; but he does not ultimately control the conclusions drawn by faith. Faith is *a plus*, a gift from God that sees beyond the external facts and interprets their meaning.

The very existence of God is a matter of faith. We can neither prove nor disprove the opening sentence of Genesis, that in the beginning God created the heavens and the earth (Gen. 1:1); we understand it by faith (Heb. 11:3). We might say that we have *evidence* that is sufficient for faith, *but not proof* which makes faith unnecessary. We cannot prove historically that God chose Israel to be His very own, with whom He entered into a *berith olam,* an everlasting covenant; we have simply the evidence of Israel's faith that they were such an elect or chosen people. As Kurt Galling says, the question of the *objectivity* of the election of Israel by God belongs to the judgment of faith (Glaubensurteile) with which we receive or regard the Bible as the Word of God.[26] "Archaeology can neither affirm nor disprove the 'truth' of the Bible," says S. H. Hooke; "its ultimate truth is spiritual and lies beyond the region with which archaeology is concerned."[27]

The point that we would make is that *even if we could prove the existence* of the man named Abraham, *we would not thereby prove the objectivity of the divine election and covenant and mission* to which Genesis bears witness. Historicity cannot be equated with revelation. There may be a self-revelation of God in history; but if we are to understand such a revelation there is need of something more: there must be also an interpretation of the acts of God given by the Spirit and received by faith.

The corollary to what we have just said is this, that there may be a revelation of the mind of God by the Spirit and an accompanying confession of faith without attachment to a specific or concrete event in history. We think of the variety of human literary forms found within the Bible through which, according to Christian faith, God speaks. Jesus, for example, made extensive use of the parable in His teaching. The parable has been defined as "a method of speech in which moral or religious truth is illustrated from the analogy of common experience." Common experience is not the same as a specific experience. The prodigal son, or the publican in the Temple, or the rich man and Lazarus, do not lose their profound religious relevance because we cannot identify them with definite individuals who lived at a certain time and place. There is within the Bible religious teaching by means of story and fable as well as by prophetic interpretation of the facts of history or of a biographical experience; and we must not forget that the historical event, where it can be proved, is religiously irrelevant without the prophetic interpretation. Whatever our personal opinion may be as to the historicity of the Book of Job, the book is not dependent on the historicity of its characters to be an effective lesson in the divine-human relationship. Would there be any serious religious loss if the same were said about the Genesis narratives, and specifically now about the story of Abraham?

There is, however, a significant difference between the Book of Job and the story of Abraham. It is not only a difference in character; rather, the difference in character is due to a difference of position in relation to the total Biblical witness as to what God has done. The Book of Job, significant as it may be theologically, contributes little or nothing to that unity and continuity of Biblical teaching which we call "the saving acts of the Lord." (See Mic. 6:5.) The story of Abraham claims to be the record of an act of God which is united in the most intimate and permanent way with the whole Biblical witness to *a God who acts* redemptively in relation to the world. Gillis Gerleman has well said that according to the Bible's own testimony "it is in history that God reveals himself. . . . God has not revealed himself in timeless myths or in a system of norms and dogmas, but in the historical event (det historiska skeendet)."[28]

There hovers over the Old Testament throughout, and in a very special way over the story of Abraham, what the same writer calls "the wing-strokes of a great happening" (vingslagen av ett stort skeende).[29] The Bible bears witness to an event; and this event is really *a series of events* leading up to *the supreme event:* it is a history of salvation (Swedish, "frälsningshistoria"; German, "Heilsgeschichte") whose goal is the coming of Jesus Christ into the world for judgment and for salvation. It makes a difference *for the content of Christian faith* whether God really acted or not in the calling of Abraham, in the covenant with Israel, in the coming of the Lord Jesus Christ. If He did not act in these significant "faith-events" the religious "truth" in the narrative loses its concreteness; it belongs in the realm of religious ideas rather than of historical events. We do not say "in the realm of faith," for that is true even if God has really acted in the event. It is by faith, and faith alone, that we know that He has acted: that God *loved* the world and *sent* His Son to be the Savior of the world (1 Jn. 4:14), and through Him *has visited* and *redeemed* His people (Lk. 1:68). But mark, it is *faith in the God who acts,* and in what He has done for the salvation of the world. Christian faith cannot surrender the objective reality or do without the concrete saving act of God; for in so doing it ceases to be the Biblical faith of which it is the spiritual heir.

It may be objected that what we have just said is quite true of God's redeeming act in Jesus Christ but does not apply to Abraham. How valid is the objection?

If we were concerned with the story of Abraham *as an historical basis* for Christian faith we would rightly hesitate to put it in the same category with the life of Christ. Our concern, however, is with *the content of the Christian faith.* It will make a difference in the content of our faith, if we read the Abraham story as fact rather than fiction, as essentially historical rather than unhistorical, or as a personal religious experience rather than the personification of the national religion of Israel. It will affect our faith in three ways.

1. It will affect our whole attitude toward the Biblical witness concerning the way of salvation. Abraham is a key figure in the Biblical story of the saving acts of God. If we recognize him for what he is, or is said to be, our faith will move within the framework of the Biblical tradition, which in the Old Testament and the New Testament alike is predicated on the conviction that God acted redemptively in relation to Abraham and through him in relation to the world. We will see by faith a unity and continuity in the Sacred Scriptures as they have been given to us, with the saving act of God in Christ as its heart and center: but belonging to that heart and center, as being also a part of the saving acts of God, is the blessing of Abraham. The same God acts and with the same ultimate purpose in the calling of Abraham and in the sending of Jesus Christ.

2. It will affect also our whole concept of God, or our basic theology. According to the Biblical witness our God is the God "of the saving *act*," by which we mean that "God was in Christ reconciling the world to himself" (2 Cor. 5:19); but according to the same witness there are also "saving *acts* of the Lord" (Mic. 6:5). He is not a God who acted only once, without preparation and without continuation, like a bolt of lightning from the blue. He is a God who acts continually; a Creator who has not abandoned His universe like some absentee landlord, a Redeemer who has been actively engaged in redemption from the beginning, a Sanctifier who did not begin with the Confederacy of the Twelve Tribes in Palestine to prepare for himself a people.

Such is the clear witness of the Bible as given. To this witness belongs the call of Abraham. If we are persuaded that God did call this man even as He did the prophets, or even as He sent Jesus Christ into the world and spoke by Him, it will help us to see and to know our God as one who acts continually within the world of men, in relation to men, for the purpose of bringing blessing and salvation to all men. Why should it be regarded as unbelievable that God confronted a man named Abraham if we believe that He confronts men today; and that out of this confrontation came a few simple but significant spiritual insights and a real spiritual experience, which became the steppingstone to greater saving acts of God in the future? In what kind of God do we believe? Is He living or not? Is He only a tribal deity, or is He the Lord of the whole earth? Is He a God who sees "the end from the beginning" (Is. 46:10) *and works towards a divine goal,* or is He limited in His activity as to both time and place? Above all, does He ever use human individuals in His redemptive service; and if so, why not an Abraham? As Wilhelm Vischer so pertinently asks, "Is Abraham, 'the Father of faith,' really more remote from me than the Christians of today? It is remarkable how many Christians and free religious spirits of our day regard it as self-evident that they know more about God than Abraham, 'the friend of God,' simply because they live a few thousand years later. Have they perhaps never reflected that, however creative they may be in such matters, what they say and write concerning God can be at best but a few drops by the side of the living spring which flows joyously through the chapters about Abraham in Genesis, from which through the ages men have allayed the thirst of their hearts?"[30] The greatness of the Abraham story and of the Abraham experience is that it reflects the greatness of the God of Abraham to whose call he responded in the obedience of faith. In what we are saying we are not trying to prove that there was an Abraham as a basis for faith, but to illustrate what a difference it makes if we believe that he was, and that God did something with him and through him.

Olof Olson, a pioneer Swedish Lutheran theologian in America, has given a fine description of this life relationship between the living God and the man named Abraham: "God gave His promise whenever it was possible, whenever men would listen to Him. He had to wait two thousand years to find a man like Abraham. The promise given to Abraham He would gladly have given before if there had been some one ready to receive it; but there was none until the Lord found Abraham in Ur of Chaldea."[31] There is quite a difference between a simple faith like this, that God really acted with redemptive purpose in the life of a man named Abraham, and a mere theoretical idea about a God who acts, without concrete illustration from life. The Bible witnesses to a God *who has acted* in specific situations, of which the life of Abraham is one.

3. It will affect also our preaching and teaching, not only from the Book of Genesis but from the Bible as a whole. The issue involved is not one of biographical details but of the saving acts of God. We can preach and teach what God has done only if we firmly believe that it has been done by Him. That is true of His work of crea-

tion. It is true also of His work of redemption. It is true of the call of Abraham, with all the spiritual significance that the Bible witness ascribes to this call from God to this man. It is true of the vocation of Israel to be a people for God's own possession and use. It is true of the life and ministry of Jesus Christ. It is true of the continuing activity of the Holy Spirit in creating the Christian church in our midst today. If we believe that these things are indeed *God at work,* we will preach Him not as a theoretical deity but as the living God and Savior. There will be a note of objective reality in our preaching.

It makes a difference *in our faith* whether there actually was a man named Abraham or not. The testimony of Scripture is unanimous that there was, and that God did something for him and through him that is of religious significance still.

4

What this religious significance is we shall try to set forth in the chapters that follow. We shall do so from the viewpoint that there was a man named Abraham, and that the Abraham story is essentially historical. We shall not ignore the possibility of a history of oral transmission of the narratives which may affect our understanding of both content and form. We shall not deny that in form the Genesis stories bear a resemblance to what is called "Sage" or legend; but we keep in mind the dictum of Gunkel that "Sage ist nicht Lüge" (legend is not falsehood).[32] Even if the literary form should be in part that of "saga," this does not rule out the "substantial historicity" of the narrative which has been so convincingly attested by recent archaeological discoveries in the Near East. Not that the case for such "substantial historicity" rests with archaeology alone! We need to remember Woolley's warning: on the one hand, against *an uncritical doubt* of the Old Testament on the part of its defenders, and on the other hand, against *an uncritical acceptance*: a doubt that they would not entertain in the case of any other ancient history, and an acceptance that ignores the fact that the Old Testament authors wrote "with a didactic purpose" which colors the narrative. "The historical books of the Old Testament, which are for most of the things recorded in them, the only authority that we possess, must by any sane school of criticism be accorded due weight as authorities."[33]

Above all, we would proceed in the conviction that there is in the Abraham story something more than biography or history: something that can best be described as a self-revelation of God, or a manifestation of the redemptive purpose and of the saving acts of the Lord. We would listen for "the wing-strokes of a great happening," as Gerleman so aptly puts it.[34] We would be keenly aware always that the Abraham story belongs to God's "history of salvation." We shall look for the *central ideas* that express the fundamental significance of this man in Bible history and religion; and if we let the Bible speak for itself, we shall soon see that he had no significance apart from his relationship to his God, and to his role as a servant in the working out of the divine plan of redemption for all mankind. We shall be confronted with the truth not only that there was a man named Abraham, but *that God made a covenant with him.*

NOTES

[1] Bernard Stade, *Biblische Theologie des alten Testaments.* Tübingen: J. C. B. Mohr. 1905-11. Vol. I, p. 66.

[2] *Ibid.*

[3] J. Coppens, *The Old Testament and the Critics.* Paterson, N. J.: St. Anthony Guild Press. 1942. p. 25.

[4] H. Gunkel, "Genesis," in Nowack's *Handkommentar.* Göttingen: Vandenhoeck & Ruprecht. 1901.

[5] J. Wellhausen, *Prolegomena to the History of Israel.* Edinburgh: A. & C. Black. 1885.

[6] H. S. Nyberg, art. "Abraham," Svenskt Bibliskt Uppslagsverk. Stockholm: Nordiska Uppslagsböcker. 1948.

[7] Kurt Galling, *Die Erwählungstraditionen Israels.* Giessen: A. Töpelmann. 1928. p. 37.

[8] H. Gunkel, *op. cit.,* pp. 159, 162.

[9] From *The Westminster Dictionary of the Bible,* art. "Abraham." *op. cit.*

[10] Franz Böhl, *Das Zeitalters Abrahams.* Leipzig: J. C. Hinrichs. 1930. p. 6.

[11] Artur Weiser, art. "Abraham," *Die Religion in Geschichte und Gegenwart.* Tübingen: J. C. B. Mohr (Paul Siebeck). 3rd ed. 1957.

[12] W. F. Albright, *The Archaeology of Palestine and the Bible.* Westwood, N. J.: Fleming H. Revell Company. 1932. p. 145.

[13] W. F. Albright, "The Bible After Twenty Years of Archaeology." Pittsburgh: Biblical Colloquium. 1954. Reprint from *Religion in Life,* Vol. XXI, No. 4. 1952.

[14] S. H. Hooke, "Archaeology and the Bible" in *The Bible Today:* a Symposium. New York: Harper & Brothers. 1955. p. 35.

[15] From *The Westminster Historical Atlas to the Bible,* rev. ed. by Wright and Filson. p. 25.

[16] From *Biblical Archaeology* by G. Ernest Wright. Published 1957. Philadelphia: The Westminster Press. p. 40.

[17] H. Kremers, art. "Abraham," *Evangelisches Kirchenlexicon.* Göttingen: Vandenhoeck & Ruprecht. 1956.

[18] Martin Noth, *The History of Israel.* New York: Harper & Brothers. 1958. p. 121.

[19] *Ibid.,* p. 122.

[20] From *A History of Israel* by John Bright. Copyright 1959, W. L. Jenkins. Philadelphia: The Westminster Press. p. 82.

[21] *Ibid.*, p. 83.

[22] *Ibid.*

[23] W. F. Albright, *The Bible After Twenty Years of Archaeology. op. cit.*

[24] Leonard Woolley, *Abraham.* London: Faber & Faber, Ltd. 1936.

[25] C. H. Dodd, *op. cit.*, p. 57.

[26] Kurt Galling, *op. cit.*, p. 2.

[27] S. H. Hooke, *op. cit.*, p. 21.

[28] Gillis Gerleman, *Gamla Testamentet i Förkunnelsen.* Lund: C. W. K. Gleerup. 1956. p. 3.

[29] *Ibid.*

[30] Wilhelm Vischer, *The Witness of the Old Testament to Christ.* London: Lutterworth Press. 1949. p. 20.

[31] Olof Olsson, *Salvation in Christ.* Rock Island: Augustana Book Concern. 1942, pp. 19-20.

[32] H. Gunkel, *op. cit.*, p. VIII.

[33] Leonard Woolley, *op. cit.*, pp. 33-35.

[34] Gillis Gerleman, *op. cit.*

Chapter Four

THE CALL OF ABRAHAM

"For when he was but one I called him,
and I blessed him and made him many." (Is. 51:2b)

T HE STORY OF ABRAHAM'S CALL in Genesis 12:1-3 is simple and condensed.

We are not told where or when the call came. From the position in the narrative we might infer that it was in Haran, after the death of his father Terah. According to Stephen in the Book of Acts it was in Ur of the Chaldeans before the family moved to Haran. There are those who believe that it was a double experience, which came to Abraham in two different ways. It may have been a progressively growing conviction, which began in Ur and finally crystallized into action in Haran. If such were the case, it would conform to the nature of many a spiritual experience since the day of Abraham.

We are not told how the Lord spoke to Abraham. Theophany plays an important part in the patriarchal narrative elsewhere, but it is not necessarily implied here. It may have been true of Abraham as Sholem Asch says of the prophet in the Exile: "He had not attained to the highest sphere in which a vision of God was vouchsafed to him and speech granted him face to face. He heard it only as a voice speaking within his own heart and believed with perfect conviction that what he thus apprehended was true and right."[1] We note, however, that in Gen. 12:7 the language of theophany or of vision is used, "the Lord appeared to Abram, and said." The emphasis, nevertheless, is not on the manner but on the substance of the revelation.

We *are* told that YHWH, the Lord, was the one who spoke to him and called him. That may seem to contradict the statement in Ex. 6:3, "I appeared to Abraham, to Isaac, and to Jacob, as God Almighty [Heb. El Shaddai], but by my name the LORD [Heb. YHWH, Yahwe] I did not make myself known to them." We may not be sure that

Abraham knew God as Yahwe, with all the spiritual significance that this name suggested to Israel in its later history; but there is no mistaking the intent of the writer to say that the God of Abraham, by whatever name He may have been known, was the same as the God whom Israel knew by the name of Yahwe. We rightly stress the significance of the names *El Elyon*, God Most High, and *El Shaddai*, God Almighty, in the "theology" of Genesis. With Franz Böhl we may profess to see a certain difference between the God of Genesis, "the mild and fatherly deity" (die milde und väterliche Gottheit) and the God of Exodus, "the inaccessibly exalted Yahwe, the jealous God" (der unnahbar erhabene Jahve, der 'eifrige' Gott).[2] In this same connection Böhl refers to the character of the Genesis narrative as "allgemein menschlich," without any historical or national limitations such as we find in Exodus; and this, too, has a bearing on the doctrine of God. That there has been a progression in the revelation of the nature and will of God should be clear to every discerning Bible reader; but such growth in the knowledge of God does not contradict the basic identification of the God of Abraham with the Holy One of Israel, or with the God and Father of our Lord Jesus Christ (Eph. 1:3). It was the living God who appeared to Abraham, and the knowledge of him that Abraham had is in essential agreement with the more complete knowledge which is ours through Jesus Christ.

"Now the Lord said to Abram, Go . . ., and I will bless you, . . . so that you will be a blessing."

To Abraham God gave a command and a promise. Both command and promise are closely related to the common experience of men, and yet at the same time significantly different. It is this command and this promise that sums up for us the historical as well as the religious significance of the call of Abraham. How do we understand this experience of the man Abraham, and what is its religious relevance for us?

1

The command comes first. It is a command to "go," or to separate himself from country and kindred, and to migrate to a new and as yet unknown land.

It is tempting to let our imagination loose on this terse divine directive to Abraham. It has so much in common, for example, with the faith and hope of the men and women who in more recent centuries left Europe to settle in America. In the light of our newly acquired knowledge of the ancient Near East it is also easy to think of it as connected with the great migrations of the second millennium B.C., which vitally affected the political, cultural, and economic life of the Fertile Crescent from the Euphrates to the Nile. It may well be that there is a kinship with both ancient and modern migrations that can help us to grasp the initial significance of the command to Abraham. For the deeper ultimate significance we must look to the witness of the Scriptures.

It is obvious that this command of the Lord to Abraham involved the element of *separation*. Was it an external or physical separation only? We cannot usually account for the movements of men in that way. There are invariably other factors that enter in, such as human ambitions and aspirations, human fears, human pressures, even religious convictions. If we believe in God, we may well believe that He might use any or all of these things to persuade a man like Abraham to separate himself from a former manner of life and from a former place of abode to seek a new home and a new life. Although, as Leonard Woolley has pointed out, no reasons for the move are given in the Old Testament,[3] and the motives that actuate an individual cannot be proved by archaelogy, it is at least in harmony with the spirit of the times to suppose that Abraham's migration may have been due in part to social and economic conditions. The Genesis narrative bears witness to the effect of famine on the later movements of both Abraham and his descendants.

Were there also motivating religious factors in Abraham's decision to leave his homeland for a land unknown? Nothing is said directly about religious motivation in Gen. 12, but the whole narrative as it stands implies it. Abraham acts in response to an inner call which he believes to be the call of God. He acts in obedience to what he believes to be a divine word to him. He consecrates himself to the God who has called him, seeking to enter actively into the purpose and destiny that God has in view for him. For separation, in the sense that it has a religious aspect to it, is never wholly negative: it is always also positive in nature; it involves *separation to* as well as *separation from;* it is more than a matter of redemption, it is consecration. In the very command to "go" there is the implied claim of God to Abraham's faith and obedience, or to his commitment to the will of God for him. This becomes explicit in the course of the narrative, as Abraham is commended for his faith (Gen. 15:6) and for his obedience (Gen. 22:15-18), and as the whole tenor of the story leaves the impression of an outstanding man of faith. Faith is commitment; and Abraham believed. He proved his faith by his action in leaving Haran in obedience to the call of God. To ignore the religious aspects of this initial call to separation is to miss the mark in interpretation. It loses sight of the clear indication of purpose in the call.

From what did Abraham separate himself in leaving Haran? Can we look beyond the threefold reference in Gen. 12:1 to country and kindred and father's house? The prophet Isaiah, speaking many years after the event, refers to "the Lord who redeemed Abraham" (Is. 29:22). This would seem to agree with the picture given in Josh. 24:2, 14, of the fathers who served other gods "beyond the River," and also with the vivid picture given by archaeology of the place of idolatrous worship in the culture both of Ur and of Haran. Leonard Woolley says that "we have to think of Ur in Abraham's time as dominated by a cult the essence of which was its material magnificence, a cult absolutely inseparable from the City."[4] This was also true of Haran, "the only other important town in Mesopotamia to have the Moon-god for its special patron."[5] If Woolley be correct in his confident assertion that the worship of the Moon-god was the faith in which Abraham was brought up, it is indeed significant that, while there is clear indication of Sumerian influence in the Abraham story, "there is not the slightest trace of any Moon-god cult."

We might add that there is very little trace in the Abraham story of gross polytheism in general. If this man Abraham is not a creation of fiction, if he is not a projection into the past of later prophetic ideals, if he is a man of flesh and blood whose historical situation, according to archaeology, is that of the second millennium B.C., the difference between his religion and that of his contemporaries is so great as to require radical explanation. What other explanation is adequate than the one to which the Bible bears witness, that God himself had something to do with it; that by whatever steps, whether by gradual development or by a sudden flash of enlightenment, Abraham was led to "a new knowledge of God"? As Woolley rightly says, "The Old Testament explicitly attests something in the nature of a revelation granted to the man . . . and it would certainly seem to imply something in the nature of a conversion of the man such as later tradition has attributed to him."[6] This does not necessarily mean that he had the same spiritual insight as did his spiritual successors. It does mean that there was a change in Abraham's religious outlook; that something did happen. From out of a world of polytheism he emerges as one of the lone figures with faith in a God who is radically different, alone, the majestic El Elyon, who is the Maker of heaven and earth—an incipient monotheism. It is no accident that he is called "a prophet," even in one of the weaker moments of his faith (Gen. 20:7). Edv. Wiren, who finds in Genesis some evidences of an original monotheism as well as evidences of polytheism, characterizes Abraham as a reformer: "From this syncretistic religion or heathendom God 'redeemed' Abraham (Is. 29:22). He should become a 'reformer' or a 'protestant,' who should carry on the torch of faith in a time when religious error and moral decay threatened the world with destruction."[7]

Beneath the difference in viewpoint of Woolley and Wiren as to the exact nature of Abraham's religious experience we discern a fundamental agreement at one point: the call of Abraham, however we understand it, did involve the experience of separation from the religion of Ur and Haran, and of separation to a new faith in "the living God." It is this significant religious principle that begins to emerge in the brief, unadorned command to Abraham, "Go from your country . . . to the land that I will show you." It is a principle worth watching, not only in the life of Abraham but in the history of Israel, and in the New Testament teaching concerning Christian discipleship. We shall have more to say about it in the case of Abraham when we have looked at the promise which accompanied the command; for as we shall see, he was separated to God not only in a unique worship, but also in a unique service: and that involves the covenant of blessing. For the moment, suffice it to say that the principle of separation becomes clearer as God's redemptive purpose and will for all mankind are progressively revealed; but it is already present in the call experience of Abraham.

2

To the command given Abraham is attached a promise. We might call it simply a promise of divine blessing upon him as he went forth in obedience to the divine command; but it is really a threefold promise, and each element in the promise is profoundly significant for later Biblical history and prophecy. They grow naturally out of the human situation, yet they are pregnant with a meaning which reaches far beyond the life experience of Abraham. The language in Gen. 12 may suggest some very earthly aspects of the call, such as the land (geography), the nation (history), the great name (the fame caused by political power and prestige), perhaps even material blessing (prosperity). The emphasis in fulfillment of the promise might seem to be on Jewish nationalism, on a national kingdom and people *on this earth* and in a sense *of this world;* but even so we must not overlook the selection of this people for a special mission.

Even in terms of its fulfillment in Israel we cannot do justice to it unless we recognize from the start its religious implications. In the light of the total Biblical witness, the religious implications become unmistakable. The emphasis shifts more and more to the spiritual, until in the New Testament the picture becomes predominantly, if not wholly, spiritual: the blessing is the gospel (Gal. 3); the land is heavenly (Heb. 11:13-16); the kingdom is not of this world (Jn. 18: 36-37); the seed includes all who are Christ's (Gal. 3:28-29). For one who believes that there is a unity which binds the Old Testament and the New Testament Scriptures together into a living whole, it is manifestly unfair to neglect the New Testament in the interpretation of an Old Testament text, or of the Old Testament in its totality. That is true also of the covenant with Abraham. The Book of Genesis does not stand alone. But we look *first* at the promise as it stands in the Book of Genesis, and as a part of the recorded call-experience of Abraham.

The Promise of a Seed

We begin with the divine promise of a seed. The Hebrew word is *zera,* which AV and ASV render as *seed* and RSV as *descendants.* It is a singular-collective noun, i.e., singular in form but usually collective in meaning. It could refer to a single child or it could refer to all the future descendants that a man might have. We meet it for the first time in the Abraham story in Gen. 12:7, where it clearly has the plural connotation. It is equivalent to the promise in 12:2, "I will make of you a great nation"; and perhaps to the assurance that follows, "I will bless you, and make your name great." To have many children, and especially male children, was regarded as a great blessing. It is not necessary to date Ps. 127 to get the impact of its witness to the way of thinking in the ancient world.

> Lo, sons are a heritage from the Lord,
>   the fruit of the womb a reward.
> Like arrows in the hand of a warrior
>   are the sons of one's youth.
> Happy is the man who has
>   his quiver full of them! (Ps. 127:3-5)

What could be more natural than that Abraham should share the common hope that he might be blessed with a seed! But what the Bible declares is that there was added to the hope the conviction of a divine promise: a promise that the hope would be realized, and on a grand scale. "I will make of you a great nation" (Gen. 12:2). "I will make your descendants as the dust of the earth; so that if one can count the dust of the earth, your descendants also can be counted" (Gen. 13:16). "Look toward heaven, and number the stars, if you are able to number them. . . . So shall your descendants be" (Gen. 15:5). "I will make you exceedingly fruitful; and I will make nations of you, and kings shall come forth from you" (Gen. 17:6). "I will indeed bless you, and I will multiply your descendants as the stars of heaven and as the sand which is on the seashore" (Gen. 22:17). And the Bible further declares that the divine promise involved a divine selection, so that among the many sons of Abraham (see Gen. 25:1-6) who could in the collective sense be called his seed, the promise in its deeper divine significance and purpose attached only to one: "for through Isaac shall your descendants be named" (Gen. 21:12).

This selective purpose of God is from the Biblical point of view the really important thing in the call of Abraham. This is divine *election*, in the sense in which Edmond Jacob interprets it when he says: "Every intervention by God in history is an election: either when he chooses a place in which to make more special manifestation of his presence, or when he chooses a people to carry out his intentions, or when he chooses a man to be his representative or his messenger."[8] According to the Genesis story God chose Abraham and his seed *with divine purpose, for a divine service.* The attachment of the promise to one individual, who therefore both by his birth and in his life is a true child of promise, illustrates the singular connotation that may lie in the word *zera.* At the moment of his birth Isaac *is* the seed of Abraham. His descendants are also, in a sense, the seed of Abraham. So, according to the New Testament, are all who share Abraham's faith.

It should not seem strange that out of the matrix of such a promise there comes finally *an individual,* Jesus Christ, who fulfills both the aspect of lineal and of spiritual descent from Abraham, and who in a unique sense fulfills also the vocation of Abraham's seed, whether viewed individually as when Isaac was born or collectively as in the history of the people of Israel. According to Genesis, the initial election of Israel to be in a special sense God's servant took place not at Sinai, nor in the land of Canaan, but in Haran of Mesopotamia, when God called Abraham and gave him the promise of a seed and commissioned him to be a blessing. The New Testament, of course, goes further and gives to this promise of a seed a pure religious application; first, to Christ, and then to those who are Christ's because they share the faith of Abraham (Gal. 3:7, 16, 29).

It seems that we are confronted by two questions at this point. How much of this religious significance actually lay in the promise of a seed? How much of this significance did Abraham comprehend in his own relation to the promise?

Let us be perfectly frank and clear as to the premise from which we seek an answer to the questions raised. We are not now trying to prove the unprovable, that there *was* a divine promise involved. That was for Abraham, and for Israel, and must remain for us, a matter of faith. But even if we believe *that God acted* in this life-experience situation of Abraham, and that we have in Gen. 12:1-3 a divine word communicated to him, we face still the problem of how to understand the promise, specifically now the promise of a seed. On the surface it seems to speak only of an earthly progeny, a multitude of flesh and blood descendants, in the same sense in which the Jews of Jesus' day asserted, "We are descendants of Abraham" (Jn. 8:38). Until narrowed by Gen. 21:12 to the seed of Abraham through Isaac, it might even seem to refer to all the ethnic groups which, according to the Old Testament, were thought to derive their descent from Abraham: the Midianites (Gen. 25), and the descendants of Ishmael (Gen. 25), and the Edomites (Gen. 36). We think of the statement in Gen. 17:6, "I will make nations of you," which must be put alongside the one in Gen. 12:2, "I will make of you a great nation," and seems to indicate not one but a multitude of peoples descended from Abraham. And yet, as far as the promise of a seed is concerned, *Gen. 21:12 does narrow it down* and limit it to Isaac, or, if we look ahead, to the later people of Israel. Surely no one is so naïve as to think that the history of Israel can be fully understood *apart from its profound involvement in religion!* Somewhere there arose a deep-seated conviction of religious mission and destiny. If God really acted in the call of Abraham—and it is our theme that we may indeed believe that He did—it would seem that this spiritual aspect of the seed, though only gradually made fully clear, was involved in the promise by divine intent from the very beginning. Such is certainly the viewpoint of the New Testament. The illustration of the acorn within which is concealed a mighty oak, but which must die and live and grow before we see the oak in its glory, may help us to understand this promise, and many another where God is said to have acted and spoken in relation to men such as Abraham. The whole purpose of God in the election of Israel to be His chosen servant, the whole purpose of God in the sending of His Son to be uniquely the seed in whom Israel's vocation reached both climax and fulfillment, the whole purpose of God to redeem to himself a people from among all nations who would share Abraham's faith, lay within the promise of a seed to Abraham; but it required God, who is His own interpreter, to make it plain. For Abraham at the moment the hope and the promise centered in the birth of a son, Isaac.

It would be unfair to Abraham, however, to assume that he was given to see nothing of God's far-reaching purpose with his seed. We shall have more to say of this in connection with the promise of blessing in Gen. 12:3. For the moment we bear in mind that it is the normal thing for any man with a deep sense of religious commitment to expect great things of his God. The Genesis narrative makes it emphatically clear that Abraham was such a man of strong religious commitment. This is also the indelible impression that he has left upon all succeeding generations. Franz Böhl rightly suggests that the word translated "his trained men" in Gen. 14:14 could be translated *Eingeweihte*, that is, initiated or dedicated ones; and that Abraham stands at the head of a small religious fellowship (Kultgenossenschaft).[9] Though Luther may read too much of New Testament Christology into Gen. 12:5, he is quite correct when he speaks of Abraham's companions as being more than domestic servants: they constitute "a true holy church," who had been persuaded by Abraham's preaching to share his faith in the living God and in his redemptive mercy.[10] The "seed" is pregnant with religious significance from the beginning. Something of this far-reaching significance was revealed to Abraham and became a vital part of his religious hope and faith. To limit the promise to the material situation is wholly inadequate in the light of the Biblical witness. Herbert Alleman has summed up the case well in these words: "The purely spiritual character of Israel's religion had a slow development, but the seed was there from the days of Abram."[11] "For in Isaac shall thy seed be called" (Gen. 21:12, ASV) has a genuine fulfillment not only in the Old Testament Israel, but also through Christ in the New Testament church.

The Promise of a Land

Closely related to the promise of a seed is the promise of a land. In the working out of God's redemptive purpose through Abraham and his seed it was necessary that "the chosen people" should have "a promised land"; and this promise of a land is implied in the divine command, "Go . . . to the land that I will show you" (Gen. 12:1). After the arrival in the land of Canaan, the identification and the promise are made specific, "To your descendants [your seed] I will give this land" (Gen. 12:7).

What could be more natural than that Abraham should share the common hope of man for a home, a country to call his own! Back of all the migrations of history lies the urge to possess a better place in which to live. That was true of the perennial conflict between "the Desert and the Sown."[12] It is not difficult to see a possible relationship between the migrations of Abraham, as well as the later Israelite conquest of Canaan, and this "eternal struggle between the nomadic and the settled peoples."[13] In the case of Abraham, however, if we may trust the Bible witness, it was more than a desire and a hope; there was added to it the conviction of a definite divine promise. *This* land on which he stood, the land of Canaan, was to be the land where his seed would dwell and where God would accomplish His purpose with and through them. This land was "given" to them by the will of God. It is to be noted that the primary emphasis even in Genesis is on the gift of the land *to Abraham's seed.* He himself lived in it as a pilgrim and a sojourner; he never owned more of Canaan's soil than was needed for a burying place for himself and his family (Gen. 23). It is the promise of a seed that is to the fore in the Book of Genesis. In the Book of Exodus we find this promise in a measure fulfilled, and the emphasis shifts to the hope of inheritance which centers in the promise of a land. From here on *the land* plays a central role in Biblical history. In view of the prominent place given it in the initial promise to Abraham as well as in later history and prophecy, we can readily understand why it still looms large in the hopes and aspirations of the Jews, and why some Bible interpreters would make it the central focus of the covenant with Abraham. Wilbur Smith is perhaps correct when he says that no other divine promise in the Bible occurs as often and as insistently as this promise of a land.[14]

But questions of Biblical interpretation cannot be decided by a numerical count of Biblical references or "proof passages." The promise of the land must be seen and understood in its proper historical perspective. We mean now the perspective of Bible history as a whole. If there is any religious significance whatever to the call of Abraham—and we shall see further evidence of it in connection with the promise of blessing—the promise of a land cannot be rightly understood as an end in itself. It must be seen in the light of the total purpose of God with Abraham and with his seed. The very structure of the sentence in Gen. 12:1-3 (see punctuation in ASV) indicates that the land belongs to the preliminary and preparatory rather than to the climactic in the realization of the total promise. Abraham himself experienced the truth of the promise in spite of the fact that he must confess to the Hittites, who were then inhabitants of the land around Hebron, "I am a stranger and a sojourner among you; give me property among you for a burying place, that I may bury my dead out of my sight" (Gen. 23:4). On the other hand, his seed, the people of Israel, experienced the truth of the promise in a different way, when they took possession of the land under the blessing of God, and it became their own. That it was no permanent or unconditional possession by divine right becomes clear from the preaching of the prophets when Israel rebelled against the God of the covenant with them.

> "If you are willing and obedient,
>   you shall eat the good of the land;
> but if you refuse and rebel,
>   you shall be devoured by the sword;
>   for the mouth of the Lord has spoken." (Is. 1:19-20)

We find the same significant "if" in Deut. 30, in the divine challenge and plea to "choose life": "If you obey the commandments of the Lord your God which I command you this day, by loving the Lord your God, by walking in his ways, and by keeping his commandments and his statutes and his ordinances, then you shall live and multiply, and the Lord your God will bless you in the land which you are entering to take possession of it. But if your heart turns away, and you will not hear, but are drawn away to worship other gods and serve them, I declare to you this day, that you shall perish; you shall not live long in the land which you are going over the Jordan to enter and possess" (Deut. 30:16-18).

The possession of the land was only a steppingstone within the larger plan and program of God. As long as the literal possession of the land served this larger purpose it was important. It was so important that God promised and gave the land to Israel *twice,* in the original conquest of it which is linked with the Exodus, and in the return to it from the Babylonian Captivity. It was important in connection with that phase of the total redemptive plan of God which involved Israel, the seed of Abraham, as in a special sense His Servant. The time came when it no longer was important in this temporary and preparatory sense. Such, at least, is the witness of the New Testament; and the thought is not foreign to the Old Testament, where the earth is said to be the Lord's and not only the land of Israel. (See Ps. 24; cf. Ex. 19:5). If we once admit that there is *any* religious relevance to the call of Abraham, and that it does in some real sense foreshadow greater things to come as the New Testament testifies, we cannot give to the promise of the land a completely non-religious interpretation. It, too, stands as a symbol of and a steppingstone to something greater: the symbol of an inheritance, but an inheritance which ultimately is seen to be spiritual and universal rather than strictly material and national in nature. *For if God is active in this thing* that happened to Abraham, so that the redemption of Abraham is related by divine intent to the final redemption of all humanity, we can readily understand that the gift of a redeemed land may also be related in a preparatory and in a prophetic way to the new heavens and the new earth wherein righteousness dwells, the inheritance of the redeemed.

We may naturally ask, How much of this deeper spiritual meaning did Abraham understand? We must confess that we do not know for sure. Certainly spiritual insight at this point *grew* as God continued to act and to interpret His own thoughts by His actions. Some things that seem quite clear in retrospect may not have been nearly as clear to the forward look. That belongs to the very nature of revelation as we see it illustrated in the development from the Old Testament to the New: from the Book of Genesis to the Book of Revelation, from the Protevangelium (Gen. 3:15) to the "little Bible" (Jn. 3:16), from the old covenant to the new. If, however, we look at the situation realistically, we can easily imagine some of the thoughts of an Abraham as he neared the end of life with so much of his hope and of the divine promise seemingly unfulfilled. There is every indication that he believed in *the living God* who made heaven and earth. Would it be so strange if to a man of such a faith there should be granted a ray of hope for "a better country, that is, a heavenly one?" We know the New Testament interpretation: "These all died in faith, not having received what was promised, but having seen it and greeted it from afar, and having acknowledged that they were strangers and exiles on the earth" (Heb. 11:13). Must this interpretation be categorically rejected just because Abraham lived so long ago, before there was a Creed which said, "I believe in the resurrection of the dead"? Who shall say with authority how little or how much such a faith as Abraham's included in the way of religious hope or theological insight? Even we "walk by faith, not by sight" when it concerns this matter of life and death, and the unseen reality that lies beyond. We see only in part—but we believe. It would be presumptuous to deny to a man of faith like Abraham a similar experience, within the limitations of God's dealings with him. The promise of a geographical land, important as it was in itself, could hardly have seemed to Abraham *the end* or the goal of the promises of God; especially not in view of the promise of blessing that follows. For it is the promise of a unique blessing, not only to but through Abraham and his seed, that stands in the climactic position in relation to all that precedes.

The Promise of Blessing

According to modern literary-historical criticism, the relatively unified picture given in Genesis of Abraham as the authentic prototype of the obedience of faith must be examined in the light of the formation and composition of the Genesis-sources JEP, which in themselves are said to exhibit a long oral and written tradition. To the first stage of the formation of the tradition Artur Weiser assigns Gen. 15, and especially the promises of a seed and a land.[15] Otto Eissfeldt, in his synoptic outline of the literary sources of Genesis, assigns the whole of Gen. 12:1-4a to the relatively early source known as J. To the same source are said to belong chapters 22:15-18 and 28:13-16, in which the promise of blessing is significantly repeated. Chapter 26: 2-5 is divided between J and the closely related E. The passage in Gen. 18:17-19 is assigned to the so-called "Laienquelle" or L, which is regarded as earlier than both J and E.[16] In short, the documentary analysis gives considerable support to a relatively early origin for the tradition concerning Abraham, including his call and the covenant with him; and not least the tradition which makes him the bearer of a divine promise of blessing to all the peoples of the earth.

In the Biblical tradition outside of Genesis, of course, he is seen pre-eminently as the recipient of the divine covenant and the bearer of the promise of blessing which it contained. There is no good reason why we should hesitate to believe that such was really the case. We cannot adequately account for the origin of the tradition except on the basis of an experience that actually happened to the man named Abraham. We cannot adequately account for the Biblical faith, whether in the Old Testament or in the New, apart from an act of God which involved Abraham in a far-reaching and tremendously significant divine purpose. Here, if ever in the Old Testament, it is true that we hear, as Gillis Gerleman has so well said, "the wingstrokes of a great event."[17] We have every right to believe that the Abraham story is essentially true, and that it is a determinative factor in sound Biblical interpretation: that it belongs in a real and significant way to the saving acts of God. John Stirling has paraphrased and interpreted the Abraham-experience in these words: "Look not, says Abraham, for the story of my life in these chapters, but for the story of my God. There is none like Him. And this is His glory: He has come forward, not with a scheme merely, but with a promise for the world, and a promise which is more wonderful than anything the mind of man could possibly have conceived. More than that, He has pledged himself to see it fulfilled. This is the never-to-be-forgotten message, the news from heaven, which we are to pass on to the children of men in all generations."[18] Or as Paul wrote to the churches of Galatia, "And the scripture, foreseeing that God would justify the Gentiles by faith, preached the gospel beforehand to Abraham, saying, 'In thee shall all the nations be blessed'" (Gal. 3:8).

What was the promise of blessing to Abraham?

The Hebrew word which occurs five times in connection with the call of Abraham, once as a noun and four times as a verb, twice with

God as the subject, is *barak*. (The form of the noun is berakah.) There is no better translation than "bless" and "blessing." The word is indicative of an attitude which finds expression in an act. When men bless God (see e.g. Ps. 103) it means an attitude of homage which is expressed in an act of praise. When God blesses men it means an attitude of favor which is expressed actively in the bestowal of good gifts or "blessings" on men. The word *barak* does not of itself indicate the exact nature of the blessing. It is probably true, as Herbert Alleman says, that "like most other words in the literature of the Hebrew religion, [it] originally had a material significance."[19] In the passage before us such a material content might be suggested by the reference to land and seed, which by some is taken to mean a hope of material prosperity and of future political power and national prestige. We have already pointed to some of the objections to so narrow and non-religious an interpretation of the experience of Abraham. The objections are multiplied when we consider the promise of blessing in this same context.

Let us first analyze the promise as we find it in Gen. 12, to see what are its component parts. If we follow the punctuation of RSV, there are three distinct facets to the promised blessing, which dovetail into each other because they are parts of one unified whole.

The first is in v. 2, where there is a threefold repetition of essentially the same idea, "I will make of you a great nation," "I will bless you," "I will make your name great"; leading up to this significant statement of intent and purpose, "So that you will be a blessing." It should be noted that the Hebrew verb in the last clause is in the imperative, and that the literal translation would read, "And be thou a blessing." It is so translated in the American Standard Version and in the American Jewish Version. We bear in mind that any verb form in Hebrew is very versatile and permits a great latitude in translation. S. R. Driver cites this clause as an illustration of the use of the imperative "instead of the jussive, to express with rather greater energy the intention signified by the preceding verb."[20] We find no fault with the translation in RSV, which correctly interprets the *intention* of the preceding verbs of promise; but we must note carefully what that intention is. Whatever the translation be, whether the imperative of command or a result clause, the intention indicated is that Abraham should be a blessing, not merely that he should be blessed. To render the line as Moffatt does, "I will make a great nation of you and bless you and make you famous for your bliss," is more than free; it is inaccurate.[21] The language of the original is clear and unmistakable in its emphasis upon the divine intention that Abraham (and his seed) should be a blessing. The imperative brings it out more dramatically, "And be thou a blessing." What that means we shall consider after we have completed our analysis.

The second facet of the blessing is in v. 3a, "I will bless those who bless you, and him who curses you I will curse." Abraham and his seed were to be a touchstone by which to test the attitude of all men toward Abraham's God. Perhaps we should say that Abraham's faith was to be such a touchstone; for Abraham's life and person had no special significance apart from his faith or his relationship to his God. As men share in his faith, and thereby also in his mission, they are included in the blessing. The call of Abraham from the beginning concerned others as well as himself and his immediate descendants. Every facet of the blessing implies *a mission*. What that mission was we see most clearly in the third and climactic part of the promise, the true blessing of Abraham, in the sense in which Scripture interprets it.

This third and final facet of the blessing is found in v. 3b. It is the statement to which Paul refers as "the gospel preached beforehand" (Gal. 3:8). Ed. Böhl says that Luther called this verse "the promise which one ought to write with letters of gold and to laud and praise in the language of every land, because it brings with it eternal treasures."[22] It is this promise that W. J. Beecher rightly claims to be the basis for "the doctrine of a single promise" under which the New Testament writers regarded the Messianic teaching of the Old Testament. "The biblical generalization of the matter," he says, "may be thus formulated: God gave a promise to Abraham, and through him to mankind; a promise eternally fulfilled and fulfilling in the history of Israel; and chiefly fulfilled in Jesus Christ, he being that which is principal in the history of Israel."[23]

Are these men right in their evaluation of the promise?

Before we answer, we must examine the promise itself. It poses several problems or questions, the first of which is the linguistic problem of translation. The two alternatives are indicated in the text and in the margin of RSV: the reflexive form of the verb in the text, "and by you all the families of the earth will bless themselves," and the passive form in the footnote, "in you all the families of the earth will be blessed."

There is no uncertainty as to the form of the Hebrew verb *barak* at this point. It is a Niphal form, which in the history of the Hebrew language was first used in the reflexive sense and then came to be used primarily as a passive for the simple Hebrew verb form which is called the Kal. In the four passages where the promise of blessing is repeated in Genesis the same Niphal form of the verb is found in two: Gen. 18:18 and Gen. 28:14. In the other two, Gen. 22:18 and 26:4, the form of the verb is Hithpael, which is seldom if ever used in any other than a reflexive sense. The earliest translation from the Hebrew, the Greek version known as the Septuagint, has the passive in all five Genesis passages; as does the New Testament in the two places where the promise of blessing is directly quoted, Acts 3:25 and Gal. 3:8. The older English versions follow the Septuagint and use the passive throughout. RSV indicates the modern preference for a reflexive translation in all five Genesis passages, but retains the passive in the New Testament quotations.

It would be interesting to note the many variant attempts at translation in versions and commentaries, old and new. Ronald Knox, for example, translates as "shall find a blessing" in all five passages in Genesis.[24] More significant, however, is the fact that at least one modern version, the Swedish of 1917, uses the passive translation for the Niphal and the reflexive for the Hithpael instead of translating all five passages alike.[25] This would seem to be a better approach to the problem than to try to prove that the Niphal *must* conform to the reflexive significance of the Hithpael, or that the Hithpael *can* be used as a passive in conformity with the common use of the Niphal. The interpretative argument from parallel passages can easily be overdone. There may be more than one way in which to express truth, both in Hebrew and in English. Geerhardus Vos argues for the passive sense of the Niphal, partly because of the New Testament quotation but also because of the climactic structure of the promise of blessing in the key passage in Gen. 12:1-3: the reflexive aspect of the blessing, which "is not void of religious import," is implied in v. 3a, "I will bless those who bless you," for this indicates a determination of the lot of outsiders according to their attitude toward Abraham; the third part of the promise, in v. 3b, must reach beyond the first and the second, which it clearly does if the passive significance is retained.[26] According to Otto Procksch the Niphal is related to the Hithpael in the same way as "Segen finden," or to *find blessing,* is related to "sich segnen," or to *bless oneself.* It is with definite or deliberate design, he says, that J (the source to which he assigns Gen. 12:1-3) has chosen the otherwise unusual Niphal in order to bring out the receptive sense.[27] We need not on linguistic grounds rule out either the passive or the reflexive significance of the verb *barak* in relation to the promise of blessing. There are good linguistic reasons for letting the Hithpael be reflexive and the Niphal passive; and that means, of course, a passive significance in Gen. 12:3b.

There is a deep religious, and even Messianic, significance to either translation, though the passive is the more direct of the two. Before we attempt to interpret the content of the blessing, however, we must make some further observations from its formal side. Whatever its content, to whom was the blessing to be given, and by whom was it to be mediated?

It is clear that Abraham himself is in the first instance the recipient of the promise; for God says to him, "I will bless you." The reaffirmation of the promise to Isaac (Gen. 26:2-5) and to Jacob (Gen. 28:13-14) makes it equally clear that it belonged to Abraham's seed by inheritance; especially, to Isaac, "for in Isaac shall thy seed be called" (Gen. 21:12, ASV). This line of development carries us down to the people of Israel as the children of Abraham and as heirs of the promise of blessing; for the words of 1 Peter 3:9 apply to the promise or blessing of Abraham from the beginning, "to this you have been called, that you may obtain [ASV, inherit] a blessing." No one can read the Old Testament and miss the emphasis on Israel as divinely chosen to be "a people for his own possession" (Deut. 7:6). The thought of inheritance is prominent in the Old Testament, as it is in the New; and it is closely linked with one aspect of the promise of blessing to Abraham. The promise was *to* him and to his seed; the blessing was to be received *by* him and by his descendants.

But there is another and more significant aspect of the blessing; for Abraham is not only called to obtain but *to be* a blessing. We cannot evade the central thrust of the passage as expressed in the imperative of intention in v. 2: "and be a blessing." It does not alter the situation, as we have said, if we translate as a purpose clause, "so that you will be a blessing." It is clear that in some manner or other the "Blessing of Abraham" (Gen. 28:4) was to be *shared* as well as *received*. If in the climacteric part of the promise in v. 3b we translate the verb as a reflexive, we have what Procksch calls "ein Segenswunsch," a hope or a wish to share in the blessing that God has given Abraham, and to which the life of Abraham bears witness. If, on the other hand, we translate it as a passive, we have according to Procksch "eine objektiv in Abraham vorhandene Segenskraft," or something given to Abraham by God that enables him to be in a dynamic sense a source of blessing.[28] The passive puts the emphasis on the *medium* of the promised blessing as it related to others than Abraham and his seed, who were to be the medium. The reflexive puts the emphasis on the *effect* of the witness of the blessing of God on Abraham and his seed, in that others are drawn to seek a share in it. Even without determining the *nature* of the promised blessing, it can be seen that each of these emphases may be relevant to the situation. If we believe that this is actually a divine promise there is no need, there is no good reason, to rule out either emphasis as an indication of the divine intent. This is the more true, if the promise is fundamentally religious in nature.

What is, then, the nature and content of the promise of blessing? It is customary in some circles to define it in terms of material prosperity and the closely-linked national power and prestige. It has been said to be a backward reflection from the kingdom era in Israel's history, the "golden age" of David and Solomon, and therefore in itself quite devoid of any real religious or spiritual meaning. The Genesis illustration of the blessing would be the great possessions mentioned in chapter 13; and any later illustration would be found only in the national history of Israel. Of course, religion would be *one* factor in Israel's history; but it would not be *the key* to the interpretation of the promised blessing from the beginning. The material aspects of Israel's hope takes precedence over the spiritual, just as human aspirations are regarded as more significant to an understanding of the call of Abraham than the saving acts of the Lord.

There are serious objections, however, to such an explanation of the blessing. It puts the stress almost entirely on receiving a blessing, rather than on being a blessing. The prosperity of Abraham was never so great that he could imagine himself a blessing to the world because of it. The same is true of the nation Israel; for in spite of the poetic description of it as "a land flowing with milk and honey" (Ex. 3:8), it never compared in fertility and material prosperity with the valleys of the Euphrates and the Nile, the two prongs of the Fertile Crescent where the great powers had their seat of empire centuries before the birth of Abraham. The dramatic contrast is vividly sketched by the historical novelist, Sholem Asch, in picturing the reluctance of the Jewish exiles to leave Babylon for Palestine.²⁹ As for political power and prestige, not even Solomon in all his glory (Mt. 6:29) approached the breadth of empire that belonged to Assyrian and Babylonian and Egyptian rulers before and after his time. Any hope of the Hebrew people to excel in this area to the point of becoming a blessing to the nations of the world would have bordered on megalomania. It should be added that when any nation of antiquity thought of itself as superior in the blessings of prosperity, peace, and power, the blessing was always linked in their thought with their religion, or with their gods. If Babylon was great, and its inhabitants fortunate, it was because of Bel-Merodach, the supreme deity of Babylon. By human analogy alone we would expect a similar religious emphasis in the hopes and aspirations of the man Abraham and of his seed, the people of Israel.

What we actually find in the Old Testament is not only something similar, but a *unique* emphasis on the God of Abraham, the God of the fathers, who is also the God of Israel. We repeat the relevant words of John Stirling: "Look not, says Abraham, for the story of my life in these chapters, but for the story of my God. There is none like him."³⁰ It is significant that scholars are much more inclined today, as Artur Weiser admits, to regard the patriarchs as real historical individuals, who in the time *before* the formation of the Israelite nation had acquired significance as recipients of revelation and founders of worship.³¹ Such is certainly the testimony of the Bible when seen in its wholeness. Such is also the witness of faith on the part of anyone who believes *that God acted* with divine purpose in the call of Abraham. It is from this viewpoint of faith in a God who has acted redemptively within human history, and in a Scripture which is unified by this redemptive activity of God, that we seek the answer to the question, "What was the blessing of Abraham?"

From one point of view the blessing certainly lay in Abraham's unique knowledge of God. We use the word *knowledge* in the experiential sense in which it is used in the Old Testament, where it is practically equivalent to the obedience of faith (see e.g., Prov. 1:7; Hos. 6:6; Jer. 22:15-16); but we may not speak of Abraham's faith apart from the God in whom he believed. According to Gen. 15:6, he believed *in Yahve;* a name which S. R. Driver has excellently defined on the basis of etymology and usage as "active, self-manifesting existence."[32] God is, and God manifests who he is! God not only is but acts, and in acting reveals himself. There are those who believe that it may have been a very ancient name. Guthe, for example, says, "The name Yahve, certainly of primitive antiquity, and thus no longer capable of explanation, tells us nothing as to the nature of the Godhead."[33] We may agree with him as to the antiquity without prejudging the question of definition. Whatever its etymology, its meaning in Biblical usage is clear, and the definition of Driver is correct. Whether the name Yahve was actually known and used by the patriarchs or not, that for which the name came to stand, the living God who makes himself known to men whom he chooses for the purpose of this self-revelation, "the God of revelation and grace," is sufficiently clear in the Genesis story.[34] Alleman rightly refers to Abraham as a prophet (see Gen. 20:7), who heard God speak and responded to his call.[35] For faith in the living God, who acts in relation to men whom he has created, carries with it as a corollary the conviction that he confronts and calls men into fellowship with himself, in order that they may also serve him. The Book of Genesis bears emphatic witness to such a confrontation and call of Abraham. The uniqueness of such an experience in Abraham's day is obvious; but who shall say that it is impossible for Abraham to have had it because he lived so long ago? The unanimous testimony of the Biblical writers is that he did have a personal faith in God which was unique in the world of his day; a faith based on the conviction *that God had spoken to him* in some strangely convincing and compelling way, and continued to speak. How far he had come along the way to that true and perfect knowledge of God which is ours in Jesus Christ we may not know; for admittedly there is growth in the knowledge of God as we move on from Abraham to Moses, and from Moses to the prophets, and finally to Christ and the Apostles: but there is every indication that he was *in* that way which leads to Christ, and to the perfect knowledge of God in Him. "The blessing which should come upon the peoples," says Paul Heinisch, "consists in the true faith in God."[36] Otto Procksch comments on Gen. 15:6 in somewhat similar fashion, "The whole power of the Old Testament religion lay in the certainty of (or confidence in) God"; and he adds, "In the Israelite religion lies the salvation of humanity."[37] H. E. Ryle puts it this way,

"The exercise of happiness in the personal relation to Jehovah is to be the pledge of the ultimate fulfillment of blessing to the world."[38] Even more expressive are the words of Franz Böhl, that the God of Genesis is "the mild and fatherly Deity, who in the end turns everything for the best"; and that even today we look back with "Wehmut und Heimweh" [expressive German words, which like the Swedish "vemod och hemlängtan" are poorly translated by the English "melancholy and nostalgia"; *homesickness* might express the thought best] to the spiritual world of the patriarchs.[39] Otto Eissfeldt has much the same emphasis in his brief summary of the religious-ethical contents of Genesis. He stresses first the religious relevance of the stories of the Creation and the Fall and the Flood, and then adds: "But God did not forsake the world and man. Rather, God chose for himself a man who, being united with him in a firm faith-fellowship or communion, should become the father of a people themselves blessed and appointed as a blessing for mankind."[40] The emphasis is on faith in the God who acts with intent and purpose, and who knows how to overcome all human hindrances put in the way of the fulfillment of the promise, and to bring the history to the divinely intended goal. According to Eissfeldt the view of the world and of history expressed in Joseph's words to his brethren, "As for you, you meant evil against me; but God meant it for good, to bring it about that many people should be kept alive, as they are today" (Gen. 50:20), stand on the same high level as that of Christianity.[41]

The blessing of Abraham was predominantly spiritual in character. It was the blessing of God's presence and of fellowship with God by faith in a uniquely personal sense. There is no denying that this is what Genesis in the form in which we have it ascribes to Abraham. It does not lose *all* religious value if it be regarded as the interpretative insight of a great "creative artist," as many have called the author or editor of "J," one of the sources for Genesis in the opinion of most Old Testament scholars today; but it possesses *greater* religious value if it represents the actual experience of the man Abraham and his witness to "the saving acts of the Lord." There is something both heart warming and convincing in the way John Stirling represents Abraham as saying that we should not look in these chapters for the story of his life but for the story of his God, and then adding: "And with the news pass on my own heart's witness to its truth. For I have known him of whom I speak, intimately, and this one fact he has, through all my length of days, brought me to believe: that he can be known and loved and trusted as a personal friend. . . . To me there is no other in earth or heaven; no other Living God, no other God, who speaks to man, who walks with him, through all the years of his earthly pilgrimage, that man might learn, in fellowship with him, the ways of righteousness and peace."[42] This is the heart of the blessing of Abraham; and it began as a blessing in the experience of the man Abraham, whom God called to inherit a blessing. The deepening insight and the widening fellowship which belong to the covenant history of Israel, and the fulfillment which came when "the Word became flesh and dwelt among us, full of grace and truth" (Jn. 1:14), are essentially one with this humble beginning of the mighty redemptive acts of God.

There is, however, a second point of view from which the blessing of Abraham must be examined in the light of its original wording and of the total Biblical witness. The promise as it stands is prophetic and, according to the New Testament, Messianic. Ed. Böhl has said of Abraham, that he is at the same time a prophet and a prophecy of Christ.[43] That cannot mean that he witnessed directly of the coming of the Messiah; for we have no word from him that can be called a direct prediction of a Savior or of salvation in the clear New Testament sense of those terms. The prophecy, if there be one, lay in God's word of promise to him, and in Abraham's faith and hope, or in his very life experience, based on that promise. We might say that the prophecy is inherent in the very self-revelation of God, the God in whom Abraham believed. In the progressiveness of that self-revelation it would become clear that the God of Abraham is none other than the God and Father of our Lord Jesus Christ, the God in whom we believe. The first revelation of the living God is prophetic of the last, the full and final revelation; for that is the very nature of *life*, and God lives. Moreover, the redemption of Abraham (Is. 29:22), the life experience of this one man, is prophetic of universal redemption; for every redemptive act bears witness to God as to One whose very character it is to act redemptively in relation to His creation. There is prophecy in the divine act as well as in the divine word.

It is not of these significant aspects of prophecy, however, that we would speak now. What interpretation shall we give to the prophecy *in word*, the promise that *in thee* (Gen. 12:3) and *in thy seed* (Gen. 22:18) shall all the families or nations of the earth be blessed?

It is to Abraham *and to his seed* that the divine imperative is addressed, "and be a blessing." It is in and through Abraham *and his seed* that the divine promise is fulfilled, "all the nations of the earth shall be blessed." The blessing and the seed are inseparable, both in the receiving and in the mediating of the blessing. As E. F. Kevan says, "Abram's line henceforth was to be mediatorial, and blessing to men was to flow through his seed."[44] Herbert Alleman has expressed the faith of many earnest Bible students in his comment on the repetition of the promise of blessing to Abraham in Gen. 22:18, "His seed shall be a means of blessedness to all mankind—a Messianic promise."[45] This seems to imply more than "the selection of the patriarchal family as the channel of universal blessing,"[46] and to go beyond the statement of Paul Heinisch that "it is the faith and obedience of Abraham that will be for salvation for all humanity."[47] It implies more even than the statement of S. Singer, quoted approvingly in the Pentateuch and Haftorahs, "The germ of the idea underlying the fuller conception of a Messianic Age was in existence from the time of the founders of the race of Israel."[48] According to the New Testament the divine intent with the promise to Abraham includes not only the Messianic Age, but also the Messiah. The seed to whom the promise of blessing is given, says Paul, stressing the singular form of the Hebrew noun *zera,* is Christ (Gal. 3:16).

The problem of interpretation here calls for great caution on the part of the interpreter. What does Paul mean to say in Gal. 3:16? It would be unfair to Paul to conclude that he either ignores or is ignorant of the collective sense of the word for *seed* in the Old Testament, and that he construes the Genesis passage as a direct and exclusive prophecy of the Messiah. Some scholars have called this a case of rabbinical exegesis, which fails to deal adequately with the linguistic and historical aspects of the promise. Franz Delitzsch shows a more exact insight, however, when he says that though the inference of Paul has a rabbinical character, the thought is perfectly correct, that "the singular, 'in thy seed,' includes that which a plural would precisely exclude, namely, that the seed of Abraham, which is the means of blessing, is a unity which will finally be concentrated in One; for *zera* can be just as well used of one (Gen. 4:25) as of many."[49] This is also the viewpoint of E. W. Hengstenberg. After rejecting the thought that any man who understood Hebrew, as Paul certainly did, could entertain the opinion that *only* a single individual could be signified by zera, or seed, he concludes: "Now all to which Paul intends to draw our attention is the fact that the Lord who, when He gave the promise, had already in view its fulfilment which He had himself to accomplish, did not unintentionally choose an expression which, besides the comprehensive meaning which would most naturally suggest itself to the Patriarchs, admitted also of the more restricted one which was confirmed by the fulfilment."[50] So also Ed. Böhl, in speaking of the phrase "in thy seed" in Gen. 22:18, says that a collective meaning is possible, a personal reference to Isaac is probable, and a typical reference to Christ is just as probable, and on the basis of the New Testament interpretation (Gal. 3:16), certain. The experience of Isaac as the seed becomes "a living prophecy [in the typological sense] of the coming Christ."[51]

The viewpoint just expressed is that of an older school of interpretation; but that in itself does not invalidate it. We must, however, consider the objection that this is *eisegesis* instead of *exegesis,* or that we read something into the Old Testament text from the viewpoint of the fulfillment claimed in the New Testament. Are we right in trying to exonerate Paul from the charge of misunderstanding the promise to Abraham? Are we guilty of double talk, as if we were ascribing *two unrelated meanings* to the same Scripture: the one being the meaning that the promise had for Abraham, and the other the meaning that it has for the Christian believer today?

It should be noted that Paul did not ignore the collective signficance of the seed in stressing the singular. In the same chapter of Galatians where he speaks of the seed as being Christ (3:16), he says of them who are Christ's that they are "Abraham's offspring [or seed], heirs according to promise" (3:29). Hengstenberg cites Rom. 4:13 to prove the same point, "The promise to Abraham and his descendants, that they should inherit the world, did not come through the law but through the righteousness of faith."[52] It is quite clear that Paul believed both the singular and the collective aspects of the word *zera* to be significant. To that extent the older interpreters would seem to be on solid ground when they stress the same two aspects of the original promise.

It should also be noted that this dual aspect is characteristic of other Old Testament promises which, according to the New Testament, are fulfilled in Christ and the Christian church. In Gen. 3:15, which by many is believed to be the *first* gospel promise or the Protevangelium, we have a case closely analagous to the promise to Abraham. The *seed* in both instances permits an individual as well as a plural application. The prominent Old Testament concept of Israel as the *servant* of the Lord is shown by sacred history to culminate in the Son of man, who "came not to be served but to serve, and to give his life as a ransom for many" (Mt. 20:28; cf. Phil. 2:5-8). The Old Testament offices of prophet, priest, and king, which in Israel's history were filled by many men, all have a unity of function and purpose which are finally concentrated in the one Person, Jesus Christ. There is much to be said for Ed. Böhl's thesis that the two elements of suffering and glory in the Protevangelium are *reproduced* in the life of all believers and become in this way a prophecy of Christ: in their personal experience they reproduce something of the experience of the coming Redeemer, so that what Paul says of Adam, "who was a type of the one who was to come" (Rom. 5:14), applies to them all, whether it be an Abraham, a Moses, a David, or one of the humblest of Old Testament believers. Böhl uses a fine illustration in which he compares the dewdrop and the ocean as mirrors in which the sun is reflected: the sun is the same, but the size of the mirror makes a difference in the reflection. "So also the life story of each one of the saints of God is a copy, or an impresson, of the divinely conceived plan of our salvation; this is naturally true pre-eminently of Christ, but also of all the saints before him. Christ is the ocean, they are the dewdrops. But in both instances there is present the mirror which reflects the sun. In other words, there is a wonderful similarity between Christ's path of life and that of his saints; they all go the same way, 'per aspera ad astra,' and there is only this difference that Christ goes before and all the saints follow him."[53]

It should be noted finally that life itself tends to follow the principle of unfolding and development as from a living seed. The acorn grows into an oak, but the oak in a sense already exists unseen within the acorn. The infant grows into a man, who in spite of great changes remains the same individual. Truth that emerges as a flash of insight is articulated more and more fully as its necessary implications and permissible applications become evident. There is *growth* within the Biblical religion, but not aimless growth; it is growth according to the law of life, which always sees a connection between the beginning and the end. As Alleman has so well said concerning the Hebrew religion:

"The purely spiritual character of Israel's religion had a slow development, but the seed was there from the days of Abram."[54]

The really determinative question is whether we are willing to acknowledge that the living God *had anything to do with* the call of Abraham and with the promise of blessing to him and his seed. The Biblical faith says Yes. If we have this faith, there is nothing to hinder us from seeing in the promise to, as well as in the experience of, Abraham a beginning and a preview of the redemptive purpose of God; which is later clarified and fulfilled, first, in the history of Israel, and finally, in the ministry of Jesus Christ and of His church. The divine intent is there, though not yet spelled out "in living characters" as it was later on. The call of Abraham and his seed to be a medium of blessing to the nations belongs to "the saving acts of God"; and within those saving acts there is a natural sequence, as we see the fulfillment of the promise, first, in the seed of Abraham which is Israel, called to be "a kingdom of priests" unto the Lord (Ex. 19:6); second, in the seed of Abraham which is Jesus Christ, whom God raised up and sent as his servant "to bless you in turning every one of you from your wickedness" (Acts 3:26); and third, in the spiritual seed of Abraham to which belong all who are Christ's (Gal. 3:29), and who share Abraham's faith (Rom. 4:16), and who are called both to inherit and to be a blessing. This is no artificial sequence, but the beginning of a historical process by which God purposed to bring the blessing of salvation to the world. The admonition in Isaiah 51:2 has a religious relevance that includes us all, *if* we are men of faith like Abraham:

> "Look to Abraham your father
> and to Sarah who bore you;
> for when he was but one I called him,
> and I blessed him and made him many."

The covenant of blessing with Abraham is for the world; God so intended it, and He thus fulfilled it.

NOTES

[1] Sholem Asch, *The Prophet.* *Copyright* 1955 by Sholem Asch. New York: G. P. Putnam's Sons. p. 158.

[2] Franz Böhl, *op. cit.,* p. 6.

[3] Leonard Woolley, *op. cit.,* p. 142.

[4] *Ibid.,* p. 50.

[5] *Ibid.,* p. 50.

[6] *Ibid.,* p. 50.

[7] Edv. Wiren, *Når han öppnade boken.* Stockholm: Evangeliska Fosterlandsstiftelsens Bokförlag. 1946. p. 54.

[8] Edmond Jacob, *op. cit.,* p. 201.

[9] Franz Böhl, *op. cit.,* p. 42.

[10] Martin Luther, *Sämmtliche Schriften* edited by J. G. Walch. St. Louis: Concordia Publishing House. 1880-1910. Vol. I, p. 773.

[11] Herbert C. Alleman, *"The Book of Genesis,"* in *Old Testament Commentary* edited by H. C. Alleman and Elmer E. Flack. Philadelphia: Muhlenberg Press. 1948. p. 185.

[12] Nelson Glueck, *The Other Side of the Jordan.* New Haven: American Schools of Oriental Research. 1940. p. 6.

[13] From *The Westminster Historical Atlas to the Bible, op. cit.,* p. 5.

[14] Wilbur Smith, in *Christianity Today,* December 24, 1956.

[15] Artur Weiser, *op. cit.*

[16] Otto Eissfeldt, *Die Genesis der Genesis.* Tübingen: J. C. B. Mohr (Paul Siebeck). 1958. pp. 16-27.

[17] Gillis Gerleman, *op cit.,* p. 6.

[18] John Stirling, *The Bible for Today.* London and New York: Oxford University Press. 1941. p. 18.

[19] Herbert Alleman, *op. cit.,* p. 185.

[20] S. R. Driver, *Hebrew Tenses.* Oxford: Clarendon Press. 1892. p. 69.

[21] From: The Bible: a New Translation by James Moffatt. Copyright 1922, 1935 and 1950 by Harper & Brothers. Used by permission.

[22] Ed. Böhl, *Christologie des Alten Testaments.* Wien: Wilhelm Braumüller. 1882. p. 85.

[23] Willis J. Beecher, *op. cit.,* p. 178.

[24] From the *Old Testament,* Vol. I, in the translation of Monsignor Ronald Knox. Copyright 1948, Sheed & Ward, Inc., New York.

[25] *Bibeln, eller den Heliga Skrift.* Stockholm: Evangeliska Fosterlandsstiftelsens Bokförlag. 1917.

[26] Geerhardus Vos, *Biblical Theology.* Grand Rapids: Wm. B. Eerdmans Publishing Co. 1948. pp. 91-92.

[27] Otto Procksch, *"Genesis,"* in *Sellin's Kommentar zum A.T.* Leipzig: A. Deichert. 1924.

[28] *Ibid.*

[29] Sholem Asch, *op. cit.*

[30] John Stirling, *op. cit.,* p. 18.

[31] Artur Weiser, *op. cit.*

[32] S. R. Driver, *The Book of Genesis,* Westminster Commentaries. New York: Edwin S. Gorham. London: Methven & Co. 1905. pp. 407-409.

[32] H. Guthe, art, *"Israel," Encyclopedia Biblica.* New York: The Macmillan Company. 1903. Vol. II, p. 2221.

[34] From *The Westminster Dictionary of the Bible, op. cit.,* p. 287

[35] Herbert Alleman, *op. cit.,* p. 185.

[36] Paul Heinisch, *"Genesis,"* in *Die Heilige Schrift des A.T.* edited by Feldmann & Herkenne, Bonn: P. Hanstein. 1930.

[37] Otto Procksch, *op. cit.*

[38] H. E. Ryle, *op. cit.*

[39] Franz Böhl, *op. cit.*, p. 6.
[40] Otto Eissfeldt, *op. cit.*, p. 65.
[41] *Ibid.*
[42] John Stirling, *op. cit.*, p. 18.
[43] Ed. Böhl, *op. cit.*, p. 83.
[44] E. F. Kevan, "Genesis," *The New Bible Commentary*, edited by F. Davidson, A. M. Stibbs, and E. F. Kevan. Grand Rapids: Wm. B. Eerdmans Publishing Co. 1953. p. 88.
[45] Herbert C. Alleman, *op. cit.*, p. 191.
[46] H. E. Ryle, *op. cit.*
[47] Paul Heinisch, *op. cit.*
[48] S. Singer, quoted in *Pentateuch and Haftorahs*, edited by J. H. Hertz. New York: Oxford University Press. 1929. Vol. I, p. 114.
[49] Franz Delitzsch, *Messianic Prophecies, op. cit.*
[50] E. W. Hengstenberg, *Christology of the Old Testament*. Edingurgh: T. & T. Clark. 1854. Vol. I, pp. 44-45.
[51] Ed. Böhl, *op. cit.*, p. 88.
[52] E. W. Hengstenberg, *op. cit.*
[53] Ed.Böhl, *op. cit.*, p. 9.
[54] Herbert Alleman, *op cit.*, p. 185.

Chapter Five

THE PATRIARCHAL NARRATIVE ANALYZED

T HE TERMS OF THE CALL in Genesis 12:1-3 completely control the material to the end of the book. They cut across the lines and extend into all of the so-called sources of Genesis. They constitute an intricately-interwoven fabric, through which the component threads run in a significant pattern that unifies the narrative. We are reminded by this closely-knit pattern that the terms of the call are themselves also to be understood always as a unit; so that whenever one is mentioned, it represents the whole. A special thread that runs through the pattern is the repeated emphasis on the God who acts, making and renewing and confirming and bringing to remembrance the promise given, in order that He might keep alive the faith and hope and obedience which were essential to its ultimate fulfillment. Each incident, each experience, recorded in Genesis derives its ultimate significance from its relation to the call of Abraham and to the covenant with him. For the terms of the call are also the terms of a divine covenant with Abraham and his seed. This becomes evident as we trace the terms of the call through Genesis 12-50.

1

An outline may serve to illustrate the over-all pattern just mentioned. A more graphic form of illustration would be a diagram showing the actual intertwining of the four elements of the call in the Genesis narrative. We can only give a separate listing under each of the four items, with brief explanatory notes; but a little thoughtful imagination will detect the "weaving" into a unified pattern.

Separation

The command to leave one land for another involves, as we have seen, the principle of separation: not only separation *from,* which might be called redemption, but also separation *to*, which may be called consecration. Both aspects find frequent and significant illustration in Gen. 12-50.

1.   Chapter 12:1. Go from your country and kindred—to the land that I will show you. The initial command.

2.   Chapter 13:8-9, 11, 14. The separation from Lot. The covenant of blessing was to be with Abraham, not with Abraham and Lot.

3.   Chapter 14:18-20. Consecration to God Most High, expressed in the giving of a tenth to Melchizedek.

4.   Chapter 14:21-24. Separation from the king of Sodom, by not permitting himself to be "in debt" to him.

5.   Chapter 15:13-16. Prophetically: separation to God to be achieved by oppression in Egypt and by deliverance from Egypt.

6.   Chapter 17:1. A walk before the Lord, a life of consecration.

7.   Chapter 7:9-14, 22-27. Circumcision, a sign of keeping the covenant by a separated life.

8.   Chapter 18:19. Abraham chosen to keep the way of the Lord, consecrated to a life of righteousness and justice.

9.   Chapter 19:15, 29. Lot rescued from Sodom, because God remembered Abraham and the covenant with him.

10.   Chapter 21:10. Isaac, the heir of the promise of blessing, is separated from Ishmael.

11.   Chapter 22. The burnt offering: expressive of the entire self-dedication of the offerer to God. The obedience of Abraham: complete consecration to his God.

12.   Chapter 24:2-4. Separation from the Canaanites in the matter of choosing a wife for Isaac. Go to my kindred and take a wife for my son.

13.   Chapter 24:5-8. Yet, separation also from Abraham's kindred: for Isaac must not go back to his father's former home.

14.   Chapter 25:5-6. Separation of the children of Keturah from Isaac, the child of promise.

15.   Chapter 28:1-2. Separation from the Canaanites in the matter of choosing a wife for Jacob from his mother's kindred.

16.   Chapter 34:7. The reference to "folly in Israel" implies a violation of the principle of separation.

17.   Chapter 36:6. Esau separates from Jacob, to whom the promise belongs.

18. Chapter 48:15-16. Again, a walk before God, in consecration to Him, and a walk with God, led by Him.

In one way or another, the principle of separation is to the fore constantly. It is implicit in the entire narrative; it is explicit in almost every incident. It is not to be confused with moral perfection; it is rather the spirit of consecration to God Almighty who is perfect, and who acts in righteousness and love. It is summed up in the words, "Walk before me, and be blameless." To such a walk before God Abraham was called; to such a life he was asked to consecrate himself. So also his descendants, the people of Israel, were called to be "a holy nation" (Ex. 19:6), a people set apart to God. What that meant to them, and what it means to us, we shall see later; but we mark now how deeply rooted is this principle of separation even here in the book of Genesis, in the story of Abraham, and Isaac, and Jacob, in the covenant experience of the fathers.

The Promise of a Land

The promise of a land, specifically the land of Canaan, is renewed whenever there is danger of forgetting or of losing faith in the promise. In Abraham's own experience it is renewed at such significant moments as when he separates from Lot (chapter 13), and when he in faith "offers" Isaac as a burnt offering (chapter 22). It is often linked with Abraham's seed. Whenever Isaac or Jacob leave the "promised" land, or return to it, the promise is reaffirmed. It is especially prominent in the closing chapters of Genesis, as the family of Jacob moves to Egypt to become sojourners and slaves "in a land that is not theirs" (chapter 15:13). Here it is beautifully expressed not only in the form of divine promise, but in the form of human faith, which clings to the promise and acts upon it. It represents, as we have said, the hope of inheritance; an inheritance which stands as a symbol of every blessing. It is because of this symbolism that the correspondence and the connection between their hope of inheritance and ours is not superficial, but actual and real.

1. Chapter 12:1. The initial command to go to a land "that I will show you."

2. Chapter 12:7. The land identified and the promise given, "To your descendants I will give this land."

3. Chapter 13:14-17. The promise clarified and renewed after

the separation from Lot: "for all the land which you see I will give to you and to your descendants for ever."

4. Chapter 15:7. The promise again renewed: "I am the Lord who brought you from Ur of the Chaldeans, to give you this land to possess."

5. Chapter 15:18-21. A covenant made to confirm the promise: "To your descendants I give this land." The land described in terms of its present inhabitants.

6. Chapter 17:8. Another renewal of the promise: "And I will give to you, and to your descendants after you, the land of your sojournings, all the land of Canaan, for an everlasting possession; and I will be their God."

7. Chapter 23:17-20. The purchase of a burying place showing faith in the fulfillment of the promise.

8. Chapter 24:5-8. The promise motivates Abraham's instructions to his servant that he must not take Isaac away from the land, but rather bring his bride to him in the land.

9. Chapter 26:2-4. A reminder of the promise to Isaac as he leaves the land temporarily because of a famine. Purpose: to safeguard faith in its ultimate fulfillment.

10. Chapter 28:3-4. A prayer by Isaac that Jacob might one day take possession of the land, as a part of "the blessing of Abraham."

11. Chapter 28:13-14. The promise renewed to Jacob as he is about to leave the land for Haran.

12. Chapter 28:15. The added promise at Bethel: "I will bring you back to this land."

13. Chapter 31:3. The command to return to the land after twenty years in Haran.

14. Chapter 35:12. The promise renewed to Jacob after his return from Haran.

15. Chapter 46:1-4. The promise to Jacob as he leaves Canaan to go down to Egypt: "I will go down with you to Egypt, and I will also bring you up again."

16. Chapter 47:29-31. Jacob desires to be buried in Canaan, showing faith in the fulfillment of the promise.

17. Chapter 48:3-4. Jacob reminds Joseph of the promise of both a seed and a land.

18: Chapter 48:21. Jacob's encouragement to Joseph: "Behold, I am about to die, but God will be with you, and will bring you again to the land of your fathers."

19. Chapter 49: 29-32. The dying Jacob renews his request: "Bury me with my fathers . . . in the land of Canaan."

20. Chapter 50:24-26. Joseph's faith in the promise: "I am about to die; but God will visit you, and bring you up out of this land to the land which he swore to Abraham, to Isaac, and to Jacob." The dramatic sign of his faith: before dying and being embalmed and put in a coffin in Egypt, he gives instructions and takes an oath of the sons of Israel, saying, "God will visit you, and you shall carry up my bones from here."

The promise of a land is not something that is loosely tacked on to the Genesis narrative; it is an inextricable part of it, from beginning to end. It clearly belongs to the core of the tradition in the story of Abraham. The viewpoint is always that of a divine promise to be fulfilled in the future, as a part of the working out of God's total plan in the call of Abraham and in the making of a covenant with him.

The Promise of a Seed

The promise of a seed is frequently renewed and clarified in the unfolding faith-experience of Abraham. It is progressively made clear to the childless Abraham that the promise would not be fulfilled through a legal heir, such as his steward Eliezer (chapter 15); nor through Ishmael, the son of the slave woman, by whom Sarah hoped and schemed to obtain children (chapter 16); but through Isaac, as a true child of promise: "For in Isaac shall thy seed be called" (Gen. 21:12, ASV). There is in this divine election a strong hint of the spiritual aspects of the promised seed. The fact that the beginning of the fulfillment is in an individual, Isaac, may foreshadow that concentration of the seed in one of which Delitzsch speaks;[1] although it certainly does not exclude the plural concept of descendants. The number of the seed of Abraham is variously compared with the dust of the earth (13:16; 28:14), and the stars of heaven (15:5; 22:17), and the sand on the seashore (22:17). "The great nation" in the original promise to Abraham (12:2) is repeated in the promise to Jacob (46:3). In many places the promise of a seed intertwines with that of a land, as if to show the close relationship between them in the working out of the purpose of God revealed in the choice of Abraham to be a blessing. Though the main emphasis may seem to be on the external, material aspect of the seed as well as of the land, we have already seen how inadequate is any interpretation that omits the religious implications. The seed as well as the land is by divine intent related to, and symbolic of, the emerging Biblical concept of *a people of God,* called to inherit and to be a blessing.

1. Chapter 12:2. The initial promise: "I will make of you a great nation."

2. Chapter 12:7. The land of Canaan is promised to the seed of Abraham.

3. Chapter 13:15. The promise repeated: "For all the land which you see I will give to you and to your descendants for ever." The occasion is after the separation from Lot.

4. Chapter 13:16. The promise made more specific: "I will make your descendants as the dust of the earth; so that if one can count the dust of the earth, your descendants also can be counted."

5. Chapter 15:2-4. The promise made more specific at another point: "Your own son shall be your heir."

6. Chapter 15:5. The promise illustrated in terms of the stars of heaven: "So shall your descendants be." The reference in v. 4 is to an individual son, in v. 5 to many descendants. It is in this context that we have the significant declaration in v. 6: "And he believed the Lord; and he reckoned it to him as righteousness."

7. Chapter 15:13-16. The prediction: Your descendants shall be sojourners for 400 years in another land, and there suffer oppression; but God will deliver them and bless them: "afterward they shall come out with great possessions."

8. Chapter 16:1-6. The mistaken attempt by Sarah to get children by Hagar instead of waiting for God to fulfill His promise in His own way.

9. Chapter 16:10-11, 15. Ishmael also a part of Abraham's seed, in the sense of physical sonship, with this promise from God: "I will so greatly multiply your descendants that they cannot be numbered for multitude."

10. Chapter 17:2-6. The promise repeated to Abraham: "You shall be the father of a multitude of nations. . . . and kings shall come forth from you."

11. Chapter 17:7-8. The covenant with Abraham is also with his descendants, and includes a twofold promise of blessing: to give

the land of Canaan for a possession, and "to be God to you and to your descendants after you."

12. Chapter 17:9-14. Circumcision is enjoined upon the descendants of Abraham as a sign of the covenant with them.

13. Chapter 17:15-21. The promise made more specific at another point: "Sarah your wife shall bear you a son, and you shall call his name Isaac."

14. Chapter 18:9-15. The promise of a son to Sarah is renewed and confirmed.

15. Chapter 21:1-4. The child of promise is born, circumcised, and named Isaac.

16. Chapter 21:12. An indication of election and of vocation: "In Isaac shall thy seed be called."

17. Chapter 21:13. Ishmael also Abraham's seed, in the physical but not in the spiritual sense: separated from Isaac, the child of promise.

18. Chapter 22:15-18. The promise of blessing in the comprehensive sense of a blessing *to* and a blessing *through* Abraham is given to his seed. His descendants will be in number as the stars of heaven and as the sand on the seashore. The whole chapter centers around the child of promise.

19. Chapter 26:2-4. The promise renewed to Isaac: to multiply his descendants, and to give them the land, and to bless the nations of the earth through them.

20. Chapter 26:24. The promise again renewed to Isaac, on his return from Gerar: "Fear not, for I am with you and will bless you and multiply your descendants for my servant Abraham's sake."

21. Chapter 28:3-4. Isaac blesses Jacob before he leaves home; invoking the blessing of God Almighty upon him, that he might be fruitful and become "a company of peoples," and that he (and his descendants) may take possession of the land which God gave to Abraham.

22. Chapter 28:13-14. The promise renewed to Jacob at Bethel on his way to Haran: the land to be given to his descendants, who shall be like the dust of the earth in number and spread abroad in every direction, through whom also blessing shall come to all the families of the earth.

23. Chapter 35:9-12. The promise renewed to Jacob again on his return from Haran.

24. Chapter 46:3. Jacob assured that God will make of him a great nation in Egypt.

25. Chapter 46:8-27. The descendants of Israel, "the seed" of the future nation, that came into Egypt with Jacob: seventy in number. See Exodus 1:5.

26. Chapter 48:3-4. Jacob reminds Joseph of the twofold promise of seed and land.

27. Chapter 48:15-16. In blessing Joseph and his sons Jacob gives expression to this hope: "In them let my name be perpetuated, and the name of my fathers Abraham and Isaac; and let them grow into a multitude in the midst of the earth."

28. Chapter 49:1-28. Jacob's blessing on his sons (v.1), "the twelve tribes of Israel" (v.28).

It is evident that the promise of a seed, like that of a land, is woven into the very fabric of the Genesis narrative. It, too, belongs to the core of the tradition concerning Abraham and the divine covenant with him.

The Promise of a Blessing

We have said elsewhere that the promise of blessing to Abraham and his seed may have a temporal and material as well as a spiritual aspect. Both aspects are significantly present in Gen. 12-50. It is unlikely that the Patriarchs separated sharply between the two; for to them religion was not something *apart from life*, but *a part of life*. It is characteristic of the Old Testament attitude throughout that it regards man as "a living being" (Gen. 2:7; ASV, a living soul), who is both God related and earth related at all times. There is not the same sharp distinction as with us between secular and religious, or between the bodily and the spiritual, in the human life experience. Man has a spirit as well as a body; but the distinction between the two never becomes a cleavage: man remains fundamentally a whole, "a living being." The temporal blessings experienced by Abraham as a gift of God may, therefore, rightly be taken as a part of the fulfillment of the promise of blessing to him. What we need to bear in mind is that the temporal does not constitute the only blessing, or even the chief part of it. The principle so clearly stated in Deut. 8:3, that "man does not live by bread alone, but . . . by everything that proceeds out of the mouth of the Lord," was true even before it was formally proclaimed as truth; it inheres in the very nature of man as he is created. It would be presumptuous to deny to anyone who believes in "the living God," as Abraham did, some awareness of the spiritual blessing of God received by faith. To dare to believe in God is in itself a profound spiritual blessing. What we dare to assert, however, is that there was from the beginning *a symbolic relationship* between "the blessing of Abraham" (Gen. 28:4; Gal. 3:14) in the temporal and in the spiritual sense. There is a real, not an imaginary, connection between the blessings experienced by Abraham and "every spiritual blessing in the heavenly places" with which we have been blessed in Christ (Eph. 1:3). Both belong to "the saving acts of the Lord"; both reflect as in a mirror the same redemptive will of God. Let us not be misled at this crucial point by the fact that *we* are privileged to see with clearer vision and with deeper understanding the nature and the content of the blessing promised. There is an underlying unity between the blessing of Abraham, who lived 2000 years before the coming of Christ, and the blessing of Abraham that is ours who live 2000 years after His coming. The unifying factor is *the living God who acts* in relation to men with redemptive purpose. Abraham was a man who walked with God in the obedience of faith and experienced the blessing of such a faith-fellowship, even to the point of becoming uniquely known as the friend of God (Is. 41:8; James 2:23); he *obtained* a blessing in a true spiritual sense of the word, even as God also blessed him so that he became very rich "in cattle, in silver, and in gold" (Gen. 13:2). At the same time he was called to *be* a blessing. Of this promise of blessing *through* him, and through his seed, we shall say more later on. It should be noted even now, however, in connection with our analysis of the promise of blessing in Gen. 12-50, that we can by no stretch of the imagination account for *the sense of mission* in Israel on any other than a religious basis; here a materialistic interpretation which rules out the spiritual altogether is wholly inadequate.

By way of introduction to our outline of the promise of blessing in Genesis 12-50 let us quote again the initial promise as given to Abraham. "And I will make of you a great nation, and I will bless you, and make your name great, so that you will be a blessing. I will bless those who bless you, and him who curses you I will curse; and in you all the families of the earth will be blessed." (See footnote, RSV.)

1. Chapter 13:2. Indication of temporal blessing experienced by Abraham.

2. Chapter 14:13-16. Abraham "practices being a blessing" in the rescue of Lot.

3. Chapter 14:18-20. Abraham blessed by Melchizedek, priest of God Most High.

4. Chapter 15:1. Indication of spiritual blessing experienced by Abraham. God promises to be his shield and great reward: therefore, "Fear not."

5. Chapter 15: 6. Another indication of the experience of spiritual blessing: Abraham's faith reckoned to him as righteousness.

6. Chapter 17:7-8. God's promise to Abraham and to his seed that he will be "their God." This is the heart of the promise of blessing.

7. Chapter 18:17-19. Abraham reminded of the covenant of blessing, with emphasis on the spiritual: "For I have chosen him, that he may charge his children and his household after him to keep the way of the Lord by doing righteousness and justice; so that the Lord may bring to Abraham what he has promised."

8. Chapter 18:22-23. Abraham "practices being a blessing" in his intercession for Lot.

9. Chapter 21:22-23. Abimelech seeks a covenant with Abraham in recognition of God's blessing on him.

10. Chapter 22:8, 14. By faith Abraham experiences the truth that "the Lord will provide" the lamb for a burnt offering. This truth is at the heart of the blessing of Abraham as fulfilled in Christ.

11. Chapter 22:15-18. The promise reaffirmed, with an oath for confirmation: blessing on, but also in, "your seed"—"because you have obeyed my voice."

12. Chapter 24:12, 27. Eliezer's recognition of Yahve as the covenant God of his master Abraham: a recognition also of God's hesed, or steadfast love, and of his emeth, or faithfulness, towards Abraham.

13. Chapter 24:34-36. God's temporal blessings to Abraham declared by his servant.

14. Chapter 25:11. God blesses Isaac after his father's death.

15. Chapter 26:2-4. The promise reaffirmed to Isaac, including the vocation to be a blessing.

16. Chapter 26:23-25. The promise to bless Isaac reaffirmed on his return from Gerar.

17. Chapter 27. The birthright, including the blessing, given to Jacob.

18. Chapter 28:3-4. Isaac bespeaks "the blessing of Abraham" for Jacob and his seed.

19. Chapter 32:9-12. Jacob acknowledges God as the source of blessing to him in the past, and appeals to Him on the basis of His steadfast love and faithfulness to deliver him from the hand of his brother Esau.

20. Chapter 32:22-32. Jacob blessed at Penuel; a blessing with definite spiritual overtones.

21. Chapter 39.5. Potiphar's house blessed for Joseph's sake.

22. Chapter 39: 22-23. The blessing of God makes Joseph prosper even in prison.

23. Chapter 46:2-4. God's promise to go with Jacob to Egypt and to bring him up again; stressing God's presence, an encouragement to faith, and the very heart of the spiritual promise of blessing.

24. Chapter 47:27. Temporal blessing experienced by Israel in the land of Egypt.

25. Chapter 48:3-4. Jacob recalls to Joseph how God appeared to him at Luz and blessed him there.

26. Chapter 48:15-16. The confession by Jacob of a lifelong experience of divine blessing.

27. Chapter 48:20. In blessing Joseph's sons, Jacob says, "By you Israel will pronounce blessings, saying, 'God make you as Ephraim and as Manasseh.' " The verb is *barak;* the stem is the Piel, or intensive active; but the thought illustrates the reflexive aspect of the blessing.

28. Chapter 49: 28. Jacob's blessing on his sons, especially on Judah (chapter 49:8-12) and on Joseph (chapter 49:22-26).

The promise of blessing, like that of a land and a seed, belongs to the very core of the tradition concerning Abraham. The four elements in the call are like four strands of thread of different colors, which are tightly interwoven to make up the warp and the woof of a beautiful fabric: the command to "Go" is the warp, and the threefold promise of land, seed, and blessing is the woof, of the literary pattern of the patriarchal narrative. The biographical details are incidental to the saving acts of God. The correct principle of exegesis looks always for the central idea in the history, or in the prophecy, or whatever the form of the narrative may be. The central idea in the Genesis story is clearly God's covenant of blessing with Abraham.

A shorter but equally significant outline is that of ten passages that refer most directly to the climactic element in the call of Abraham, the promise of blessing. We consider them briefly in the order of their appearance.

1. Gen. 12:1-3. We quote again the initial promise of blessing as given to Abraham: "Go from your country and your kindred and your father's house to the land that I will show you. And I will make of you a great nation, and I will bless you, and make your name great, so that you will be a blessing. I will bless those who bless you, and him who curses you I will curse; and by you all the families of the earth will bless themselves [or, as in the RSV footnote, in you all the families of the earth will be blessed]."

2. Gen. 18:17-19. The promise is repeated to Abraham as God gives him the opportunity to be a blessing by his intercession for Sodom, and for Lot. The spirit of that prayer reflects the mind of God, who is the author of every blessing. It is significant that the fulfillment of the promise to Abraham and to his seed is here made contingent on their keeping the way of the Lord by doing righteousness and justice. "The Lord said, 'Shall I hide from Abraham what I am about to do, seeing that Abraham shall become a great and mighty nation, and all the nations of the earth shall bless themselves by him? No, for I have chosen him, that he may charge his children and his household after him to keep the way of the Lord by doing righteousness and justice; so that the Lord may bring to Abraham what he has promised him."

3. Gen. 22:15-18. The promise is reaffirmed to Abraham in recognition of his obedience of faith in the Moriah experience. It is also definitely linked with his seed, who should be blessed "with the faithful Abraham" (Gal. 3:9, ASV), and should with him become a source or a medium of blessing to the rest of mankind. "By myself I have sworn, says the Lord, because you have done this, and have not withheld your son, your only son, I will indeed bless you, and I will multiply your descendants as the stars of heaven and as the sand which is on the seashore. And your descendants shall possess the gate of their enemies, and by your descendants shall all the nations of the earth bless themselves, because you have obeyed my voice."

4. Gen. 26:2-5. The promise is renewed with Isaac, when he is forced by famine to leave the land and to dwell in Gerar. This is one of several passages where the promise of seed, land and blessing are

joined together as one. The backward reference to Abraham is significant; the promise was first given to him, and because of his obedience to God's will the promise is reaffirmed to his seed. "And the Lord appeared to him, and said, 'Do not go down to Egypt; dwell in the land of which I shall tell you. Sojourn in this land, and I will be with you, and will bless you; for to you and to your descendants I will give all these lands, and I will fulfill the oath which I swore to Abraham your father. I will multiply your descendants as the stars of heaven, and will give to your descendants all these lands; and by your descendants all the nations of the earth shall bless themselves: because Abraham obeyed my voice and kept my charge, my commandments, my statutes, and my laws."

5. Gen. 26:23-25. One facet of the promise is repeated to Isaac when he returns to the land after the famine. The significant reference to Abraham makes it clear that the whole promise is reaffirmed; the part stands for the whole. "And the Lord appeared to him the same night and said, 'I am the God of Abraham your father; fear not, for I am with you and will bless you and multiply your descendants for my servant Abraham's sake.' "

6. Gen. 28:3-4. When Jacob is forced to leave home because of his brother's anger, his father Isaac sends him away with his blessing. The blessing is in the form of a prayer that God might bless him and give him "the blessing of Abraham." This is the first and only time in the Old Testament that we find this significant phrase, which we meet again in the New Testament in Gal. 3:14: "God Almighty bless you and make you fruitful and multiply you, that you may become a company of peoples. May he give the blessing of Abraham to you and to your descendants with you, that you may take possession of the land of your sojournings which God gave to Abraham!"

7. Gen. 28:13-15. The promise is reaffirmed to Jacob in a dream at Bethel, as he is on his way to Haran. Once more there is a significant union of land, seed, and blessing in the renewal of the promise. "And behold, the Lord stood above it and said, 'I am the Lord, the God of Abraham your father and the God of Isaac; the land on which you lie I will give to you and to your descendants; and your descendants shall be like the dust of the earth, and you shall spread abroad to the west and to the east and to the north and to the south; and by you and your descendants shall all the families of the earth bless themselves. Behold, I am with you and will keep you wherever you go, and will

bring you back to this land; for I will not leave you until I have done that of which I have spoken to you."

8. Gen. 35:9-12. The promise is again reaffirmed to Jacob at Bethel on his return from twenty years in Paddan-aram. Though the special emphasis is on the seed and the land, this does not exclude the blessing of Abraham in the spiritual sense. The part stands for the whole. "And God said to him, 'I am God Almighty: be fruitful and multiply; a nation and a company of nations shall come from you, and kings shall spring from you. The land which I gave to Abraham and Isaac I will give to you, and I will give the land to your descendants after you."

9. Gen. 46:1-4. The promise to Jacob once more, this time at Beer-sheba, as he is leaving the land with his family on the way to Egypt. The seed and the land are in the foreground, but the purpose is to strengthen Jacob's faith in the fulfillment of the whole promise to Abraham. "And God spoke to Israel in visions of the night, and said, 'Jacob, Jacob.' And he said, 'Here am I.' Then he said, 'I am God, the God of your father; do not be afraid to go down to Egypt; for I will there make of you a great nation. I will go down with you to Egypt, and I will also bring you up again.'"

10. Gen. 48:15-16. There is a significant reminder of the blessing of Abraham in its totality in Jacob's blessing on Joseph and his sons. The faith-experience with God had been a blessing for Abraham, Isaac, and Jacob. It is Jacob's prayer that the same God would continue His blessing and fulfill His promises in the children who stood before him.

> "The God before whom my fathers Abraham and Isaac walked,
> the God who has led me all my life long to this day,
> the angel who has redeemed me from all evil, bless the lads;
> and in them let my name be perpetuated, and the name of my fathers Abraham and Isaac;
> and let them grow into a multitude in the midst of the earth."

In v. 20, though the main verb is active rather than reflexive, we have a clear case of what Procksch calls "ein Segenswunsch," a wish to share in the blessing of Joseph's sons.[2] The material aspect of the blessing is to the fore; but that does not exclude the spiritual aspect, which we have seen to be an essential part of the original promise of blessing as given to Abraham. It is only the momentary emphasis that shifts; the heart of the promise, and God's long-range purpose with it, remains the same. We cannot separate between the promise of blessing *to* and the promise of blessing *through* Abraham and his seed. We can be a blessing only as we receive from God; we receive blessing from God, so that we might be a blessing to others. That truth is deeply ingrained in the call of Abraham, and in the life story of the Patriarchs, even as it is in the history of Israel as God's chosen people, and in the Christian life experience today.

We note also how closely the promise of blessing is tied in with the promise of land and of the seed. The promise is reaffirmed on each occasion when the "seed," in the person of Isaac or Jacob, or in terms of Jacob's family, left or returned to the Promised Land. The inheritance of the land is an important preparatory part of the blessing. So is the development of the seed into a chosen people. Unless this preliminary fulfillment of the promise to Abraham be carefully safeguarded the divine mission of being a blessing to the nations could not be fulfilled.

3

There are three chapters in the story of Abraham that call for a closer examination. They are the chapters in which mention is made of *a covenant* of God with Abraham. What is the relationship between the terms of the call and the covenant? What is the added significance, if any, of the divine covenant with Abraham?

The three chapters that speak of the covenant are 15, 17, and 22. In terms of the documentary analysis of Genesis chapters 15 and 22 are usually assigned to J and chapter 17 to P. It is significant that *all four elements of the call* are represented *in each of the three chapters.* If there be two sources involved, there is a markable unity of tradition between them. In the Genesis arrangement of the material from these sources there is not only unity but a definite forward movement. Chapters 12, 15, 17, and 22 appear as four major incidents in Abraham's life, which are also successive steps in God's revelation of his will and purpose to him.

The first reference to a covenant with Abraham is in Gen. 15:18. This does not imply that there was no covenant relationship earlier, nor that this was a new or a second covenant with him. God made one covenant with Abraham. The contents or the terms of that covenant were stated in the call; as we see from the manner in which they are repeated and reaffirmed in significant connections in the following narrative. It is this one covenant which is the key to the explanation of the whole story of Abraham's life and of the divine communication with him; but there is progress in the unfolding of the full nature of the contents and of the significance of Abraham in relation to it. It is such a forward movement that makes chapter 15 so significant.

Genesis 15

Of the four terms of the call, two are easily discernible in chapter 15, the promise of a seed and the promise of a land. The chapter is constructed around them as an outline, leading up to the formal enactment of a covenant in v. 18, "To your descendants I [will] give this land." The element of blessing is present also, however, if we think of the blessing *to* Abraham; a temporal blessing in connection with the seed and the land, and a spiritual blessing as indicated by the promise in v. 1 and by the experience of Abraham in v. 6. The blessing *through* Abraham is not to the fore at the moment; the emphasis is on those things which must come first. It is impossible, however, to divorce the promise of the seed from the divine intent that Abraham was to be a blessing. The whole concept of a promised seed implies divine election, and hand in hand with election goes the divine intent which is expressed in mission. In the chapter before us the element of separation is not stressed, but it is involved in the prediction of the Egyptian sojourn when seen from the viewpoint of its purpose and of its result.

The chapter is introduced by a great word of the Lord to Abraham: "Fear not, Abram, I am your shield; your reward shall be very great" (v. 1). The purpose is evidently the confirmation of faith; for faith is the antithesis of fear, and the "fear not" of God is ever designed to create faith. The basis for this fearless faith lies in what God is willing to be for those who believe in Him; and Abraham was one who believed. "I am your shield" is a beautiful way of saying that "I am your protector or defender." I am your exceeding great reward" (see ASV) is a vivid way of saying that God is the source of all true joy and satisfaction, the giver of the promise of blessing and of every good gift; for the promised blessing includes this fellowship with God by faith which is a reward in itself, and which brings other blessings with it. The thought is essentially the same as in Gen. 17:7, 8, "I will be their God." It links up eventually with the prophetic message of Immanuel, God with us (Is. 7:14); and this in turn with the gospel message of the Word of God which "became flesh and dwelt among us, full of grace and truth" (Jn. 1:14). We do not mean to say that the Genesis passage is as clearly formulated or as far advanced as the Isaiah prophecy and the New Testament gospel; but it does express the same fundamental truth of the blessedness of the presence of God in human lives. How general, and yet how specific, is the word of God to Abraham! How rich and relevant it is as an assurance for us even today! "Do not fear, only believe" (Mk. 5:36).

Yet the life of faith may still have its problems. It is not easy to resolve the tension between a walk by faith and the natural human desire to walk by sight. In Abraham's case it involved the seeming contradiction between the divine promise of a seed and his own continuing childlessness. How was the promise to be fulfilled? Did God perhaps intend that Eliezer, Abraham's servant who was set over his household as a steward, should be his heir, and heir also of the promise of blessing? The tone of the question is not sceptical. It is the question of *faith seeking guidance*, that it may know how to act. Abraham wanted to know just what God meant by the promise of a seed, so that he could act accordingly.

In reply, the promise given in the call is made more specific with respect to the seed, as had already been done in regard to the land. This gradual clarification of the promise is characteristic of the Genesis narrative and seems to reflect an actual growing experience; for life is like that, and God deals with men on the human level, within the framework of a genuine human experience. It was made clear to Abraham that it was a son of his own flesh and blood, not a servant, who should be the seed and the heir of the promised blessing. For Abraham that cleared the point that puzzled his faith. There were other points that had to be clarified later; for example, that the son to be born should be a child of Sarah as well as of Abraham, and not the son of the slave woman Hagar: and that "in Isaac shall thy seed be called" (21:12, ASV). For the moment it was sufficient for Abraham to know that "this man (Eliezer) shall not be your heir; your own son shall be your heir" (v. 4). With this clarification went a reaffirmation of the promise of a seed so numerous as to make it almost numberless. In chapter 13:16 the comparison was with the dust of the earth. Here it is with the stars of heaven. The emphasis is on the collective aspect of the seed, and on the physical rather than on the spiritual descendants of Abraham.

How fully Abraham understood what this promise of a seed ultimately included, we do not know. It did include Christ, as Paul says in Gal. 3:16. That does not mean that it was a direct and exclusive reference to Christ. Christ is included in the seed, and in Christ the seed is fully realized; but in the beginning the promise moves on this collective, and historically unfolding, basis. In its spiritual aspects it might seem to be a prophetic type of the people of God, they who are Christ's (Gal. 3:29), rather than of the Christ himself (Gal. 3:16). If we believe, however, that the New Testament in some real sense fulfills the Old, we cannot escape the conviction that Christ is at the center of every divine promise that concerns God's people; and that is true of the promise to Abraham. However enigmatic the form of the promise may be, the divine intent with it is clarified by redemptive history. The beginning and the end do not contradict each other. The fact that at a certain stage we see only the husk does not deny the existence of the kernel of wheat within. That is why faith in the Lord who gives the promise, and who knows what he intends by it, *can be saving faith*, even when the human insight must wait for God to act as His own interpreter and to make the promise plain.

According to v. 6 Abraham responded to the renewed promise with renewed faith. "And he believed the Lord; and he reckoned it to him as righteousness." This prophetic interpretation of the experience of Abraham represents one of the high points in Old Testament religion. There is no good reason for doubting that it was a real experience. Abraham believed in the Lord; he trusted in Him. In all of Scripture he stands out as the pre-eminent example of a true man of faith. How much he understood of what God had in mind to do is not as important as this, that he believed in God on the basis of what God had done, and he believed His word of promise. "He was ready to wait God's time, without doubting God's truth. That is the mark of true faith—steadfast trust in God, despite darkness and disappointment, and despite the fact that circumstances all point in the opposite direction."[3] By such a faith man is justified; or in the expressive language of v. 6, "he reckoned it to him as righteousness." According to Moffatt, "Abram believed the Eternal, who counted his trust as real religion."[4] The Douay version, "Abraham believed God, and it was reputed to him for justice," is hopelessly inadequate; because the change of the verb in the last clause from active to passive obscures the Hebrew emphasis on God as the active agent, and because justice is not an equivalent of righteousness.[5] God *reckons* faith as righteousness. It does not at all imply that there is something meritorious about faith itself, but only this, that God seeks from man the response of faith and chooses to reckon it as righteousness. New Testament conscious as we are, we instinctively ask, "Apart from Christ?" No; for whether Abraham fully understood it or not Christ was included by divine intent in the promise of a seed, the promise which Abraham believed; and when Abraham believed "that God was able to do what he had promised" (Rom. 4:21), we may rightly say that he believed also in Christ, through whom the fullness of the blessing should come to all mankind. There can be true faith without perfect knowledge; but true faith must be ready to act on the basis of the knowledge that it has. Such a faith Abraham had: both a quiet confidence in God and a dynamic readiness to obey His will; and it qualified him to become "the father of all who believe" (Rom. 4:11). "We are not merely told that Abram believed the testimony of him who promised," says Franz Delitzsch, "but that he relied upon his person, and believingly rested in or upon him."[6] This faith the Lord reckoned to him as righteousness and confirmed by making a covenant with him.

For the first part of the chapter may not be arbitrarily separated from the latter part, which speaks of the making of a covenant. The chapter as it stands is a literary unit, with a natural sequence of thought. This sequence is not disturbed by the change to the vision form of revelation from v. 12 on. The new light shed on the promise of a seed and of a blessing in vv. 1-6 prepares the way for a new emphasis on the seed and the land in vv. 7-21. The divine act which reckons faith as righteousness is closely related to the divine act in making a covenant. Delitzsch sees in Abraham's readiness to prepare a sacrifice as commanded by God "a practical proof" that he believed, and in the symbolic divine action related to the sacrifice "a practical declaration" that he reckoned this faith to Abraham as righteousness. Such an interpretation seems to be true to the spirit and intent of the chapter.[7] The covenant is clearly unilateral in origin; it is made by God to confirm a promise, and Abraham can make it mutual only by the response of faith. The covenant is a renewal of the promise, an added assurance that the divine promise stands firm. The promise of the land as an inheritance was true, even though the fulfillment would not come until after a severe testing of faith; for Abraham's descendants must spend 400 years as sojourners and slaves "in a land that is not theirs" (v. 13). The covenant, however, is sure: "To your descendants I give this land" (v. 18). The land is in the foreground of the promise at the moment, together with the seed in the sense of the people of Israel (v. 18) and the material side of the blessing (v. 14); for these must come first in the working out of the divine purpose of blessing for the world, and they are a concrete symbol of greater blessing to come. We bear in mind always that beneath the material present aspect there is a deeper spiritual significance, which finds its fulfillment not in the history of Israel alone, but in the New Testament covenant, and in the history of the Christian church, and in the possession finally of heaven as our homeland. (See Heb. 11:13-16.) There is in the blessing of Abraham a double emphasis, both true; the one like a seedling, from which shall grow the other, a mighty fruit-bearing tree. The covenant to give the land is a guarantee of God's faithfulness to perform the whole promise, in all its far-reaching implications which bring us finally to Jesus Christ as the seed of Abraham and the source of every blessing.

The formal side of the covenant in chapter 15 may illustrate one way in which human covenants were made. Some scholars believe it to be the oldest form. The Hebrew verb used with berith is *karath*, meaning "to cut"; so that the literal translation would be, "the Lord cut a covenant with Abram." The covenant here, however, is not strictly a covenant by sacrifice (see Ps. 50:5); for the slain animals were not placed on an altar and consumed by fire. It is commonly believed that the parties to a human covenant enacted in this way passed between the parts of the slain animals and invoked upon themselves a like fate (that is, death) if they should prove guilty of breaking the covenant. In Abraham's vision God accommodates himself to this human form of covenant making; with this conspicuous difference, that He alone (as represented by the symbol of fire) passed between the pieces. This harmonizes with Begrich's contention that *berith* originally always denoted a relationship between two unequal parties wherein one who is mightier guarantees to one who is not mighty a covenant relationship; a relationship in which only the former is bound by oath to keep the covenant, whereas the latter is completely passive, as one who receives.[8] Whether we agree with Begrich or with those who hold that *berith* originally represented a reciprocal relationship, with mutual rights and privileges, there can be no doubt that the covenant in Gen. 15 is unilateral in form. It is a divine promise to be believed, and a covenant by which God binds himself and gives Abraham a claim upon Him. To the objection that self-imprecation seems out of question when it is the Lord who binds himself by a covenant Delitzsch rightly replies, "But it is just this which is essential in this custom, and that this was the case in Israel also is shown by Jer. 34:18, where Jahveh gives this reference to the trangression of the covenant. The passing of Jahveh between the pieces is an act of deepest condescension, to the same effect as his elsewhere swearing by himself, Gen. 22:16, or by his life, Deut. 32:40, or still more anthropomorphically by his soul, Amos 6:8; Jer. 51:14."[9]

Genesis 17

According to the documentary analysis of Genesis, chapter 17 belongs to the priestly source known as P. If this be correct, it is highly significant that we find the same basic outline in terms of the four elements of the call as in chapter 15, which is said to belong to J. The two sources do not contradict but rather supplement each other. "Both sources," as Alleman has said, "give a necessary element of the full account. . . . This is not a renewal of the covenant, but a parallel account."[10] The present literary structure of Genesis, however, suggests a forward movement between the two chapters; so that while chapter 17 does not refer to a new covenant with Abraham, it does shed new light on a covenant already made. The new emphasis on circumcision as a sign of the covenant clarifies the original emphasis on *separation* in the call. It does not change the substance of the covenant or, if we prefer, of the tradition concerning the covenant.

The chapter begins with another great word of the Lord, "I am God Almighty; walk before me, and be blameless." This is the same principle of consecration as we have seen to be involved in the call of Abraham from the beginning. In terms of the covenant with Abraham, however, it marks a new and stronger emphasis on the human response to the divine covenant. For though the covenant originates as a sovereign disposition of the divine will, and is, therefore, with respect to its origin unilateral, it seeks always a certain response from man which in effect makes it a mutual agreement. One-sided in origin, the divine covenant is designed to become reciprocal in experience: a covenant on God's terms, but binding on both parties.

For what response does God rightly look in order to seal the covenant on man's part? If the covenant be a covenant of promise, as it was with Abraham, he looks for *faith*. That is clear from chapter 15:6. If the covenant be also a covenant of mission, and it was with Abraham, he looks for *obedience* in a walk before Him. That we see from chapter 17:1. Putting the two together, we may say that God looks for the attitude of the obedience of faith (see Rom. 1:4). This is the proper response to the divine covenant always. In terms of the original call of Abraham, the call to be a blessing, the response sought is that of the separated or consecrated life. It is this aspect of the call and of the covenant that is to the fore in chapter 17 in the sign of circumcision.

The keynote is struck in v. 1, "Walk before me, and be blameless"; but before this human side of the covenant is stressed further, God reaffirms his own gracious purpose and promises, with some important additions in the way of clarification. The unified structure of the chapter makes it clear that the covenant of which it speaks is more than a covenant of circumcision. It is a covenant with the same four basic terms which we have seen in chapters 12 and 15. Only the point of emphasis is different.

The first reference to covenant is linked with the promise of a seed. "And I will make my covenant between me and you, and will multiply you exceedingly" (v. 2). We are on familiar ground so far. This is the promise of a seed that should be numerous as the stars of heaven and as the dust of the earth. The new illustration is that Abraham shall become "the father of a multitude of nations" (v. 4). The reference to earthly nations that claim Abraham as ancestor is obvious; in this earthly or physical sense it was literally true. In the light of redemptive history, and on the basis of New Testament interpretation (see Rom. 4:16, 17), we see that it has also a spiritual reference; it is a promise that is spiritually as well as physically fulfilled. Therefore we watch for clarification of the promise in the progressive self-revelation of God as to His purpose in making it.

The next reference to covenant is more comprehensive, and reaffirms the threefold promise of a seed, a land, and a blessing. "And I will establish my covenant between me and you and your descendants after you throughout their generations for an everlasting covenant, to be God to you and to your descendants after you. And I will give to you, and to your descendants after you, the land of your sojournings, all the land of Canaan, for an everlasting possession; and I will be their God" (vv. 7, 8). The promise of a land is to Abraham and to his descendants after him (it is so stated three times). The land that is promised them is Canaan; the promise had a geographical aspect that was literally fulfilled. In the light of redemptive history we see that it also had a spiritual reference, as the symbol of a hope of inheritance that cannot be satisfied with any mere earthly possession. Such is certainly the interpretation of the writer of the Epistle to the Hebrews (11:13-16). The pledge of Canaan as an earthly possession to Abraham and his seed is important. In the light of the total Biblical witness, however, it is only preparatory in purpose in relation to the divine promise of a heavenly possession for those who are the seed of Abraham because they share his faith. The promise in Gen. 17:7-8 is not without spiritual emphasis, as we see from the twice-repeated promise to be their God. This is the beginning of the experience of blessing as an experience not only of material prosperity but of religious fellowship with the living God. The later promise of Immanuel, God with us, and the fulfillment of that promise in the unique event of the Incarnation, and the living presence of God in Christ with His believing people, only carries through to the ultimate goal of the covenant in this matter of divine fellowship with His people. The chief thought in the whole covenant may be said to be this assurance and this experience, "I will be their God." With this faith-experience Abraham was equipped and qualified to be a blessing. Within this promise, "to be God to you and to your descendants after you," lies hidden the whole mystery of the gospel.

In connection with the third reference to covenant there is a new emphasis on the principle of separation, or on what God expected of Abraham in response to the covenant made with him. The theme of the chapter is restated in v. 9, "As for you, you shall keep my covenant, you and your descendants after you throughout their generations"; for there is an obvious parallelism between "walk before me" in v. 1 and "you shall keep my covenant" in v. 9. The natural impression is that both refer to a way of life. The thought is closely akin to the New Testament concept of a walk in the newness of life. The primary emphasis in v. 1, if we may judge by the use of such language elsewhere, is spiritual and ethical rather than ritual or ceremonial: it is the summons to a life in the obedience of faith. At first glance it may seem otherwise in vv. 9-14, for here the keeping of the covenant is definitely connected with the rite of circumcision. Circumcision was indeed a ritual mark of the covenant, but it was also a spiritual symbol. The real separation at which the covenant with Abraham aimed was spiritual (faith) and moral (obedience). To these requirements God added circumcision as an external sign of their status as a religiously separated people. It was to be the mark of a people in covenant with the Lord; a sign of their covenant relation and a constant reminder in their flesh of their covenant obligations. Circumcision was not an uncommon practice among Semites in antiquity. It was seemingly practiced even among the Egyptians, though for other reasons than indicated for the family of Abraham in Gen. 17. God selected a rite already known to be a sign of covenant position and of covenant duty. If the sequence of the Biblical narrative means anything, it would seem to represent what we call sanctification, or the separated life, the consecrated obedience of the believer; for in Abraham's experience it came after the faith that was reckoned to him as righteousness. Paul in Rom. 4, confirms this spiritual interpretation of circumcision in Abraham's life as "a sign or seal" of the righteousness of faith. The Apology for the Augsburg Confession speaks at length of circumcision and, in agreement with Paul, classifies it under "works," the outward evidence of the inward attitude of faith.[11] It is interesting, and perhaps significant, that there is little emphasis on circumcision in the Priestly Code. It is given as a commandment only in Lev. 12:3. In Deut. 10:16 the commandment is given a spiritual application, "Circumcise therefore the foreskin of your heart, and be no longer stubborn." According to Gen. 17 circumcision was the sign of the covenant with Abraham, which was essentially a covenant of promise. The sign of the Mosaic covenant at Sinai was the sabbath (see Ex. 31:16). Circumcision later became almost identical with the requirement of keeping the Mosaic Law (see Acts 15; Gal. 2); but in the original appointment, if we may believe the Book of Genesis, which has most to say about circumcision, it was simply a sign or seal of consecration to God in true faith and in dedication of life. Such is also the prophetic interpretation of it, as we see from Jer. 4:4,

> "Circumcise yourselves to the Lord,
>   remove the foreskin of your hearts,
>   O men of Judah and inhabitants of Jerusalem."

In Abraham's experience the place of circumcision was *after faith* in the promise given to him. He was asked to seal his faith by his obedience to the law of circumcision, in order to show thereby his willingness to be separated unto the Lord and to live in accordance with the covenant. We should remember that God's new covenant of grace in Jesus Christ also calls for separation, from sin and from the world, unto God, in true sanctification as a fruit of justification. Paul is quite right in saying that the covenant of blessing with Abraham reveals an experience of faith and obedience, of promise and outward commandment, in that order—a genuine spiritual experience.

From the formal side the references to a covenant or berith in this chapter are sightly different from those in chapter 15. Nevertheless it is the same covenant, with the same basic terms. We must not infer from the English translation of v. 2, "I will make my covenant between me and you," that this is either a new covenant or a covenant to be made in the future. The Hebrew imperfect can also be translated as a present, "I make," or "I am making." The emphasis is on the covenant as being *continually* affirmed. See v. 4, where we have a nominal sentence, "My covenant is with you." The Hebrew verb in v. 2 *is nathan,* with the basic meaning of *giving,* instead of *karath* as in chapter 15. In v. 7 the Hebrew has the causative form of the verb *qum,* which means to *set* or to *establish.* The thought of a continuing or an enduring covenant is discernible in the verb as well as in the accompanying phrase *berith olam,* an everlasting covenant. The primary meaning of the word *olam* is that of "indefinite time of long duration" rather than "never ending time"; but the phrase does stress the divine faithfulness to the covenant purpose. The command, "You shall keep my covenant," points to the human response to the covenant, of which circumcision is the outward symbol or sign. The purpose of the sign was partly as a reminder to the seed of Abraham that they were the covenant people of God, in order thereby to strengthen their faith and to challenge their obedience. "So shall my covenant be in your flesh an everlasting covenant" (v. 13). The seriousness of the demand for separation to the Lord can be seen from v. 14: the man who is not circumcised "has broken my covenant" and "shall be cut off from his people." Whether this implies a sentence of excommunication or of death is unclear. It is interpreting the verse too narrowly, however, to conclude that it has only a ritual significance. God's real concern is expressed in v. 1, "Walk before me, and be blameless." The same ready obedience of faith on the part of Abraham is seen here as in chapter 12:4 and in chapter 15:10. "Then Abraham took Ishmael his son and all the slaves born in his house or bought with his money, every male among the men of Abraham's house, and he circumcised the flesh of their foreskins that very day, as God had said to him. . . . That very day Abraham and his son Ishmael were circumcised; and all the men of his house, . . . were circumcised with him" (vv. 23, 26, 27).

Genesis 22

Ishmael, as the seed of Abraham according to the flesh, was included in the covenant of circumcision; but the Genesis narrative distinguishes carefully between him and Isaac in relation to God's ultimate purpose with the promise of a seed. This distinction comes to the fore in chapters 21 and 22, which relate in a special way to Isaac as the child of promise (see 21:12). The word *berith* or covenant does not occur in these chapters, except in 21:27 where we are told that Abraham and Abimelech made a covenant with one another; but the oath of God in chapter 22:16 singles out one unique feature often associated with the divine covenant. See, for example, the parallelism in Ps. 105: 9,

> "the covenant which he made with Abraham,
> his sworn promise to Isaac."

The four distinctive terms of the call are all present in chapter 22, as we have seen them to be in chapters 12, 15, and 17. At the same time there is something significantly new in the way of clarification.

The theme of chapter 21 is the birth of Isaac, the child of promise. It must have been a wonderful event, a glorious experience for Abraham as the recipient of the covenant promise of a seed; and yet the Bible narrative does not dwell upon it at any great length. Of the three events recorded in the chapter, all covenant related, the birth story is told in the fewest words. We may recall that it did not require many words for the evangelists to record the birth of Jesus either! The birth of Isaac marked the beginning of the fulfillment of the promise of a seed. The writer's concern seems to be to present the event as a fulfillment of promise and as a realization of faith: "The Lord visited Sarah *as he had said,* and the Lord did to Sarah *as he had promised.* And Sarah conceived, and bore Abraham a son in his old age *at the time of which God had spoken to him*" (21:1-2) [italics the author's]. The primary emphasis is on God's word and activity in the matter; Abraham's response in the obedience of faith, with respect to the circumcision of the child, is significant, but nevertheless secondary. The same is true in the tangled skein of resentment, jealousy, and injustice on the part of Sarah, and of reluctance, grief, and helpless acquiescence on the part of Abraham, in the casting out of Hagar and Ishmael. It is not the ethical aspect of this story that commends it to us, as if it were meant to be our example; but the story is relevant, because we hear in it "the wingstrokes of a great happening or event," and through it we catch a glimpse of the manner of the fulfillment of that which *God had promised,* and was even now moving to perform. The key verse is 21:12b, the word of God to Abraham, "For through Isaac shall your descendants be named." It was through Isaac that "the blessing of Abraham" in its deep inner sense should be mediated to the nations; it was to him that God purposed to entrust the vocation of being a blessing. This divine purpose must be accomplished, whether with man's co-operation and help or in spite of man's foolishness and sin. God's hands are clean, even when He must resort to drastic measures to safeguard His own covenant purpose from the results of human sin, impatience, and unbelief. This is the lesson of Gen. 21; but we bear in mind *that God seeks always* the faith which co-operates with His purpose and furthers it, because it is obedient to His will. In the long run His covenant of blessing requires men who are willing to walk before him, in faith that trusts and in obedience that acts according to His will. In comparison with others, Abraham was such a man; but he, too, had his moments of weakness. The story of Abraham is not that of a perfect man, but of a gracious God, who seeks in every way to strengthen Abraham's faith in the covenant of promise so closely linked with the birth of the child Isaac.

It is this interplay between the divine covenant purpose and the human faith response that is so important in a right interpretation of Gen. 22 as an experience of the man Abraham. The keynote is sounded at the very outset of the chapter: "After these things God tested Abraham." The birth of the child of promise after a long time of waiting is followed by the test of faith and obedience in the command to offer him again to God as a burnt offering!

We move quickly to the heart of the matter, the nature of the test. The time is indefinite, and unimportant, except that Isaac was seemingly old enough to understand what went on. His attitude, therefore, as well as his father's, must receive consideration in reading the story. The Hebrew verb *nasah* can be translated as "tested" or as "tempted," depending on the context; here it is clearly a case of testing, for God never tempts men. (See James 1:13, the definite formulation of a truth implied in all of Biblical theology.) He does, however, prove or test them. He tested Abraham. We do not know just how God gave the command or put the thought in his mind, but Abraham knew it to be from God. It has been suggested that Abraham simply faced with convicting honesty the question of whether he was ready to give as much to his God as did some of his neighbors who practiced child-sacrifice to their gods. What is the price of true religious consecration, the ultimate in dedication to God? We do not deny that something akin to this question may be involved in the incident before us; but if we take the witness of Gen. 22 seriously, there is more involved than this.

What was the exact nature of the test that confronted Abraham? Two things were involved.

The first was his love for his son, his natural parental feeling and affection. The wording of the divine command in v. 2 seems to play upon that string: "Take your son, your only son Isaac, whom you love, and go to the land of Moriah, and offer him there as a burnt offering upon one of the mountains of which I shall tell you." The sacrifice asked for was that of a beloved and only son (Isaac); the other son (Ishmael) had been sent away under the most painful circumstances of finality. Was Abraham's devotion to his God such that he was prepared to give such a supreme sacrifice? The test that confronted him was strangely similar to that laid down by Jesus in His instructions to His disciples as He sent them forth to preach: "He who loves son or daughter more than me is not worthy of me" (Mt. 10:37). Would he fail or pass the test of such supreme devotion?

The second was his faith in God's covenant promise of blessing, his spiritual hopes, as they were expressed in the promise of a seed through which blessing should come to all men. The very covenant of God seemed at stake; for had not God said, "In Isaac shall thy seed be called" (21:12)? This beloved and only son was also the son of promise, given as by a miracle, and the heir of the promise, the medium of divine blessing. Would not the promise perish with the child? Was Abraham's faith in his God such that he was prepared to trust Him even when his tired mind gave up all attempt to understand? Once more there is a strange similarity to a word of Jesus, spoken to his disciple Thomas, "Blessed are those who have not seen and yet believe." (Jn. 20:29). Would Abraham fail or pass this searching test of his faith?

"We should fear, love, and trust God above all things," says Martin Luther in his Small Catechism, echoing the words of both the Old Testament and the New.[12] Abraham stood the test in obedience and faith. He feared God in the right sense of the word (v. 12). Hebrews 11:19 stresses his faith. Gen. 22:18 stresses his obedience. We have a right to stress both, or the combination of the two in the obedience of faith. On this occasion, at least, it is not too much to say of him that he acted according to the great commandment later given to Israel, "Hear, O Israel: The Lord our God is one Lord; and you shall love the Lord your God with all your heart, and with all your soul, and with all your might" (Deut. 6:4, 5). He passed the test of faith and devotion with flying colors! God is witness.

There is something greater and more wonderful in this chapter, however, than Abraham's remarkable faith. The whole experience led to a signal lesson in relation to the covenant and to the way of salvation.

It begins with the burnt offering (the Hebrew *olah*). There was nothing new in the thought of bringing a burnt offering to God. It was an ancient form of sacrifice with which Abraham may have been perfectly familiar. It was sometimes called a "whole burnt offering," because all of the sacrificial animal was consumed by fire on the altar. There is a natural symbolism with every kind of sacrifice; and if, as A. B. Davidson suggests, the essential idea of all sacrifice is that of "a *gift* or offering to God,"[13] the symbolism of the burnt offering is not difficult to see. It signified "the entire self-dedication of the offerer to God."[14] It expressed "the ascent of the whole soul of man in worship."[15] Such self-dedication, such wholehearted worship, should certainly characterize the response of man to a divine covenant of blessing such as God made with Abraham. God asks for nothing less than my life, my all. Such was the symbolism of the burnt offering; and symbolism in worship without some corresponding reality in life is meaningless. How wholehearted was Abraham's devotion to God?

The test, as we have seen, lay just in this: Was he willing to give *his all* to God?

But in this case it was Isaac's life, not his own, that Abraham was asked to offer. That suggests another aspect of the burnt offering, and indeed of every form of sacrifice to God. Instead of actually giving his own life, the worshiper substituted something that represented him, such as the sacrificial animal. It may be said that in so doing he acted in the belief that this substitution was acceptable, either by divine permission or by divine provision. In v. 8 Abraham alludes to such a divine provision when he answers Isaac's question, "Where is the lamb for a burnt offering?" by saying, "God will provide himself the lamb for a burnt offering." There is nothing necessarily new or unique in such a faith: it inheres in every sacrifice where man brings a substitute gift for himself to the altar of God; but what is significant in this instance is that, as far as Abraham knew, Isaac was the burnt offering that God would provide. To the father it must have seemed like giving himself in giving his son; but he seems to have been ready for so great a sacrifice. He acknowledged by his act that God had a right to all, and that he was ready to give his all to God.

Then came the moment when God stopped him in the very act of beginning to make the required sacrifice. We are told nothing about Abraham's emotional response; we can imagine that it must have been an overwhelming surge of happiness and thankfulness and love! But we are told in vv. 13 and 14 of his religious response, and it reveals that he had learned a great religious truth in a far deeper sense than he had known it hitherto. Through the ram caught in the thicket, which he now offered as a burnt offering instead of his son, he learned in a new way the truth of "Jehovah-jireth" (v. 14, ASV), "The Lord will provide" (RSV). Here we catch a definite glimpse, not only of the truth of vicarious sacrifice, but of the even more fundamental truth of a gracious divine provision of the sacrifice that becomes our acceptable offering. How closely it is all related to the unfolding covenant of blessing; for this covenant is the redemptive covenant of God, which is ultimately fulfilled in Christ; and even here in the Abraham story it is seen to be related to, if not rooted in, this truth that God himself will provide the lamb for a burnt offering. We need not claim for Abraham the same clear vision of the cross of Christ that is ours, in order to recognize the unifying truth of divine grace in his experience and in ours. "On the mount of the Lord it shall be provided!" Such is the message of the gospel still.

It may be that through this experience Abraham learned another lesson, a vivid object lesson, that God does not require nor desire "human sacrifices." There are some scholars who stress this as if it were the chief point of religious relevance in the story in Gen. 22. That is wide of the mark, and misses the basic significance of the covenant in the life of Abraham; but there does seem to be a definite rejection of the common heathenish practice of child sacrifice. The strong renunciation of this vicious practice by the prophets in times of religious apostasy reflects the spirit of the Biblical religion from the beginning. See Mic. 6:6-8; Jer. 7:30, 31; 2 Kings 21:6. Child sacrifice was never a divine requirement; but it may have been one purpose with the dramatic experience of Abraham in relation to his son to indicate an emphatic rejection of the widely prevailing practice. It was not the only purpose, however; nor, if we may trust the witness of the story as we have it, the primary purpose. Its real relevance is much more definitely connected with the religious significance of the covenant of blessing with Abraham.

The reward for Abraham's faith and obedience is a renewal of the promise of blessing. It is now confirmed by an oath, "By myself I have sworn, says the Lord, because you have done this, and have not withheld your son, your only son, I will indeed bless you, and I will multiply your descendants as the stars of heaven and as the sand which is on the seashore. And your descendants shall possess the gate of their enemies, and by your descendants shall all the nations of the earth bless themselves (or, be blessed)" (vv. 16-18). By this declaration the whole chapter is related to the covenant. It is a renewal or a reaffirmation of the covenant, but at the same time there is progress within the covenant revelation. The promise of blessing is clarified once more by being connected definitely with the seed, "in thy seed shall all the nations of the earth be blessed" (v. 18, ASV). In the light of the context there can be little doubt that Isaac, the child of promise so wonderfully "sacrificed" and yet "spared," is the point of departure for this new reference to Abraham's seed; "for in Isaac shall thy seed be called" (21:12, ASV). It is not necessary to choose between the singular reference to Isaac and a plural reference to his descendants; both are included in the promise of blessing. Included also is a final fulfillment in Christ, who "redeemed us" in order that "in Christ Jesus the blessing of Abraham might come upon the Gentiles" (Gal. 3:14), and that all who are Christ's might be "Abraham's offspring, heirs according to promise" (Gal. 3:29). The promise carries through by divine intent from Abraham to Christ.

The condition for experiencing and for being a blessing in the sense of the covenant with Abraham is *obedience*. That is made crystal clear by the words, "because you have obeyed my voice." Abraham obeyed, and he became the bearer of a promise of blessing to the nations. When God renewed the covenant with Israel at Sinai he again asked for obedience: "Now therefore, if you will obey my voice and keep my covenant, you shall be my own possession among all peoples; for all the earth is mine, and you shall be to me a kingdom of priests and a holy nation" (Ex. 19:5, 6). One of the great prophetic words of the Old Testament is the word of the Lord spoken by Samuel to Saul about obedience:

> "Has the Lord as great delight in burnt offerings and sacrifices, as in obeying the voice of the Lord?
> Behold, to obey is better than sacrifice,
> and to hearken than the fat of rams." (1 Sam. 15:22)

The supreme witness of the New Testament to Christ is that He "became obedient unto death" (Phil. 2:8), and by His obedience became the Savior in whom is "every spiritual blessing" (Eph. 1:3) for all who believe. Because Paul was not disobedient to the heavenly vision (Acts 26:19), he became the apostle who brought blessing to the Gentile world by preaching the gospel of Christ. The secret is always the same: they believed, and they obeyed. For the obedience of which we speak is the obedience of faith (Rom. 1:5, ASV), which is the human response to the divine covenant, both in receiving and in being a blessing. It has been so since the time of Abraham.

We have said that the oath of God in v. 16 is equivalent to his covenant. The purpose of the divine oath is the same as that of the covenant, to give to the heirs of the promise a *double assurance* of "the unchangeable character of his purpose." (See Heb. 6:13-18.) Neither the oath nor the covenant, of course, actually made the promise *more sure;* for all the promises of God are faithful and true. The covenant is a condescension on God's part to the human need and desire for such a solemn confirmation of the divine promise. It is His way of assuring man that He really means and will surely perform what He has promised. The divine promise remains the central feature of the divine covenant. In the case of the covenant with Abraham that means especially the promise that in him and in his seed all the nations of the earth will be blessed. At the heart of the covenant is "the blessing of Abraham," which is pregnant with the promise of "every spiritual blessing in Christ."

IV

The Genesis story of Abraham gives the impression of a great human personality, a man of outstanding faith in God, with a unique religious experience. More important, it bears witness to a divine covenant with this man to which he responded in obedient faith. By the simple device of a fivefold repetition, it emphasizes that at the heart of this covenant was a promise of divine blessing; and that this blessing included a divine appointment to be a blessing: "In thee [and in thy seed] shall all the families of the earth be blessed." The Genesis story is remarkably clear and unified in this central emphasis on the covenant of blessing, with the material controlled throughout by the constant interweaving of the four fundamental elements from the call of Abraham in chapter 12. There is a remarkable harmony also with the rest of Scripture, in the Old Testament as well as in the New. Of this we shall speak further as we go along; but we have already seen something of the Biblical claim to a fulfillment of the covenant with Abraham in two stages: first, in the history of Israel as the chosen people, called to be in a peculiar sense "the servant of the Lord"; and secondly, in the life and ministry of Jesus Christ and in the history of the Christian church, with the gospel of Christ as the supreme proclamation of "every spiritual blessing" for all who believe in Christ.

How shall we account for it? How shall we explain this remarkable story of Abraham and of the divine covenant with him? Is it fact or fiction? Does it make any real difference to Christian faith which of the two it is?

We want to make it clear that we are not now concerned with the literal inerrancy of the narrative in all its details, but only with *its essential historicity*. There may well be a complicated historical process back of the formation of the Book of Genesis. There are human factors to be taken into consideration in the interpretation: linguistic forms peculiar to the Hebrew language, literary "thought" forms peculiar to the Semitic people, historical "times coloring" that reflects the religion and culture of the ancient world. There is a human aspect to all Biblical literature, which must be seriously and honestly considered as we study it. There is also a divine aspect which must be given equally serious and honest consideration by the Bible reader and exegete. Therefore "we reject all rationalizing processes which would explain away either the divine or the human factor in the Bible."[16] To this declaration of principle we would subscribe without hesitation, as a statement of personal conviction.

When we begin to apply this principle honestly to the material in the Book of Genesis, we may find ourselves agreeing that the stories do have something of "the universal quality of folk tales";[17] that they bear a resemblance *as to form* to what is called Saga or legend;[18] and that they have something of the "allgemein menschlich," the universal human character of a parable.[19] We may admit the possibility of oral tradition in handing down these stories through many generations, until they were given permanent written form either in Genesis itself or in sources of which the writer of Genesis made use.[20] We may come to think of them as cherished stories handed down from generation to generation within the patriarchal family, and then used with didactic purpose within the covenant community of Israel; and, as with the parables of Jesus, we may not always be able to say how many of the details represent an actual original experience and how much is the religious interpretation of a later age, perhaps the prophetic interpretation of "the great artist" who is often credited with the composition of the documentary source known as J, or of the unknown author-editor of our present book of Genesis.[21] We may reach the conclusion so well stated by Frederick L. Moriarty: "It would be unfair to judge the patriarchal history according to the standards of modern historical writing. History in Genesis is written in the popular, anecdotal style proper to the ancient Near East; unlike most of our modern history, it is written from a profoundly religious viewpoint, seeking to find in every event the directing hand of God. . . . Nevertheless, the patriarchal narrative is truly historical in that it records, in its own popular way, real events, centering around real persons who lived in the early centuries of the second millennium before Christ."[22]

Whatever its literary history or form, the story of Abraham reflects the fundamental life experience of a man named Abraham; but more significant, it represents a fundmental self-revelation of God.

Just as the narrative is too closely related to the second millennium B.C. to deny its essential historicity, so the unified emphasis on the divine promise to Abraham reflects a tradition which must go back to an original happening or event. It is too deeply ingrained in the narrative to be lightly denied. There is no real convincing historical or archaeological evidence to the contrary. The Biblical evidence, especially in the New Testament, is unanimous in favor of a historical as well as a spiritual connection between the blessing of Abraham and the fullness of the gospel, between the call of Abraham and the coming of Christ. There is nothing to hinder faith that this is really so. We need only understand the relationship between Abraham and Christ, between the blessing and the gospel, in accordance with the principle of a progressive revelation, wherein God himself acts with a redemptive purpose in relation to men: then each event becomes significant in its own right and in relation to the other, God being His own interpreter of His own saving acts whereby He brings "the blessing of Abraham" to all men in Christ.

For the Abraham story is more than a product of human thought and religious imagination. It is the record of an actual experience of personal faith based on a unique knowledge of God. Whatever literary or didactic additions may have been made as the story was told and retold within the family of Abraham, the fundamental lines of the original experience stand out with a compelling clarity: the call to *go* to a new land, and to *enter* on a new life, with faith and hope inspired by the threefold promise of a seed, a land, and a blessing. Upon this part of the Abraham story, that which constitutes the heart of it, the New Testament has written its "imprimatur," which far transcends the personal conviction of any prelate, scholar, or theologian. It was God who acted in the call of Abraham, and the covenant of blessing made with him is no more the figment of imagination than when God acted in the sending of Jesus Christ. Both belong to "the saving acts of the Lord."

NOTES

[1] Franz Delitzsch, *Messianic Prophecies, op. cit.*

[2] Otto Procksch, *op. cit.*

[3] J. H. Hertz, *Pentateuch and Haftorahs, op. cit.*

[4] James Moffatt, *The Bible: a New Translation, op. cit.*

[5] The Douay Version of the Holy Bible. New York: P. J. Kennedy & Sons.

[6] Franz Delitzsch, *A New Commentary on Genesis.* Edinburgh: T. & T. Clark. 1888-89. Vol. II, pp. 6-7.

[7] *Ibid.*

[8] J. Begrich, *op. cit.*

[9] Franz Delitzsch, *A New Commentary on Genesis, op. cit.,* p. 14.

[10] Herbert Alleman, *op. cit.,* p. 188.

[11] "The Apology of the Augsburg Confession"; see *The Book of Concord,* edited by Henry Eyster Jacobs. Philadelphia: General Council Publication Board. 1916.

[12] Martin Luther, *The Small Catechism, op. cit.*

[13] A. B. Davidson, *The Theology of the Old Testament.* New York: Charles Scribner's Sons. 1904. pp. 311-315.

[14] From *The Westminster Dictionary of the Bible, op. cit.*

[15] William Gesenius, *A Hebrew and English Lexicon of the Old Testament,* edited by Brown, Driver, and Briggs, *op. cit.*

[16] See *United Testimony on Faith and Life,* approved by the Uniting Churches of the American Lutheran Church. 1952.

[17] C. H. Dodd, *op. cit.*

[18] H. Gunkel, *op. cit.*

[19] Franz Böhl, *op. cit.*

[20] Eduard Nielsen, *Oral Tradition.* Chicago: Alec R. Alleson, Inc. 1954.

[21] Franz Böhl, *op. cit.*

[22] Frederick Moriarty, *Foreword to the Old Testament.* Weston, Mass.; Weston College Press. 1954. p. 15.

Chapter Six

THE SPIRITUAL INTERPRETATION
OF THE COVENANT

WHAT DO WE MEAN by a *spiritual* interpretation of the covenant with Abraham?

Lest we be guilty of deliberate "double talk," as some say that all spiritual interpretation of the Old Testament is, we must make clear what we understand spiritual interpretation to be—and what it is not.

Spiritual interpretation does not mean that we attribute two completely unrelated meanings to a passage: one being the plain sense of the passage in the light of the historical situation, and therefore the one intended by the writer and understood by those for whom he wrote; and the other a hidden spiritual meaning, which is later arbitrarily assigned to it in its use in a new and wholly different situation. For such an arbitrary procedure there is no justification either on the basis of Scripture or of scientific historical research. This would be to indulge in the kind of double talk which inevitably leaves the Bible reader in confusion as to how to understand anything that he reads. There are at least two good reasons for denying that this is what a spiritual interpretation really means.

1. For one thing, life is not that sharply divided or separated into what we call spiritual and secular. There is a spiritual aspect, good or bad, to all that happens in human life; for the simple reason that man is created a living being with body and soul, earth related and God related in all that he is and does. The failure to see or to recognize the spiritual aspect of life does not eliminate it, as if it did not exist. The natural hope of having children or of possessing a home can have profound spiritual implications, especially for the religious man. That must be borne in mind when we speak of the promise of a land and a seed to Abraham. Was Abraham a dull clod who

102

never looked beyond the things that could be seen; or was he a man of unusual religious sensitivity, who walked with God by faith and in faith looked upward to catch a glimpse of things that are not seen? It is remarkable, as Wilhelm Vischer has said, how many people to-day regard it as self-evident "that they know more about God than Abraham—simply because they live a few thousand years later."[1] But do they? What is there about the human situation in the twentieth century A.D. that would be more likely to produce an Abraham than that of the twentieth century B.C.? And if we believe at all in divine revelation, could not the living God speak then as well as now? And if the living God does speak at all to men, would we not expect a deep inner harmony in the revelation, however much the form may be adapted to the human situation? We see this harmony not least in *the divine concern for the whole of man's life,* to which the Bible bears witness from beginning to end; never separating as sharply as we are wont to do between physical and spiritual, between secular and sacred, between temporal and eternal. There is a religious implication to the most earthy things in human life; and we may be sure that this was true in the case of Abraham.

2. There is another thing to be borne in mind as we try to understand what we mean by a true spiritual interpretation of the covenant of blessing. We think of the law of growth in life, with its living continuity which gives evidence both of unity and of change. If we speak of the acorn and the oak as essentially *one,* we are not indulging in double talk, for there is a life relationship between the two. The same is true in a slightly different way of the child who grows into a man. We do not see the mature man in the child, but the identity is there nevertheless. This is the same law of growth that we see illustrated in the Bible with respect to the redemptive purpose of God. It is not all revealed at once in a blinding flash of lightning; it resembles rather the gradual illumination of the sun, from the moment when we see the first faint streaks of light that precede the dawn until it rises over the horizon, and finally reaches its zenith at noonday. The first gospel promise (Gen. 3:15) becomes the little Bible (Jn. 3:16); the presence of God within a tabernacle, in the midst of His people, becomes the Word made flesh and dwelling among us "full of grace and truth"; the word that God spoke by the prophets "in many fragments" (Heb. 1:1, Weymouth)[2] becomes the living word spoken in the very person, the life-mission, the manner of life, as well as the teaching, of

God's Son, the Lord Jesus Christ. It is this sort of thing that is characteristic of all of Scripture, and that we believe to be true also of the covenant with Abraham. There may be far more of spiritual content and of divine intent in it than Abraham could see; yet what he did see, and that to which he responded in faith and obedience, is spiritually related to that which we see and that to which we respond in the same obedience of faith. God implanted in the acorn the life which becomes the oak. God also implanted in the promise of blessing to Abraham the seed which became the Christian gospel. God acted in the case of both acorn and promise according to the law of growth which He himself has established.

In attempting a spiritual interpretation of the covenant of blessing we shall look at both ends of the historical process that unites Abraham with Christ, the blessing of Abraham as given to him and as interpreted by Paul, the beginning with the end, the promise with the fulfillment. We shall try to show that there is in the Genesis account something that forms a real basis for faith in something of the New Testament sense; that the language suggests a spiritual significance which transcends Abraham's insight, and yet is one with it. We shall try to retain the historical contemporaneity of the promise as given to Abraham, and yet relate it to its eschatological fulfillment in Jesus Christ. For we firmly believe that only such an interpretation can do justice to the promise.

A Covenant of Blessing

The covenant with Abraham was a covenant of divine blessing. It centered in a great and glorious and gracious promise; and at the heart of the promise was a threefold assurance of blessing. There was the promise of a personal blessing to Abraham, in the words, "I will make of you a great nation, and I will bless you, and make your name great" (Gen. 12:2a). There followed what seems at first to be a pure commandment, "And be thou a blessing" (Gen. 12:2b, ASV), or a statement of divine intention, "So that you will be a blessing" (RSV); an impossible commission, if it were not for the accompanying divine promise which turned the commandment into a predictive statement of future fact, "And in you all the families of the earth will be blessed" (Gen. 12:3b, RSV mg.). Abraham and his seed, personally blessed, should become the source of a universal blessing, embracing men "from every nation, from all tribes and peoples and tongues" (Rev.

7:9). Moreover, in the exercise of this calling to be a blessing, the family of Abraham would become a touchstone of blessing to others, according to the attitude taken by those others toward them; for God said, "I will bless those who bless you, and him who curses you I will curse" (Gen. 12:3a).

Such were the provisions of the covenant of blessing made with Abraham; and they have never been repealed, nor has the covenant itself ever been superseded. The covenant of blessing continues in effect to this day; for though the Scriptures speak of a "new" and of a "better" covenant (see Jer. 31:31-34; 1 Cor. 11:25; Heb. 8:6), the antithesis is not with the covenant of blessing as being "old" and "inferior." Paul speaks of it as a preaching of the gospel beforehand to Abraham (Gal. 3:8). Peter says to the people in Solomon's porch, to whom he preached Christ, "You are the sons of the prophets and of the covenant which God gave to your fathers, saying to Abraham, 'And in your posterity shall all the families of the earth be blessed.' God, having raised up his servant, sent him to you first, to bless you in turning every one of you from your wickedness" (Acts 3:25,26). There is something about this covenant that seems to indicate from the start an everlasting and universal spiritual covenant. It continued in effect, and undergirded, the national covenant at Sinai; nor was it disannulled by the fact that the law was added "because of transgressions" (Gal. 3:15-19) and for "hardness of heart" (Mt. 19:8). If we may believe the testimony of Scripture in its wholeness, God has never had more than one way of salvation; and the covenant of grace and blessing made with Abraham is essentially one with the spiritual fellowship into which we are called through Christ in the New Testament church.

Let us carry the comparison a step further.

A Spiritual Covenant

The covenant of blessing was at its inception a spiritual covenant. It depended for its validity upon a divine promise received in faith. It had as its basis a word of the Lord which Abraham believed and obeyed. It involved for Abraham a genuine religious experience.

The thing promised was not, of course, exclusively spiritual. There was a material aspect to the promise, and we would not minimize its importance in relation to the future fulfillment of the covenant. The promise, like Abraham himself in his own person, had a body of earth.

It was clothed in the easily understandable terms of a land to be possessed as an inheritance, and of a seed that would be like the stars of heaven and like the sand of the sea for multitude. This material side of the blessing found a significant fulfillment in the history of Israel, in their inheritance of the Promised Land, and in their experience of God's blessings upon them as a people. They often forgot that these temporal blessings were a gift from God, a fulfillment of His covenant promise. The prophet Hosea in the eighth century indicts the people because they forgot the Lord and misused his blessings:

> *And she [Israel] did not know*
> *that it was I who gave her*
> *the grain, the wine, and the oil,*
> *and who lavished upon her silver*
> *and gold which they used for Baal.* (2:8)

It is not difficult to show from both the Old Testament and the New that every good gift is from God, temporal blessings included. It is not strange that the promise to Abraham should begin with such concrete material blessings as the gift of children and the inheritance of a land. It would have been strange if this were not the case, for such is the very nature of human life and aspirations.

But is that all there is to the promise? Was the author of Deuteronomy the first one to discover that "man does not live by bread alone," or that any purely materialistic interpretation of life is a perversion of its meaning? We cannot take the promise of blessing as in any sense whatsoever *a word of God* and fail to see that the blessing must involve a sense of relationship to God as the giver, an acknowledgment of dependence upon Him, an experience of fellowship with Him. This is one compelling reason why we say that within the material husk of the promise lay a spiritual kernel: a soul within the body, an inner spirit which illumines the whole with a genuinely spiritual radiance; an implicit witness to the blessedness of an intimate personal faith experience of the presence of the living God, whether in the life of a man (like Abraham), or in the life of a nation (like Israel), or in the life of a redeemed humanity (such as within the Christian church). Abraham experienced the spiritual as well as the material blessing of God in his life; and of the two, the spiritual was the greater and the more wonderful. Such was the divine intent with the promise in which he believed. The blessing *on* or *to* Abraham was at heart a spiritual blessing. It was the blessing which comes whenever a man experiences the presence of the living God in his life.

The focal point in the promise, however, lay elsewhere, in the blessing that should come *through Abraham* and his seed *to others*. It is here that we really see the spiritual nature of the promise, which according to the New Testament is Messianic. The blessing was not intended to be a selfish one. It is only when we look too narrowly at the promise of a land and of a great nation that it seems quite selfish and materialistic, just as a narrow nationalism can be today. When, however, our attention is turned to the coming seed *as the source of blessing to others,* the true spiritual nature of the promise begins to appear. Just as the blessing on or to Abraham was essentially the spiritual blessing of a unique knowledge of God, so also the blessing to be mediated to others must be spiritual; and let us add, there is something spiritual about the very concept of *sharing* the gifts of God. When we consider who the seed of Abraham ultimately is, the spiritual nature of the whole promise becomes abundantly clear; we cannot disallow it without denying the whole witness of sacred history. For "the seed of Abraham" is a developing concept, reaching a fulfillment first in Isaac as the original child of promise, then in Israel as the chosen people, and finally in Christ and those who are Christ's, men of faith, who are Abraham's offspring and heirs according to promise (Gal. 3). According to the witness of sacred history the promise to Abraham reached its goal in Jesus Christ as the mediator of "every spiritual blessing" to the nations of the world. (See Acts 3:25, 26; Gal. 3:8, 16; Eph. 1:3.) There is nothing in the original promise that rules out such an interpretation as being inherently impossible or untruthful. There is much in the promise that would rather suggest that such an interpretation is probable and may be assumed to be correct. From the New Testament point of view, of course, the interpretation is conclusive. We need not assume that Abraham understood all that lay within the promise given him; but we may be sure that a man as deeply religious as this man is seen to be in his later life must have apprehended something of the spiritual significance of what God had promised him. He certainly knew the blessing of the presence of God in his own life—the same gracious presence more gloriously experienced through Christ, who is Immanuel, God with us. It is this blessing of the knowledge and of the presence of the living God that constitutes the heart of the covenant with Abraham, and of all true religion. This is what makes it fundamentally spiritual. This is what transforms every other facet of the covenant. It is in this light that we begin to see the possibility of a deeper significance to the very promise of a country as an inheritance. We know, of course, the interpretation in Heb. 11:13-16: "These all died in faith, not having received what was promised, but having seen it and greeted it from afar, and having acknowledged that they were strangers and exiles on the earth. For people who speak thus make it clear that they are seeking a homeland. . . . A better country, that is, a heavenly one." There is nothing in the situation in Genesis to make such a hope seem incredible. Who shall say with authority *when men first began to hope* for life after death? We need not assume that the doctrine of resurrection was known to Abraham as a truth of revelation; but the words of Delitzsch with reference to David are apropos also here, that there may well have been a *hope* rising out of the very life situation, "a view that, by reason of the already existing revelation of God, lights up out of his consciousness of fellowship with him."[3]

The covenant with Abraham was essentially a spiritual covenant. It did not depend upon ordinances. It was not limited to a single nation. It was not even circumscribed by earth, though the earth is the Lord's (Ex. 19:5). It came from heaven and pointed heavenward. It was a part of the saving acts of God. It rested on faithful promises, which were also received in faith. It was true of Abraham, as it is true of us, that "faith comes from what is heard, and what is heard comes by the preaching of Christ" (Rom. 10:17); and such a faith-relationship with God is a spiritual relationship, resting on a spiritual covenant, even as God who made it is Spirit (Jn. 4:24).

A Spiritual Experience—Justification

For this faith in the divine promise which looked forward to Christ led in the case of Abraham, as in our own case, to a genuine spiritual experience. It put him in a right spiritual relationship to God. In the language of the New Testament, it became the basis for his justification, in the sense of his acceptance with God, who approved his faith. For it is written of him, the first man of whom it is so written, "And he believed the Lord; and he reckoned it to him as righteousness" (Gen. 15:6).

Faith reckoned as righteousness! That is indeed a true spiritual experience. Though there is nothing said about that other element in justification in the New Testament sense, the blessing of the experience of the forgiveness of sins, we may safely assume its presence also; for there can be no righteousness without cleansing from sin. The Lord cannot at the same time reckon sin to us and also reckon our faith to us as righteousness! From Abraham's frequent practice of building an altar to the Lord and calling on the name of the Lord (see e.g., Gen. 12:7, 8) we know that he was not lacking in that sense of need and consciousness of sin which is common to all worship. From Paul's interpretation in Romans 4 we see that Abraham's experience, like that of David later on, was an experience of the full spiritual blessing of a gracious God. "So also David pronounces a blessing upon the man to whom God reckons righteousness apart from works:

> 'Blessed are those whose iniquities are forgiven, and whose sins are covered;
> blessed is the man against whom the Lord will not reckon his sin' " (Rom 4:6-8).

The positive and the negative side of the blessing belong together always. God did not reckon sin to Abraham, though he was a sinner. He did reckon his faith to him as righteousness. Surely, if that be true we must say of him that he was justified by faith even as we; and of the covenant of blessing, that it was indeed a preaching of the gospel beforehand, with the same saving effect as with us. The only difference is that our faith has a broader base of the knowledge of God as befits those who have seen the fulfillment of the promise in Christ; but it is the same God who acts in fundamentally the same way and with the same ultimate purpose.

A Life of Obedience—Sanctification

The analysis and interpretation of this spiritual experience of Abraham under the covenant of blessing is still not complete, however. On the basis of his experience of righteousness by faith, Abraham was also called in the most direct and personal way to a life of obedience. The intent of God is clear: faith should be expressed in obedience; the life in God should lead to a consecrated walk before Him; theologically speaking, justification should issue in sanctification.

The relationship between these two basic elements in the spiritual life could not be illustrated more graphically than it is in the story of Abraham. The sequence is significant. The experience of righteousness by faith came first (Gen. 15:6). The summons to sanctification of life in the obedience of faith came much later (Gen. 17:1). We speak now of the narrative as it stands, assuming that there is some reason why the sequence is what it is; and inclined to believe that the only adequate reason is that it corresponds to the actual sequence in Abraham's life. Is perhaps the long interlude of time between the statement in Gen. 15:6, "And he believed the Lord; and he reckoned it to him as righteousness," and the next appearance of the Lord to Abraham with the words, "I am God Almighty; walk before me, and be blameless" (Gen. 17:1), God's way of making clear to Abraham, and to us, the right sequence of faith and life, of grace and works, of justification and sanctification?

It undeniably serves that purpose in the New Testament interpretation and in Christian teaching; and rightly so, if we think in terms of a true spiritual experience based on the gospel. Faith, confident trust, comes first, as the divinely wrought answer to the divine promise of grace and blessing. Nevertheless faith without works is dead. True faith is obedient to the will of God. True faith is willing to be separated from the world of evil to live in fellowship with God and to walk as before Him. True faith becomes the motivation to a new manner of life, a spiritual life, which is a life unto God. So it was in the covenant of blessing with Abraham; and so it is with us, according to the terms of the full-orbed Christian gospel. It is significant that it is Paul, with his deep insight into the gospel of salvation by grace, who so often admonishes the Christian to walk worthily of his calling; who emphasizes most clearly the obedience of faith; who points to the ultimate goal of God for the believer in these words, "May the God of peace himself sanctify you wholly; and may your spirit and soul and body be kept sound and blameless at the coming of our Lord Jesus Christ" (1 Thess. 5:23). That is also the spirit of the original covenant of blessing in the Book of Genesis. "As for you, you shall keep my covenant, you and your descendants after you throughout their generations," God said to Abraham (Gen. 17:9); "walk before me, and be blameless" (17:1). The covenant had its origin in the grace of God, but it had its obligations for Abraham as the recipient of grace; it sought the fruit of faith in a consecrated life.

The Sign and the Seal—Circumcision

Of this consecrated life God set circumcision as an external symbol and seal. The words in Genesis are specific as to its purpose: "This is my covenant, which you shall keep, between me and you and your descendants after you: Every male among you shall be circumcised. You shall be circumcised in the flesh of your foreskins, and it shall be a sign of the covenant between me and you. . . . So shall my covenant be in your flesh an everlasting covenant" (Gen. 17:10, 11, 13b). Circumcision was to be a sign of the covenant. With this agrees the New Testament explanation as given by Paul in Rom. 4:11, "He received circumcision as a sign or seal of the righteousness which he had by faith while he was still uncircumcised." Circumcision was a seal of an already existing covenant relationship and of covenant blessings already experienced. It belonged to the human response to the divine covenant. It did not change the spiritual character of the covenant of blessing. It did not substitute a ritual law for the righteousness of faith. It added something to the covenant observance, but the addition did not contradict the spirit of the covenant: it too had a spiritual significance.

It is true that the documentary analysis assigns Gen. 17 to the priestly source or P, because it is said to reflect a ritual influence and emphasis. We need not deny this ritual aspect in order to assert that it had also a genuine spiritual character. The ritual and the ethical, or the spiritual, aspects of religion do not necessarily contradict each other. The alleged conflict between priestly and prophetic religion has often been grossly exaggerated; what the prophets denounce, and rightly so, is not ritual per se but a ritual religion devoid of ethical content: where the symbol has crowded out the spiritual reality which it is meant to express. The covenant of circumcision with Abraham must be interpreted in the context of Genesis, not of Leviticus. It is true that the rite of circumcision became a part of the later Mosaic law, although, as we have shown elsewhere, it receives surprisingly little attention in the ritual law. As far as the Old Testament is concerned, circumcision is associated more closely with the Abrahamic covenant than it is with the Mosaic law. There is nothing in the story in Genesis that indicates any change in the fundamental character of the covenant of blessing when God added the sign of circumcision as a seal. The ritual command in chapter 17:9-14 must be taken together with the spiritual-ethical command in v. 1, the keynote to the teaching of the chapter. Then circumcision is seen to be an external testimony to the faith in the heart and to the obedient attitude of the life of Abraham. It was a confession of the covenant relationship with God; a confession which had much in common with the Christian's membership in the external organization of the church today. Abraham was not declared to be righteous because of circumcision; neither is the Christian saved by his church membership. But the one as well as the other may be the external confirmation of an inner spiritual experience growing out of faith in the promises of God.

By circumcision Abraham and his descendants confessed themselves to belong to the people of God. The outward act was meaningless, and even hypocritical, if it did not actually represent an inner faith and a sincere dedication to the will of God for them as His people. With Abraham circumcision did express such a sincere devotion to his God. The outward symbol faithfully reflected the inward consecration. It was in complete harmony with that circumcision of the heart which was later emphasized both by the prophet Jeremiah and by the Apostle Paul. It is true that later on, in connection with the Mosaic legislation, circumcision came to stand for "the law of commandments and ordinances"; and it became for many an external substitute for the inner experience, the ritual emphasis crowding out the spiritual. There is no indication that it was so with Abraham; nor, as we shall see, is there any indication that the addition of the law in the renewal of the covenant with Israel as a nation at Sinai altered the original spiritual purpose of the divine covenant of blessing. It was an everlasting and universal spiritual covenant; a true covenant of grace intended for all nations and for all generations. Even circumcision must be seen and understood in the light of the central idea of the covenant, the universal promise of blessing.

A Universal Covenant

The covenant of blessing with Abraham and his seed was intended to be a universal covenant. However national in scope and form the Sinaitic covenant may be, there can be no serious question of the ecumenicity of the covenant with Abraham. The very spirit of the narrative in Genesis is, as F. Böhl has well said, "allgemein menschlich": there are no national limitations in evidence; Abraham is a citizen of the world.[4] As for the divine covenant with him, it too from the very beginning included the world. "In you all the families of the earth will be blessed" (Gen. 12:3b, RSV mg.), and "by your descendants shall all the nations of the earth bless themselves" (Gen. 22:18, RSV text): such was the divine promise. It was not a sort of after thought with God to include the Gentiles in the covenant of redemption. It was His primary purpose in calling this man Abraham and in establishing His covenant of blessing with him. Genesis reveals that God has *always* thought in terms of the world or of all humanity, even when He has chosen individual persons and nations for some special service, commissioning them to be a blessing by being the privileged bearers of the personally experienced good news of His grace.

The covenant of blessing with Abraham, whose first stage of fulfillment was in the history and mission of Israel, was never intended to be a purely Hebrew or Jewish covenant. From the first it aimed at the goal "that in Christ Jesus the blessing of Abraham might come upon the Gentiles" (Gal. 3:14); that all men might eventually learn to know what it means to be able to say, "Blessed be the God and Father of our Lord Jesus Christ, who has blessed us in Christ with every spiritual blessing in the heavenly places" (Eph. 1:3). Paul simply puts into plain words that which the Abraham story in Genesis implies, when he says that it is "men of faith" everywhere, irrespective of nation or race, who are "the sons of Abraham" (Gal. 3:7) and "blessed with Abraham" (Gal. 3:9) and "heirs according to promise" (Gal. 3:29). For "the scripture, foreseeing that God would justify the Gentiles by faith, preached the gospel beforehand to Abraham, saying, 'In thee shall all the nations be blessed'" (Gal. 3:8). There is a more personal way of expressing the same truth: *God knew his own purpose* to justify the Gentiles by faith, and He called Abraham to be His servant in the accomplishment of this purpose, and for the encouragement of his faith (and ours) He gave him in His promise a preview of the breadth of His purpose. The covenant of blessing was beautifully catholic or ecumenical as well as genuinely spiritual in nature and intent from the beginning.

An Everlasting Covenant

It was also an everlasting covenant. God said to Abraham, "And I will establish my covenant between me and you and your descendants after you throughout their generations for an everlasting covenant [berith olam], to be God to you and to your descendants after you. And I will give to you, and to your descendants after you, the land of your sojournings, all the land of Canaan, for an everlasting possession (achuzath olam); and I will be their God" (Gen. 17:7-8). Now it is true that the Hebrew word *olam* does not always and necessarily mean *everlasting,* in the sense of never-ending time. It means rather *indefinite time of long duration.* It often seems that the connotation of *time* is subordinate to that of fulfillment; as if to say that the *berith olam* shall be in force until God has accomplished His covenant purpose, or until it has been fulfilled. That brings us right back to the heart of the covenant promise, the so-called "blessing of Abraham." The promise of a land in the geographical sense of the land of Canaan may have a strictly temporary purpose, and may even be conditioned on Israel's faithfulness to the covenant in the years to come; but that does not touch the heart of the covenant. The promise of a seed in the historical sense of Israel as a nation may be regarded as fulfilled when God's mission for Israel as His chosen servant has been accomplished; but once more, that does not affect the covenant at its heart or center. A *berith olam* implies that God will accomplish *all* that He has set out to do, that He will perform *all* that He has promised; and what this means we see from the gospel part of the promise, to which the New Testament interpretation rightly attaches itself. God has never abrogated the covenant of blessing! He has never altered its essential terms. It stands as an unchangeable declaration of the gracious will and purpose of God to bless all humanity with the blessing experienced by Abraham, and with every spiritual blessing.

Someone may ask, Did not Sinai change the nature of the covenant? Did not the coming of Christ usher in an altogether new covenant of grace? Does not even the prophet Jeremiah speak of a new covenant which God would make with the house of Israel? Does not the New Testament contrast *two* covenants, the first and the second, the old and the new; and does it not say of the first, "what is becoming obsolete and growing old is ready to vanish away" (Heb. 8:13)? How can we speak of the covenant with Abraham as an everlasting covenant in the light of the witness of Scripture to other covenants that seem to supersede it? Specifically, what is the relation between the covenant with Abraham and the Mosaic covenant, and the relation of both to the new covenant mediated by Jesus Christ?

The questions are pertinent to a spiritual interpretation of the covenant with Abraham. They call for an incisive answer. When the answer has been given, we shall see that the covenant of blessing has not been disannulled but fulfilled. The fulfillment may be greater and more glorious than the promise indicates; but nevertheless promise and fulfillment are essentially one.

A Law Added

We shall speak at length of the covenant with Israel in a subsequent chapter. One thing is clear, however, that in the formal application of the covenant with Abraham to Israel as a nation *something was added*. We refer, of course, to the Torah, or the Law. The promise, and the commission to be a blessing, was given through Abraham; the law was given through Moses. Why was it added?

Jesus suggested one reason when He said, "For your hardness of heart" (Mt. 19:8). According to Paul, "it was added because of transgressions" (Gal. 3:19). The educational function of the law can be seen from the New Testament statement that "through the law comes the knowledge of sin" (Rom. 3:20); and from the Old Testament concept of Torah as loving guidance "in the good and the right way" within the covenant relationship. (See e.g., 1 Sam. 2:23; Deut. 6:24; 10:12, 13.) We can readily see its usefulness as a standard for the guidance of human behavior, and especially for the conduct of those already within the covenant relationship by an act of God's redeeming grace. We can understand also its function as "our schoolmaster" or "our tutor" or "our custodian" to help us realize the depth of our need of God's grace in Christ. But there is nothing in the Mosaic law that sets aside the original covenant of grace and blessing in its universal and spiritual character. There is nothing to indicate that the covenant with Israel was not also a covenant of grace and blessing. The law was *added;* it did not take the place of the covenant with Abraham. It was added for a temporary educational purpose (spiritual pedagogy) as God dealt with His people on a national level. When this temporary purpose had been achieved there was "a disannulling of the foregoing commandment" (Heb. 7:18, ASV), because it had done all that it could do; but the covenant of promise, the covenant of blessing, made with Abraham and his seed was never annulled (see Gal. 3:15-18). It found instead a still greater fulfillment than in the covenant with Israel and lives on in the fulfillment.

Christ the Fulfillment

The fulfillment is in Christ. His coming and His ministry of eternal redemption did not set the covenant of blessing aside as if it were

115

outworn or outmoded. By His coming He brought the covenant to full fruition and established it. He gave objective reality to the promise; He gave substance to the promised spiritual blessings; He "spelled out" for us all that lay in the intent of God from the beginning. But it was still the same covenant: the covenant given to Abraham by promise, and received by him in faith, now fulfilled by Jesus the Christ as the mediator of a new covenant. It is true that we make no mistake in calling this covenant *new*. Just as Jesus by His death on the cross gave to the commandment of love such a new depth of meaning that He could rightly call it "a new commandment" (Jn. 13:34), even though the law had said long before that "you shall love your neighbor as yourself" (Lev. 19:18), so also it is with the covenant of blessing: in its essential outlines it is an old covenant, that goes back to the days of Abraham; but it pointed forward to the Christ who should make the promise come fully true, and in so doing, while retaining 'the terms of the original covenant, would make it as new.

The Covenant and Atonement

That this is so becomes doubly clear when we note that God did not leave Abraham in ignorance as to the eternal redemptive basis for this covenant of blessing. Through his experience on Mt. Moriah, when he was told to offer his beloved son as a burnt offering to God, and in obedient faith stood ready to make even this supreme sacrifice, only to be stopped in the last moment by God's voice from heaven, Abraham learned something more than the truth that "to obey is better than sacrifice" (1 Sam. 15:22); he learned something of the basic truth involved in what we call *vicarious atonement*. It was perhaps not so much the truth that "without the shedding of blood there is no forgiveness of sins" (Heb. 9:22), for of this truth every bloody sacrifice was a vivid symbol; it was rather the truth that the Lord will provide the lamb for a truly acceptable burnt offering, with its symbolism of complete self-dedication to God. "So Abraham called the name of that place The Lord will provide" (Gen. 22:14). The object lesson was well learned. It was a fundamentally spiritual lesson in divine grace. On that basis the covenant of blessing was repeated and confirmed with an oath, as if to impress upon Abraham that He who makes the promise and the provision is faithful and true. The Epistle to the Hebrews does not miss the mark in its interpretation: "So when God desired to show more convincingly to the heirs of the promise the unchangeable character of his purpose, he interposed with an oath, so that through two unchangable things, in which it is impossible that God should prove false, we who have fled for refuge might have strong encouragement to seize the hope set before us" (6:17-18).

A Divine Mission

We have stressed *the spiritual experience* of Abraham in this spiritual interpretation of the covenant with him, because as we read the Book of Genesis it is this personal experience with God that first meets the eye. It was an experience with far-reaching spiritual implications for us all as an example in faith and obedience. Its spiritual significance, however, is more than a matter of example. Spiritual experience in the Scriptural sense is never limited to being on the receiving end of the blessings of God; it involves giving, or sharing, or serving, as well. There is in the call of Abraham and in the covenant with him a clear indication of *mission* in the divine imperative, "Be a blessing." The five times repeated formula of blessing, especially when the verb is translated passively, puts special emphasis on a blessing which is to come to all nations *by* or *in* Abraham and his seed. This would seem to involve an active servant status on their part, or a divine mission of sharing the blessing received with others. God's universal purpose of blessing would not be realized if Abraham and his descendants remained completely passive, content to enjoy the spiritual privileges of a "friend of God" and of "a chosen people," with no thought of sharing. The covenant called for dynamic participation in God's plan of blessing for the world. How faithfully or how well Abraham and Israel fulfilled their vocation to be a blessing is not for us to judge. It is far more significant to note that this vocation leads at last to Him who came in the form of a servant (Phil. 2:7) and said of himself, "The Son of man came not to be served but to serve, and to give his life as a ransom for many" (Mt. 20:28). The context of Jesus' words makes it clear that we, too, are called to have the same servant spirit; or, in the words of Gen. 12:2, to be a blessing by sharing the blessing of the gospel given to us. The mission of Abraham reaches through Israel to Christ, and through Christ to us; for we, too, belong to the seed of Abraham and share his vocation.

Conclusion

Of the tremendous influence of this initial covenant of blessing in the history of Israel and in New Testament preaching much more could be said. It found a twofold fulfillment: first, in the spiritual mission of Israel as the chosen people, and second, in the ministry of Christ and of His church. It has a unique and powerful unifying influence throughout the Old Testament revelation, as does the root of a tree: uniting into one message with a single purpose the many words spoken by God to the fathers in so many and various ways (Heb. 1: 1). And because the focal point of the promise is Christ, whom God sent "when the time had fully come" (Gal. 4:4) to bring this covenant of blessing to its full fruition, it becomes the unifying bond between the Old Testament and the New, the silver cord on which the message both of prophets and apostles is strung. It is true, as W. J. Beecher has pointed out, that "the New Testament men regard the Messianic teaching of the Old Testament as mainly the unfolding of a single promise," the promise first given to Abraham as initiating the covenant of blessing.[5] The unity carries over into the area of the Christian life, as Paul and Luther both testify, the one echoing the other; for the truth that God reckons faith as righteousness is the very heart of Scripture and of Christian experience, and the unifying principle of Christian theology. In proportion as the church in all its denominational parts grasps with mind and heart this spiritual significance of the covenant of blessing it will also be unified, in the unity of the Spirit and of faith, and in the experience of our father Abraham: an experience originating in a gracious divine promise which centers in Christ, expressing itself in a faith born of the promise and reckoned as righteousness, and issuing in a consecrated way of life, a life lived in the fellowship and presence of God.

When all has been said, this is the heart of the gospel. If we stand fast in this covenant of grace and blessing, we shall not make the mistake of those who look only at the periphery of divine truth and fail to grasp that truth at its center; who go off on spiritual tangents and bypaths, and lose themselves in endless mental speculations, moral vagaries, sentimental emotionalism, cold formalism, and (or) sensational prophesyings. We shall know the truth and, set free by it, shall walk in the way of the blessing of God. For this is the way illumined by "the saving acts of God," which culminated in Him who is "the Savior of the world" (Jn. 4:42).

NOTES

1 Wilhelm Vischer, *op. cit.*, p. 20.
2 Francis Weymouth, *The New Testament in Modern Speech*. Boston. The Pilgrim Press. London: James Clarke & Co. 4th ed. 1924.
3 Franz Delitzsch, *Biblical Commentary on the Psalms*. Edinburgh: T. & T. Clark. Tr. from German 1871. pp. 244-245.
4 Franz Böhl, *op. cit.*, p. 6.
5 Willis J. Beecher, *op. cit.*, p. 179.

Chapter Seven

THE ABRAHAM COVENANT AND THE EXODUS REDEMPTION

THE VIEWPOINT OF THE BOOK OF GENESIS is forward looking. The story revolves around the promise to Abraham and looks to the future with a strong hope of fulfillment. The Book of Exodus looks backward as well as forward. It, too, revolves around the promise to Abraham and finds in it the key to the explanation of the events currently taking place. In reading the two books as they stand, we cannot escape the impression of natural sequence between the two, from the giving of a great promise to the real beginning of its fulfillment. With the Exodus-redemption we enter on *the First Act* of the two-act historical drama of the consummation of the covenant with Abraham: the history and mission of Israel, including the divine covenant relationship with her which from here to the end of the Old Testament is never out of sight, be the writer a poet, a historian, or a prophet.

Before we look at the nature and significance of the covenant with Israel let us take a good look at the way in which the redemption from the bondage in Egypt is linked with the story of Abraham in the Old Testament tradition.

In the Book of Exodus

The literary strands that unite the events of the exodus with the blessing of Abraham are too many and too strategically placed to be accidental.

The opening paragraph is such a connecting link. The reference to the offspring of Jacob as seventy persons (Ex. 1:5) has the same purpose as the similar but more detailed account in Gen. 46 (see the number "70" in v. 27): it indicates the "seed" out of which under the blessing of God grew "a great nation" (Gen. 12:2). There is intentional

120

contrast between the seventy persons who "comprehended the whole of the nation of God" at the time of the descent into Egypt and the situation described in v. 7, "But the descendants of Israel were fruitful and increased greatly; they multiplied and grew exceedingly strong; so that the land was filled with them."[1] The promise to Abraham of a numerous seed is well on the way to its fulfillment. The writer of the Book of Deuteronomy notes the same contrast: "Your fathers went down to Egypt seventy persons; and now the Lord your God has made you as the stars of heaven for multitude" (Deut. 10: 22). The illustration employed is reminiscent of the terminology of the promise in the Abraham story (Gen. 15:5; 22:17; 26:4). The promise of a seed has found a significant measure of fulfillment. Such is the viewpoint with which the Book of Exodus begins. It says in effect that what has already taken place is in fulfillment of God's promise.

The promised seed is, however, still far from inheriting the fullness of the blessing. In the temporal sense of the blessing, as including the promise of a land, they seem to belong to the disinherited. They are sojourners and slaves in a foreign land. It is improbable that many remembered the fact that this contradictory situation had been foretold to Abraham at the time when God entered into formal covenant with him to give to his descendants the land of Canaan (Gen. 15). Perhaps the promise that "you shall return" lingered with some of them through the years; but it must have become for many a forlorn, if not a lost, hope. The promise of blessing in all its incipient richness, as faith and hope had tried to imagine it, seemed far away. Here is contrast of a different kind: not between promise and fulfillment, but between promise and disappointed hope. Where was the God of their fathers now? What was His promise worth in their prolonged distress? Was He able and faithful to keep this promise that He had given to Abraham? Such questions must have thrust themselves upon even the few devout souls who had faithfully preserved the traditions and had tried to keep the faith. Here was a test of faith which in intensity resembles that of Abraham on Mt. Moriah. Now as then faith needed a signal demonstration of the truth that "the Lord will provide" for the needs of His people; there was need of a saving act of God.

Actually God was already at work on many fronts to bring about the deliverance of His people. The birth of Moses, and his preparation for his life work as leader and lawgiver, may be seen as human symbols of the divine activity which reaches a climax in the exodus and in the covenant at Sinai. It is not our purpose here, however, to go into all the details of the history itself. What we want to note is the interpretative comment in Ex. 2:23-25, which is the key to the writer's understanding and interpretation of the whole series of events in the Book of Exodus. "In the course of those many days the king of Egypt died. And the people of Israel groaned under their bondage, and cried out for help, and their cry under bondage came up to God. And God heard their groaning, and God remembered his covenant with Abraham, with Isaac, and with Jacob. And God saw the people of Israel, and God knew their condition." This passage is a good example of the way in which men naturally think and speak of God. The language is anthropomorphic; but how would we improve upon it for simple, direct appeal, or even theologically? God is a God who knows the condition of His people and is moved to act in their behalf. He is presented in simple human language, so that simple human hearts might understand, as one who is *about to manifest* all this gracious activity in relation to His people Israel. It is a vitally personal and satisfying theology. God is aware of the sufferings of His people. He hears their cry for help, even if He seems slow to act. He knows best how to time the answer. He is not deaf to the cry of any sufferer. It says of Israel that "God knew their condition" (RSV) or "took knowledge of them" (ASV). Luther's version is this: "God accepted them." He knew them in the sense of not being ashamed to know them as His own. He acknowledged them, knowledge leading to action, in the usual sense of the Hebrew verb "know," and implying for His people an active experience of His saving power now about to begin.

But why did God take knowledge of them? It was not only because of the claim that human suffering always has upon a gracious and merciful God. We do not wish to minimize *this* significant religious truth; but there is another that is more significant still. It is this, that "God remembered his covenant." The statement stands at a strategic spot where it clearly ties in the coming redemption with the previous covenant, "his covenant with Abraham, with Isaac, and with Jacob." God remembered a covenant which He had already made, and this remembrance is given as the motivation for what He is now about to do. He remembered the covenant with the fathers, the covenant of blessing. We remember the nature of this covenant: a covenant partly material and partly spiritual in its content and character, with these as its essential elements: separation unto God, and the promise of a land, and of a seed, and of a blessing; the appointment to be a blessing; a covenant calling for the response of faith and of obedience to Him who made it. God remembered His promise to Abraham. It was time now to act, to fulfill one more portion of the promise, to take one more step toward the final consummation of the covenant purpose. God had promised Abraham that his seed should be numerous as the stars and as the sand on the seashore. This promise had been fulfilled: the descendants of Israel had multiplied "so that the land was filled with them" (chapter 1:7); although even here a greater fulfillment lay ahead, in the spiritual sense of all those who were to become the children of Abraham by an experience of faith like his. God had also promised Abraham that he would give to him and to his seed the land of Canaan as a possession and as an inheritance. It was this facet of the promise that should now be fulfilled through the events of the exodus and the conquest. Each stage in the fulfillment becomes a steppingstone to something future and far greater; for God had promised above all that Abraham and his seed should *both receive and be* a blessing: that they should become the medium of blessing to all the nations of the earth. Toward the fulfillment of this promise and the attainment of this goal God is ever moving. He began to fulfill it through the ministry of the Old Testament Israel in giving to mankind a true revelation of God. He took a mighty stride forward in the fulfillment of it when Jesus Christ came as the seed of Abraham to be a blessing, in the unique sense in which He as the Savior of the world mediates to all men "every spiritual blessing." He is still moving on toward the final realization of this promise as through the preaching of the gospel the blessing of Abraham is being brought in ever-widening circles also to the Gentiles. God still remembers His covenant with Abraham. He remembered it when Israel was suffering oppression in Egypt, and His remembrance of the covenant motivated His saving acts in the Exodus redemption.

It is significant that in the theophany of the burning bush God identified himself to Moses as "the God of your father, the God of Abraham, the God of Isaac, and the God of Jacob" (Ex. 3:6). Evidently Moses knew something of this God of the fathers. God does not come to him as a total stranger. He identifies himself as the God of previous acts of grace and of still present promises. He connects His present purpose with the relationship into which He had entered with Abraham and Isaac and Jacob, to be "their God"; that is to say, with the heart of the covenant of blessing. By this reminder of the covenant relationship with Abraham He shows himself to be a God to be trusted, even while He is to be feared.

The reference to "the God of your fathers" is repeated four times in chapters 3 and 4. (See Ex. 3:13, 15, 16; 4:5). It is linked in chapter 3:13-15 with the profound religious insight into the character of Israel's God given in the name YHWH, or the LORD. The Hebrew verb from which this sacred name of the God of Israel, Yahve or Jehovah, seems to be derived is *hayah,* which can be used to express either *being* or *becoming.* The explanation given by S. R. Driver still commends itself, that it represents fundamentally the concept of "self-manifesting existence."[2] God is! God manifests His existence! The name Yahve therefore means "he who in the absolute sense exists and who manifests his existence and his character."[3] By interpretation in the light of Israel's faith we may say that it stands for "the God of revelation and grace,"[4] who dwells with His people and makes himself known to them by what He does (i.e., in experience) and by what He says (i.e., in the prophetic or revealed word). It indicates a self-revelation of God which moves within the sphere of redemption, the experience through which Israel learned to know Him in a unique sense as their God. If not itself the original name for the God of the covenant with Abraham (See Ex. 6:2-3), it does designate the continuing self-manifestation of the covenant God in redemptive acts such as those of the exodus. It is really quite irrelevant to argue from Ex. 6:2-3 that the name Yahve was altogether unknown to the patriarchs. The point of the assertion is simply this, that God as "self-manifesting existence" was now about to act in such a signal, epoch-making way in the redemption of His people from centuries of enslavement so that in comparison it was as if He had not been known at all up to this time by His name Yahve. In the thought of the author of Exodus, He who acts now is certainly the same God as the God of the fathers, the God of Abraham; and He acts in accordance with the covenant with the fathers.

There is a strong reminder of God's covenant with Abraham in Ex. 6:2-9. From a literary point of view it stands in a significant context. It follows the first abortive attempt to persuade Pharaoh to let the people of Israel go (chapter 5). It links the present crisis with the faith experience of the fathers and with the divine promise given to them. The purpose is to strengthen Moses' faith; but it serves also to keep the Exodus situation within the framework of the covenant of blessing with the patriarchs. The past tense faithfully reflects the sense of the Hebrew verbs: "I appeared to Abraham, to Isaac, and to Jacob, as God Almighty, . . . I also established my covenant with them, to give them the land of Canaan, the land in which they dwelt as sojourners. . . . the land which I swore to give to Abraham, to Isaac, and to Jacob." What God proposes to do now is consistently presented as the fulfillment of a covenant from the past. The seed is now represented by the people of Israel. The promise to give them the land of Canaan is singled out for emphasis because it was now to be fulfilled through the exodus and the conquest. This was the most significant part of the promise just then. The promise of blessing is reaffirmed in v. 7 in language reminiscent of Gen. 17:7-8, "And I will take you for my people, and I will be your God; and you shall know that I am the Lord your God, who has brought you out from under the burdens of the Egyptians." The call to be a blessing is implied in the "your God" and "my people" relationship; for God's people must share His spirit. The covenant remembrance is worded in the same beautiful anthropomorphic language as in Ex. 2:24, "I have remembered my covenant" (v. 5); it is in my mind right now, and I am ready to do something about it. The covenant assurances in vv. 6-8 might well be called the Ten Encouragements, growing out of the covenant from the past and given as "new" promises for the present situation. Three times God says, "I am the Lord (Yahve)." Seven times he says, "I will." Listed in outline form the ten statements are these:

1. "I am the Lord" (v. 6).

2. "I will bring you out" from the Egyptian oppression (v. 6).

3. "I will deliver you" from your bondage (v. 6).

4. "I will redeem you" with power and with great acts of judgment (v. 6).

5. "I will take you for my people" (v. 7).

6. "I will be your God" (v. 7).

7. "You shall know that I am the Lord your God" and your redeemer (v. 7).

8. "I will bring you into" the promised land (v. 8).

9. "I will give it to you" for a possession (v. 8).
10. "I am the LORD." (v. 8).

How could it be more clearly and emphatically stated, that God intended to keep the covenant with Abraham by redeeming His people and thereby revealing as never before what it really means that "I am Yahve (the LORD)": I am He "who in the absolute sense exists and who manifests his existence and his character"![5] The saving acts of God in the exodus are seen as proceeding from out of His saving purpose in the calling of Abraham and in the making of a covenant with him, a covenant of blessing.

There are other indications in the Exodus narrative of its orientation to the fundamental beginnings to be seen in the Abraham story. They take us through that which is the heart of the narrative, the Exodus redemption, to the double experience in which redemption issues: the formal making of a covenant with the nation and the giving to them of the Torah or the law. Of these we shall speak further in a subsequent chapter. Nothing more need be said, however, to show how deeply the tradition of the exodus is rooted in the previous covenant with the fathers. It requires a skillful knife or a ruthless force to separate the one from the other. To the author of Exodus the saving acts of God that he narrates give evidence that God remembered His covenant made long ago with Abraham. Such was also the faith of Moses, as we see from his prayer in behalf of the "stiff-necked people" of Israel when the Lord threatened to consume them in his righteous wrath because of their great sin, and to make of Moses instead "a great nation" (see Gen. 12:2): "Remember Abraham, Isaac, and Israel, thy servants, to whom thou didst swear by thine own self, and didst say to them, 'I will multiply your descendants as the stars of heaven, and all this land that I have promised I will give to your descendants, and they shall inherit it for ever'" (Ex. 32:13). In response to his prayer "the Lord repented of the evil which he thought to do his people" (v. 14). The writer could just as well have paraphrased the words in Gen. 19:29, when God saved Lot from the overthrow of the wicked cities in which he dwelt: "God remembered Abraham, and therefore Israel was not destroyed." For God had given a promise of blessing *to* and *through* Abraham and his seed; and Moses rightly believed that He who promised is faithful.

The author of Deuteronomy has essentially the same tradition as the author of Exodus with respect to the patriarchal antecedents of the history of Israel. In chapter 1:8 the people are encouraged to go in and take possession of the land "which the Lord swore to your fathers, to Abraham, to Isaac, and to Jacob, to give to them and to their descendants after them." References to "the God of your fathers" intermingle with references to "the Lord our God" or "the Lord your God." See, for example, chapter 1:20-21. The promise of the land is to the fore, as we might expect in a book written from the viewpoint of the approaching conquest and inheritance. In chapter 9:27 we find a parallel to the prayer in Ex. 32:13, "Remember thy servants, Abraham, Isaac, and Jacob; do not regard the stubbornness of this people, or their wickedness, or their sin, lest the land from which thou didst bring us say, 'Because the Lord was not able to bring them into the land which he promised them, and because he hated them, he has brought them out to slay them in the wilderness.'" The message of Deuteronomy is a strong encouragement to believe that God, who made the covenant with the fathers and renewed it with the people of Israel at Sinai, is both willing and able to do what He has promised. It is from this book that Luther has taken the key words in his explanation to the First Commandment, with which he motivates the keeping of all the commandments: "We should fear, love, and trust in God above all things."[6] The Christian hymn writer reflects the spirit of Deuteronomy as well as of the fortieth chapter of the Book of Isaiah, which comes to us from a comparable situation, in these stirring words:

> "O God of mercy, God of might,
> In love and pity infinite,
> Teach us, as ever in thy sight,
> To live our life to thee."[7]

It is in Deuteronomy 7 that we see most clearly this God of mercy and of might, and the relationship between His faithfulness to the covenant with the fathers and the redemption of Israel from Egypt. We read in verses six to eight: "For you are a people holy to the Lord your God; the Lord your God has chosen you to be a people for his own possession, out of all the peoples that are on the face of the earth. It was not because you were more in number than any other people that the Lord set his love upon you and chose you, for you were the fewest of all peoples; but it is because the Lord loves you, and is keeping the oath which he swore to your fathers, that the Lord has brought you out with a mighty hand, and redeemed you from the house of bondage, from the hand of Pharaoh king of Egypt." What a significant combination: "because the Lord loves you, and is keeping the oath which he swore to your fathers"! These are the two reasons for the redemption of Israel and their election to be "a people for his own posession." They were not chosen because of numbers that made them one of the great powers among the nations of the earth, for politically they were relatively insignificant; nor were they given possession of the land because of their own righteousness or uprightness of heart, for religiously they were "a stubborn people" (Deut. 9:4-6). God acted in the deliverance from Egypt and in the conquest of Canaan in order to "confirm the word which the Lord swore to your fathers, to Abraham, to Isaac, and to Jacob" (Deut. 9:5b). The tradition is clear and consistent at this point. It is the point of attachment for the great theological passage in chapter 7:9-10, "Know therefore that the Lord your God is God, the faithful God who keeps covenant and steadfast love with those who love him and keep his commandments, to a thousand generations, and requites to their face those who hate him, by destroying them; he will not be slack with him who hates him, he will requite him to his face." It is the point of departure for the summons to renew the covenant in the land of Moab: "You stand this day all of you before the Lord your God; . . . that you may enter into the sworn covenant of the Lord your God, which the Lord your God makes with you this day; that he may establish you this day as his people, and that he may be your God, as he promised you, and as he swore to your fathers, to Abraham, to Isaac, and to Jacob" (Deut. 29:10-13). It is the motivating conclusion to the dramatic choice between life and death, between blessing and curse, between good and evil, in chapter 30:15-20. "I call heaven and earth to witness against you this day, that I have set before you life and death, blessing and curse; therefore choose life, that you and your descendants may live, loving the Lord your God, obeying his voice, and cleaving to him; for that means life to you and length of days, that you may dwell in the land which the Lord swore to your fathers, to Abraham, to Isaac, and to Jacob, to give them" (v. 19-20). It is woven into the preaching framework within which is set the Deuteronomic Code. The point of beginning for the history of Israel as God's covenanted people is not with Moses, according to the Book of Deuteronomy, but with Abraham. God acted to keep His promise to Abraham by redeeming Israel. In so doing He moved toward the fulfillment of the covenant in its wholeness. However much the emphasis may seem to be upon the promise of a land, the whole covenant promise and purpose of God is involved, including the mission of being a blessing.

In the Historical Books—Kings and Chronicles

It is not our intention to review every reference to Abraham or to the fathers in the Old Testament. The intention is to illustrate something of the extent of the tradition concerning the covenant with Abraham in the Old Testament as a whole. The tradition may be more deeply ingrained in the Old Testament message than is indicated by the direct references to the man Abraham. Such direct references are fewer in the historical books than in Exodus and Deuteronomy. In the Books of Samuel there are none at all. There are two significant passages in 1 and 2 Kings. We shall look at one in 2 Chronicles, and another in the closely related Book of Nehemiah.

The first passage in Kings is Elijah's prayer on Mount Carmel. "O Lord, God of Abraham, Isaac, and Israel, let it be known this day that thou art God in Israel, and that I am thy servant, and that I have done all these things at thy word. Answer me, O Lord, answer me, that this people may know that thou, O Lord, art God, and that thou hast turned their hearts back" (1 Kings 18: 36b-37). It is certainly interesting that so long after the time of Abraham the prophet should address God as the God of Abraham, and ask that He let it be known in unmistakable fashion that He is the God of the fathers, living still in Israel.

The second passage is a declaration by the historian with reference to the situation in Israel after the death of Elisha. "Now Hazael king of Syria oppressed Israel all the days of Jehoahaz. But the Lord was gracious to them and had compassion on them, and he turned toward them, because of his covenant with Abraham, Isaac, and Jacob, and would not destroy them; nor has he cast them from his presence until now" (2 Kings 13:22-23). The covenant with Abraham and his seed still carried weight with God! He had not forgotten it. Such was the conviction of the writer; and present events must still be interpreted in accordance with the clearly expressed purpose of that ancient covenant of blessing.

This is also the attitude expressed in several places in the Book of the Chronicles. The prayer of David in 1 Chron. 29:18, like that of Elijah on Carmel, is addressed to the Lord as "the God of Abraham, Isaac, and Israel, our fathers." The prayer of Jehoshaphat in 2 Chron. 20 is also directed to Yahve, "God of our fathers" (v. 6), who is also said to be "God in heaven," and who rules with power and might over all the kingdoms of the nations, and who has given a land to Israel as "the descendants of Abraham thy friend" (v. 7). This is one of two passages in the Old Testament where Abraham is called *the friend of God*. (See Is. 41:8; cf. James 2:23.) The phrase takes on new meaning when we consider Jesus' definition of *his* friends, "You are my friends if you do what I command you" (Jn. 15:14). Abraham obeyed God in faith, and God blessed him for it with a unique experience of His fellowship or friendship.

The tradition of this unique experience lingered in Israel way down into the time of the Exile. After the Exile we hear Ezra confessing in his public confession of sin, "Thou art the Lord, the God who didst choose Abram and bring him forth out of Ur of the Chaldees and give him the name Abraham; and thou didst find his heart faithful before thee, and didst make with him the covenant to give to his descendants the land of the Canaanite, the Hittite, the Amorite, the Perizzite, the Jebusite, and the Girgashite; and thou hast fulfilled thy promise, for thou art righteous" (Neh. 9:7-8). Abraham was faithful; yet, the emphasis is not so much on the faithfulness of Abraham as on the faithfulness and righteousness of God. The real theme of the covenant remembrance everywhere is beautifully stated in the great covenant passage in Deut. 7:9, "Know therefore that the Lord your God is God, the faithful God who keeps covenant and steadfast love [berith and hesed] with those who love him and keep his commandments." In the context is the covenant with Abraham and the confirmation of this covenant in the redemption of Israel to be God's segullah, or priceless treasure. God is faithful to His covenant always. It is in this conviction that Hezekiah sent couriers with letters not only to Judah but to the few who remained in Israel after the Assyrian conquest, saying, "O people of Israel, return to the Lord, the God of Abraham, Isaac, and Israel, that he may turn again to the remnant of you who have escaped from the hand of the kings of Assyria" (2 Chron.

30:6). Return to the God of Abraham who is true to his covenant! Return in the faith of Abraham, who also was faithful to God's covenant with him. Then the blessing of God promised to Abraham can move on to its fruition or final consummation, which we know to be in Jesus Christ, himself "the son of Abraham" (Mt. 1:1).

In the Prophets

There are only a few direct references to Abraham in the prophetic books; but that does not mean that there is no influence of the Abraham covenant on the prophetic message in more indirect ways. We shall see more of this influence on prophetic thought when we look at the covenant between God and Israel as a first stage in the fulfillment of the covenant of blessing. For the moment we restrict ourselves to the prophetic passages where Abraham is mentioned by name. We have already noted Is. 29:22, with its reference to "the Lord, who redeemed Abraham"; and also Is. 41:8, where Israel is called "the offspring of Abraham, my friend." In Micah 7:20 we have one instance where the name seems to designate the people descended from Abraham; the only instance in the Old Testament, according to Franz Böhl, where it does not designate the man.[8]

> Thou wilt show faithfulness to Jacob
> and steadfast love to Abraham,
> as thou hast sworn to our fathers
> from the days of old.

The three most significant passages are all from prophets who deal in one way or another with the problem of the Babylonian Exile. In Is. 51:1-2 there is a strong encouragement for the believing remnant from the remembrance of the call of Abraham.

> "Hearken to me, you who pursue deliverance,
> you who seek the Lord;
> look to the rock from which you were hewn,
> and to the quarry from which you were digged.
> Look to Abraham your father
> and to Sarah who bore you;
> for when he was but one I called him,
> and I blessed him and made him many."

What God has done once he can do again; and he will do it, if we seek the Lord as Abraham did and share his faith. Such is the continuing promise still. On the other hand, Ezekiel is told to warn the people who remained in the land after the destruction of Jerusalem in 586 B.C. against a false faith that uses almost identical language, but without seeking the Lord: "Son of man, the inhabitants of these waste places in the land of Israel keep saying, 'Abraham was only one man, yet he got possession of the land; but we are many; the land is surely given us to possess.' Therefore say to them, Thus says the Lord God: You eat flesh with the blood, and lift up your eyes to your idols, and shed blood; shall you then possess the land? You resort to the sword, you commit abominations and each of you defiles his neighbor's wife; shall you then possess the land?" (Ezek. 33:24-25) In Is. 51 we have the divine viewpoint; in Ezek. 33 we have the popular viewpoint, which bordered on sheer presumption. They wished to claim the material blessings of land and seed and inheritance, but scorned the spiritual blessing of living in devoted fellowship with God and consecration to His will. They wanted nothing to do with His Torah, as a guide in "the good and the right way"; they wanted nothing to do with covenant obligations; they were indifferent to their vocation to be "a holy nation." They did not really know the Lord; but "they will know that I am the Lord, when I have made the land a desolation and a waste because of all their abominations which they have committed" (v. 29). What a reverse twist that gives to the Genesis story of covenant and the Exodus story of redemption! And yet, the original plan of God with the covenant is not changed. It simply becomes clearer that the enjoyment of the blessings promised, be they material or spiritual in nature, is dependent on faith and obedience as a response to the covenant grace of God. Ezekiel teaches the same truth as Paul, only in different language: "So you see that it is men of faith who are the sons of Abraham" (Gal. 3:7). For Abraham believed God and obeyed His will; and so must all who would either inherit or be a blessing.

The reference to "the seed of Abraham, Isaac, and Jacob" in Jer. 33:26 is significant because it stands in a Messianic context. God will raise up "a righteous Branch" for David, who will rule in righteousness over the house of Israel (v. 15). This is in fulfillment of His covenant with the house of David, which is a part of the larger covenant with Israel, and this in turn of the covenant with Abraham. In the background we seem to sense the concept of the new covenant spoken of in Jer. 31:31-34. The blending of all the so-called covenants, Noachian, Abrahamic, Mosaic, and Davidic, in one picture of future restoration and consummation of the covenant purpose is an illustration of the essential oneness of God's covenant with men: "Thus says the Lord: If I have not established my covenant with day and night and the ordinances of heaven and earth, then I will reject the descendants of Jacob and David my servant and will not choose one of his descendants to rule over the seed of Abraham, Isaac, and Jacob. For I will restore their fortunes, and will have mercy upon them" (Jer. 33:25-26). All "the covenants" are simply so many facets of the *one* covenant, which is fundamentally a covenant of blessing, and which leads ultimately to Christ through whom we have every blessing. From one aspect of the promise to Abraham, Jesus Christ is the seed who mediates blessing to all; from another aspect the seed is seen to be His people, over whom He rules with grace and blessing, and through whom He continues to mediate blessing to others by the preaching of the gospel. Paul senses no contradiction, nor should we, in stressing first that the promise of a seed refers to one, "which is Christ" (Gal. 3:16), and then adding, "if you are Christ's, then you are Abraham's offspring [or seed], heirs according to promise" (Gal. 3:29). These two aspects of the fulfillment inhere in the promise of blessing from the beginning. They witness to the fundamental unity of purpose in the mission or vocation of the Lord's Christ and of His people.

In the Psalms

There are two passages in the Book of Psalms that speak with special clarity of the covenant with Abraham.

The one is in Ps. 47:9, "The princes of the peoples gather as the people of the God of Abraham." This is a striking assertion of the universality, and impliedly of the spiritual character, of the covenant of blessing. The God of Abraham is, of course, also the God of Israel; but the psalm celebrates the fact that He is also the God of the whole earth. To call him "the God of Abraham" brings this truth to mind much more readily than if he were called "the God of Israel." Furthermore, the verse as translated in RSV is really a declaration that *the peoples share with the people* of the God of Abraham in the promised blessing under the covenant. It is shallow exegesis to interpret this verse as meaning nothing more than the hope of conquest of Israel's enemies and their incorporation in Israel as a part of a political entity. It reflects the promise to Abraham that "in thee and in thy seed shall all the peoples of the earth be blessed"; and it anticipates the pronouncement of Paul that "in Christ Jesus the blessing of Abraham might come upon the Gentiles" (Gal. 3:14). We must not do violence to the religious character of the psalm, nor to the spiritual aspect of the covenant with Abraham which it reflects. "For God is the king of all the earth. . . . God reigns over the nations": such is the witness of the psalm; and the reign of the God of Abraham must be interpreted in the light of the covenant of God with Abraham, a covenant of blessing.

The second passage is in Ps. 105, a historical psalm, which opens with the exhortation,

> O give thanks to the Lord, call on his name,
> make known his deeds among the peoples! (v. 1)

The first paragraph is devoted to exhortation, which is addressed to the "offspring of Abraham his servant, sons of Jacob, his chosen ones" (v.5). Then follows a recital of some of the wonderful works of God, beginning with the covenant rather than with creation.

> He is the Lord our God;
> his judgments are in all the earth.
> He is mindful of his covenant forever,
> of the word that he commanded, for a thousand
> generations,
> the covenant which he made with Abraham,
> his sworn promise to Isaac,
> which he confirmed to Jacob as a statute,
> to Israel as an everlasting covenant,
> saying, "To you I will give the land of Canaan
> as your portion for an inheritance." (vv. 7-11)

The recital of God's wonderful works which follows includes a selection from patriarchal as well as national history, with special emphasis upon the exodus redemption. Near the end of the psalm we find this significant motivation for his mighty acts in relation to Israel, "For he remembered his holy promise, and Abraham his servant" (v. 42). The first fifteen verses of the psalm are identical with the first half of the psalm of thanksgiving in 1 Chron. 16, which is said to have been appointed by David to be sung to the Lord by Asaph and his brethren (v. 7). Regardless of date or authorship, the psalm illustrates the place that the covenant with Abraham had in the worship tradition of Israel. This was the starting point of God's blessings, according to Israelite faith and thought. Without the covenant with Abraham, with its broad universalism and deep spirituality, there is no adequate explanation of Israel's election and redemption to be a chosen people and a servant of God in relation to the nations of the earth; and when we say "without the covenant," we mean actually "without the saving act of God in making the covenant." The covenant with Abraham is the real beginning of the redemptive plan which culminates in Jesus Christ and in His mission of grace and truth to the world. For the statement in Deut. 7:8, "It is because the Lord loves you, and is keeping the oath which he swore to your fathers, that the Lord has brought you out with a mighty hand, and redeemed you from the house of bondage, from the hand of Pharaoh king of Egypt," applies equally to the redemption in Christ. Both the exodus redemption and the cross redemption belong to the saving acts of the Lord by which He fulfilled the promise of blessing to Abraham.

"And God heard their groaning, and God remembered his covenant with Abraham, with Isaac, and with Jacob" (Ex. 2:24).[9]

"For all the promises of God find their Yes in him. That is why we utter the Amen through him, to the glory of God" (2 Cor. 1:20).

NOTES

[1] C. F. Keil and Franz Delitzsch, *Biblical Commentary on the Old Testament*. Edinburgh: T. and T. Clark. 1864. Vol. I, pp. 373-4.

[2] S. R. Driver, *The Book of Genesis, op. cit.,* p. 408.

[3] From *The Westminster Dictionary of the Bible, op. cit.,* p. 287.

[4] *Ibid.*

[5] *Ibid.*

[6] Martin Luther, *The Small Catechism, op. cit.*

[7] Godfrey Thring, "O God of Mercy, God of Might," in The Augustana Hymnal. Rock Island: Augustana Book Concern. 1925.

[8] Franz Böhl, *op. cit.*

[9] See James Orr, *The Problem of the Old Testament,* for the natural deduction: "Israel's God was the God of Abraham, of Isaac, and of Jacob. The starting-point in its covenant history was not Moses, but Abraham." New York: Charles Scribner's Sons. 1926. p. 38.

Chapter Eight

THE ABRAHAM COVENANT AND THE
COVENANT AT SINAI

W HEN THE OLD TESTAMENT speaks of a series of covenants this does not mean that they are unrelated to each other, nor that a "new" covenant necessarily replaces the "old." There is rather an element of fulfillment in each new covenant in relation to that which precedes; and also an element of adaptation, which is designed to further the coming of the final consummation of the central purpose of the divine covenant, in "the period of the great Restoration" (Acts 3:21, Moffat's translation).[1] It is quite correct to speak with Paul of "the covenants" and of "the promises" (Rom. 9:4), as if they were plural; it is also correct to speak of *two* covenants, comparing the "first" with the "second," as does the writer of the Epistle to the Hebrews (Heb. 8:7); but it is equally correct to speak of "the covenant," as if God had made *one* covenant with men, of which the several "covenants" are so many facets, or so many stages in the historical working out of a single covenant of grace and blessing.

The first major stage in the fulfillment of the covenant with Abraham is in the great covenant with Israel at Mount Sinai. Millar Burrows rightly says that among the many covenants in the Old Testament "the covenant with the nation at Sinai remains central; it is usually what is meant when the covenant is mentioned."[2] We cannot rightly speak of the centrality of the Sinai covenant, however, without at the same time acknowledging its connection with the earlier Abraham covenant; for this covenant with the nation is essentially the same in content and purpose with the covenant of which we have been speaking, the covenant of blessing with Abraham and his seed. From one point of view it may rightly be called *new*, for there is a certain newness in every life situation and in every human experience; from another point of view it is simply an affirmation and an adaptation *of the old* to a changed or a new situation. If we think of it as a new covenant, it is because we believe that there is a goal to redemptive history, toward which the covenant with Israel was a mighty forward step; it is because we recognize a law of growth in life, according to which

> "The best is yet to be,
> The last of life, for which the first was made."[3]

The newness is not that of substitution, but of completion. The Sinai covenant did not annul the covenant of promise; it was a step forward in its fulfillment. In the same way the new covenant in Jesus' blood did not annul the covenant with Israel: it brought this covenant to fulfillment. There is a radical newness in any fulfillment, whether it be of a hope, or of a promise, or of a covenant, or of an ambition, or of a mission; but in order to be a genuine fulfillment, there must also be a fundamental oneness with the thing fulfilled. It is this kind of newness that we would assert for the covenant with the people of Israel in relation to the covenant with the man Abraham.

1

The Basic Provisions of the Covenant

The basic provisions of the covenant with Israel are set forth in Ex. 19:3-6. Two months after leaving Egypt the people of Israel come to Sinai and encamp before the mountain. Moses turns to God, as if to find out what to do next, and God says to him, as if in answer to his prayer: "Thus you shall say to the house of Jacob, and tell the people of Israel: You have seen what I did to the Egyptians, and how I bore you on eagles' wings and brought you to myself. Now therefore, if you will obey my voice and keep my covenant, you shall be my own possession among all peoples; for all the earth is mine, and you shall be to me a kingdom of priests and a holy nation. These are the words which you shall speak to the children of Israel."

From a strictly historical point of view the time and place, if authentic, are sufficient to indicate that these are significant words. From a literary point of view they serve as the introduction to the Sinai experience as narrated in the Book of Exodus. From the religious point of view they seem to be the key to the interpretation of the whole covenant relationship of God with Israel.

The passage begins with a reminder of the wonderful experience of redemption that preceded and prepared the way for the experience that now confronted them; serving as the historical and the spiritual foundation for their present status (v. 4). "You have seen what I did!" The position of the pronoun before the verb in Hebrew makes it emphatic, "*You* have seen." They had personally experienced "the saving acts of the Lord"; they were witnesses of His power and grace in their behalf. They had seen God's judgments, "what I did to the Egyptians"; judgments directed against Egypt for the deliverance of Israel; the righteous, but also the redeeming, acts of God. They had seen God's saving grace, "how I bore you on eagles' wings"; a symbol of initial deliverance, but also of the subsequent experience of God's upholding power on the dangerous and arduous journey: "eagles' wings" suggesting strength and security. Israel had experienced both of these, in a physical as well as in a spiritual sense, since leaving Egypt. We learn something of the spiritual symbolism of the events from 1 Cor. 10:1-4: "I want you to know, brethren, that our fathers were all under the cloud, and all passed through the sea, and all were baptized into Moses in the cloud and in the sea, and all ate the same supernatural food and all drank the same supernatural drink. For they drank from the supernatural Rock which followed them, and the Rock was Christ." In Old Testament language let it suffice to say that they had experienced in a very concrete way the gracious presence of God. They had experienced a divine fellowship, "how I brought you to myself"; that is, how I took you into my protecting love and care, into a relationship of blessing akin to that of Abraham. It is too limited an interpretation to make these beautiful words mean only that God had brought them to this meeting with Him at Sinai; that is included, but He had also brought them into a daily experience of His presence, into a spiritual fellowship with Him as His people. This experience had already begun. It began in the Passover. It was evidenced during the march from the Red Sea to Sinai. It was an experience of the love and faithfulness (hesed and emeth) of God on the basis of the covenant of blessing made with the fathers. Everything that follows is oriented from out of this redemption experience, which was itself an expression of covenant faithfulness and love on the part of God.

Three questions may serve to bring out the essential terms of the covenant as summed up in Ex. 19:5-6.

The Condition

The first question concerns the human response to the divine covenant. What did God ask of the people of Israel as the condition to be fulfilled on their part, if they were to live in covenant with Him? We note the significant words, "If you will obey my voice and keep my covenant." They were to keep His covenant by obeying His voice; so that we may rightly say that *obedience* was the condition for the continued enjoyment of the blessing of the covenant relationship.

The stress on obedience should not surprise us, for we have seen its importance already in the Abraham story. Nor should we be confused as to the nature and origin of this obedience. We shall not understand the "if" of God, if we forget the context in which it stands: the immediate framework of the redemption from Egypt, as one of the great "saving acts of God"; and the larger framework of the covenant of blessing already initiated with the fathers. The obedience required did not initiate the covenant; it belongs to the response of man to the covenant. It does not alter in any way the fundamental character of the covenant with Abraham as a divine covenant of grace and blessing. It does not transform the covenant of promise into a covenant of human works. The introductory words, "Now therefore," suggests the same sequence here as in Rom. 12:1-2, "I appeal to you therefore, brethren, by the mercies of God": we begin with the experience of the unmerited love of God (see the fine interpretative comment in Deut. 7:6-11), and this experience becomes the motivation for the obedient life of His people. This is the obedience of faith. This is the obedience of the heart. This is the childlike obedience of the redeemed, who know by experience something of the wonderful love of God in making and keeping covenant. It is a condition only in the sense that without it God is thwarted in His love and hindered in His purpose. He can do nothing for, nor can He accomplish anything through, a wilfully disobedient people. Abraham believed and obeyed the voice of God; therefore he could become the bearer of the promise of blessing to others, he could be a blessing. The conditions remained exactly the same for Israel as his seed if they were to fulfill the vocation which the covenant set before them. God acted first. He looked for a response from His redeemed people.

If we look at the condition from the New Testament point of view the conclusion remains the same. If the passover redemption is a spiritual type of the redemption through the blood of Christ (see 1

Cor. 5:7), there should certainly be room here for an analogy between this faith obedience of Israel as God's ransomed people and the faith obedience of the Christian in relation to Christ. It has its roots in either case in an act of redemption by God; the one symbolic and preparatory, the other "an eternal redemption" (Heb. 9:12), but both related to the same ultimate purpose of God. It is not to be understood as the external obedience to ordinances imposed from without, but as the inward response of the heart to the will of God who has graciously made a covenant into which we are called. It is this inwardness of the obedience that is stressed in the basic provisions of the covenant at Sinai. There were external ordinances given later on, as we shall see; for what purpose we shall also see. Of these the New Testament has much to say; but when it sets aside the ordinances as insufficient (Heb. 10:1) and "becoming obsolete" (Heb. 8:13), it by no means sets aside God's call to obedience of faith on the part of His people. The obedience of faith is something permanent, a fruit that God always seeks in His redeemed people; for without it there can be no real appropriation of His blessings, nor can there be any sharing of them with others. We know from the New Testament that only the Holy Spirit working within man's heart can bring forth such fruit. Though this is not stated in Ex. 19, we need not therefore rule out "his holy Spirit" (Is. 63:10, 11), the Spirit of His presence, as being active also in this situation. At any rate the tone of the divine "if" in Ex. 19:5 is definitely not legalistic but spiritual, in harmony with the spirit of the covenant with Abraham.

The Promise

The second question concerns the divine promise as a part of the covenant. What did God promise the people of Israel "if" they were willing to accept the covenant on God's terms? We note the words, "you shall be my own possession among all peoples." The translation is not quite adequate. "You shall be my *segullah*," says the Hebrew text. It is a unique and significant word, which is found several times in the Book of Deuteronomy in combination with the word for people: "a people for his own possession" (see Deut. 7:6; 14:2; 26:18). According to the lexicon *segullah* means "valued property, peculiar treasure."[4] The English versions generally follow the Septuagint and translate as "my own possession," which is weak because it omits the concept of "treasure." The American Jewish version renders it as "mine own treasure."[5] See also Moffatt's translation, "my own prized possession."[6] In the American translation of Smith-Goodspeed it is rendered as "my very own."[7] R. D. Wilson explains it from the Arabic for the treasure of jewels which a woman kept in her bosom as if it were her bank for the safe keeping of her valuables.[8] What a wonderful thought! "God's treasure," and "God's possession"; His prized possession and His peculiar treasure, His very own: that is what He called Israel, or promised that they could be "if" obedient to His voice. The same is true of the Christian, and of the church of Jesus Christ, today. They are precious in the sight of God because of His love; He regards them as His valued property. It is not a valuation that is conditioned by their obedience in the sense that the obedience creates or calls forth God's grace, but in the sense that God's grace calls forth and is received by the obedience of faith. There is nothing higher in God's scale of values than a humble, obedient faith. It was so in the covenant with Abraham. It was so in the covenant with Israel. It is so in the new covenant in Jesus Christ. We must not forget, however, that in each instance it is God who in grace makes the covenant to which faith responds and is obedient. We become His *segullah* not by merit but by mercy. It has never been otherwise.

The phrase "among all peoples" clearly suggests a special place for Israel among the nations of earth, or an election of grace; but it may also suggest a special purpose, in relation to those others among whom it was at the moment uniquely privileged. There is nothing here to indicate that these others were excluded from God's love and concern; there is no indication that Yahve was regarded as the God of Israel only, or as a tribal deity. For God adds, as if to correct any possible misconception at this point, "for all the earth is mine"; that is, it belongs to me, it is also my possession. Surely God must value all the earth if it belongs to Him! The Hebrew "ki" clause is often an explanatory clause, and such seems to be the case here. The punctuation of the sentence in RSV is significant, in that it joins this clause with the following statement of Israel's mission to be a kingdom of priests; making the latter half of the sentence in vv. 5-6 an explanation of the first half. There can be only one explanation of the uniqueness of Israel's position as God's "very own": it was never intended to be a selfish privilege, but rather a special opportunity; or, in God's words to Abraham, "and be a blessing." Israel was chosen and called to be God's servant in relation to all humanity. The same is true of the Christian church today; it is called to be a blessing by sharing the blessing which it has received from God as His people, the blessing of a personal experience of the truth of the gospel.

The Mission

The third question concerns this commission of God to His people. What was to be Israel's character and mission as God's very own from among the peoples of the earth?

The answer is given in the form of a great declaration, which in many ways resembles the great commission of Jesus in the New Testament: "You shall be to me a kingdom of priests and a holy nation." Theirs was to be a position of "kingship over and priesthood in behalf of the nations." The thought conveyed is that of a spiritual ministry or service that will lead to a spiritual dominion or rule over mankind. There is a marked similarity between this concept of "a kingdom of priests" and the New Testament concept of the priesthood of all believers. The connecting link between the two, however, is forged by the consummation of this vocation of Israel "in Christ"; for every reference to Israel's priestly-royal position and function must include the Christ that should come (and came) out of Israel. It is on the basis of this fulfillment in Christ that the whole picture of "a chosen race, a royal priesthood, a holy nation, God's own people" is in the New Testament transferred to the church; see Titus 2:14; 1 Peter 2: 5, 9-10; Rev. 1:6 and 5:9-10. The purpose of it all, says Peter, is "that you may declare the wonderful deeds of him who called you out of darkness into his marvelous light" (1 Peter 2:9). A spiritual ministry to the world is the goal of the covenant: a ministry such as was exercised in a measure by Israel through her witness to Yahve as the living God, who is both Creator and Redeemer, the God of Israel and the God of the whole earth; a ministry such as we see in a unique sense in Jesus Christ, our prophet, priest, and king, who is the source of "every spiritual blessing," the Savior of the world; a ministry such as now is being performed by the Christian church, the body of Christ, commissioned by Him to preach the gospel, the good news, to all the world.

Such a mission demands a holy character of those who are called to perform it. "You shall be to me a holy nation"; holy in the sense of being "set apart" as the possession of the holy God, but holy also in the sense of being "transformed" into the likeness of the holiness,

142

the purity, the perfection, of God (see Rom. 12:1-2). "You shall be holy; for I the Lord your God am holy" (Lev. 19:2). The New Testament requirement is the same: "As obedient children, do not be conformed to the passions of your former ignorance, but as he who called you is holy, be holy yourselves in all your conduct; since it is written, 'You shall be holy, for I am holy'" (1 Peter 1:14-16). Such is his goal for His people always. Something of this character there must be in those who shall serve him in the ministry of blessing. But first things first! This fine quotation from the commentary by Keil and Delitzsch with reference to Israel may help us at this point: "It was not made this (i.e., holy) however, by being separated from the other nations, for that was merely the means of attaining the divine end, but by the fact that God placed the chosen people in the relation of covenant fellowship with himself, founded his kingdom in Israel, established in the covenant relationship an institution of salvation, which furnished the covenant people with the means of obtaining the expiation of their sins and securing righteousness before God and holiness of life with God, in order that by the discipline of his holy commandments, under the guidance of his holy arm, he might train and guide them to the holiness and glory of the divine life."[9] There is truth in the saying, that what God demands He also provides; for He provided within the covenant the means by which Israel could attain to that which was required for its great mission. But there could be no attaining without the heart attitude of the obedience of faith. The Old Testament teaching at this point is so very similar to that of the New: we are redeemed in order that we might be God's own and serve him with a glad heart and a willing mind in the holiness of life.[10]

2

The Torah or the Law

If we were to judge only by the basic provisions of the covenant with Israel as found in Ex. 19:4-6, we would quickly conclude that this was no new covenant, but a reaffirmation of the everlasting and universal spiritual covenant with Abraham. The content is essentially the same, even if expressed in slightly different language. Both seek a spiritual relationship with God in faith and obedience, in response to the covenant initiative or grace of God. Both have as their goal a spiritual ministry of blessing to the peoples of the world. Both seem to be essentially a covenant of promise. In both instances the response sought is that of the obedience of faith. The tone is not legalistic but spiritual. The covenant reflects a broad universalism rather than a narrow nationalism: it seems to encompass the earth through the ministry of a nation called for the purpose of being a blessing.

What happens to the covenant when the Torah or the law becomes a part of it? For a law was added to the covenant of promise at Sinai. Whether we think of the Ten Commandments, which are called "his covenant" (see Deut. 4:13); or of "the book of the covenant," which was read in the hearing of the people, and to which they responded by promising obedience (Ex. 24:7-8); or of "the law of commandments and ordinances" (Eph. 2:15), which is customarily referred to as "the law of Moses," the Biblical witness is clear: a significant addition *was* made to the covenant that we have thus far consistently interpreted as a covenant of promise, grace, and blessing. Did the law change the nature of the covenant made with Abraham? Is the addition so radical as to make the Sinai covenant a wholly new covenant, a covenant of law rather than of promise? Did the giving of the law serve to annul the promise previously given by God?

In Gal. 3:19, after discussing the covenant of promise with Abraham, Paul asks a similar question, "Why then the law?" Obviously he was concerned with the same problem that confronts us, the relation between the covenant at Sinai and the earlier covenant of blessing with the patriarchs. From our study of the introductory statement in Ex. 19: 3-6 we have concluded that they are basically one covenant: a covenant extended now to include formally, as it always had in principle, the whole nation; even as we believe that in Christ and through the Christian gospel and within the Christian church it is made inclusive of all nations. With this conclusion Paul would seem to be in complete agreement. At least we know from Gal. 3:15-18 that the promise was not annulled by the law; the basic provisions of the covenant with Abraham remain unchanged. "For if the inheritance is by the law, it is no longer by promise; but God gave it to Abraham by a promise" (Gal. 3:18). If Paul is right in his interpretation we, too, stand on solid ground in our interpretation of the Abraham covenant.

And yet, a law was added. We see that in Ex. 24:7, with its reference to "the book of the covenant"; a reference which seems to include chapters 21-23 of the Book of Exodus, and possibly also the Ten Commandments in chapter 20—the fundamental law of the covenant, which elsewhere is referred to as "his covenant" (Deut. 4:13). The response sought and given when the book of the covenant was read was the pledge of obedience to its provisions: "All that the Lord has spoken we will do, and we will be obedient." In chapter 24:8, the covenant is said to have been made with them "in accordance with all these words." (See ASV mg., "upon all these conditions.") In short, to the general spiritual proviso for an attitude of heart obedience, or of the obedience of faith, there are added specific statutes and ordinances to be obeyed, often with equally specific penalties attached to them for disobedience. The initial legislation given through Moses may have been quite simple in form; it may have grown through the centuries of Israel's history, always within the framework of the covenant, into the complex codes of the Old Testament; but according to the clear and consistent witness of the Scriptures it was added by divine authority. It is not the problem of origin, however, that concerns us now. We are concerned with the fact that a law was given, and with its effect on the covenant of promise; or with Paul's question, "Why then the law?"

We are acquainted with Paul's own answer, in Gal. 3:19, "It was added because of transgressions, till the offspring should come to whom the promise had been made." Jesus gave a similar reply when asked why Moses permitted divorce: "For your hardness of heart Moses allowed you to divorce your wives, but from the beginning it was not so" (Mt. 19: 8). The addition of the law had a specific purpose, which is closely connected with the transition from a covenant relationship with an individual or with a family to a covenant relationship with a nation. Ideally its goal within the covenant was to guide God's people in "the good and the right way" (1 Sam. 12:23); and when they failed or refused to walk in this way, as they so often did, to convict them of sin, and so to become "our custodian," as Paul says, "until Christ came." It had an educational function in Israel, as an instrument of spiritual pedagogy; but it also had a civil function, in restraint of wickedness and as a protection of individual rights within the community, as an instrument of national righteousness. The standard of Israel's life as a nation was God's law, and the goal of the law for God's people was that they might be "a holy nation." The commandments in Lev. 19:2, "You shall be holy; for I the Lord your God am holy," sums up the spiritual-educational purpose of the law with Israel; for as Wilhelm Möller has so well said of the Book of Leviticus, it teaches that "all time, every place, all property, and every person should be sanctified unto the Lord."[11] With such a purpose the gospel has no quarrel; for the New Testament exhortation incorporates the Old Testament commandment, "as he who called you is holy, be holy yourselves in all your conduct; since it is written, 'You shall be holy, for I am holy'" (1 Peter 1:15, 16).

It is with respect to *the means* by which to achieve holiness that the law seems to depart from the original way of the covenant of blessing. The law is at best a good external discipline, as Luther has said, speaking of fasting as a religious exercise.[12] There is danger that it may become a substitute for a truly spiritual faith and obedience, for the inward devotion to God which seeks expression in the outward dedication of life. The ideal is when God's law of love is written in the heart, so that man loves to do what God wills because he knows that it is for his own good always (Deut. 6:24), and also for the good of others. We can see traces of all these tendencies in the Old Testament; and we shall say more about them later, when we discuss the Torah in connection with covenant theology. For our present purpose we would point out that the law *as an addition* to the covenant of blessing is sometimes put so sharply in the foreground of later Biblical teaching as to seem to overshadow, and even to shut out entirely, the original terms of the covenant; specifically the promise of blessing, which is a gospel preached beforehand to Abraham. This is especially true in the New Testament, with its sharp contrast between the old covenant and the new; where it seems at first glance as if the law were the very essence of the covenant which is labeled "old" and "first" and even "obsolete." It cannot be asserted too often or too strongly, however, that the law *was added*: it *was not substituted* for the covenant of promise. If we understand the ordinary laws of human speech, it is not incorrect to speak of the "first" covenant from the viewpoint of the addition, letting a part stand for the whole; but if we wish to be really exact in our speech and thought we shall look beyond the addition, recognizing that it is the promise given to Abraham which really constitutes the first covenant. The covenant with Israel, including the law, is only one significant step toward its consummation. The covenant of blessing remains fundamentally unaltered. "This is what I mean: the law, which came four hundred and thirty years afterward, does not annul a covenant previously ratified by God, so as to make the promise void" (Gal. 3:17).

146

NOTES

1 James Moffatt, *op. cit.*
2 Millar Burrows, *op. cit.*, p. 11.
3 Robert Browning, "Rabbi Ben Ezra," in *Poems of Robert Browning. New York:* Thomas Y. Crowell Co. 1896. p. 207.
4 William Gesenius, *A Hebrew and English Lexicon of the Old Testament,* ed. by Brown, Driver, and Briggs. *op. cit.*
5 The Holy Scriptures. Philadelphia: The Jewish Publication Society of America. 1917.
6 James Moffatt, *op. cit.*
7 J. M. Powis Smith and Edgar J. Goodspeed, The Bible: an American Translation. Copyright 1923, 1927, 1948 by the University of Chicago. Fifteenth impression 1951. Chicago: The University of Chicago Press.
8 Robert Dick Wilson, Lecture Notes, Princeton Seminary, 1927.
9 C. F. Keil and Franz Delitzsch, *Biblical Commentary on the Old Testament.* Vol. II, p. 100. *op. cit.*
10 Martin Luther, *The Small Catechism:* Second Article. *op. cit.*
11 Wilhelm Möller, *op. cit.*
12 Martin Luther, *The Small Catechism:* Part V. *op. cit.*

AUTHOR'S NOTE

In any discussion of the Biblical concept of covenant we must be careful not to confuse *form* with *substance*. Our primary concern is with the *substance* of the Scriptural covenant. With respect to *form* there is a significant resemblance between the covenant at Sinai and certain ancient suzerainty treaties. (See G. E. Mendenhall, *Law and Covenant in Israel and the Near East;* cf. John Bright, *A History of Israel,* p. 134 ff.). The Biblical writers naturally used thought-forms with which they were familiar, and may even have been influenced by them in the formulation of the thought; but the religious faith which is the *substance* of the Biblical covenant cannot be accounted for by such extraneous cultural influences alone. We are reminded of a statement in the *Westminster Historical Atlas to the Bible,* concerning the patriarchal covenant as "Israel's nomadic heritage": "Geography may explain the conditions of divine revelation, but cannot provide a substitute for it." The same must be said of the political suzerainty treaty in relation to the Mosaic covenant. Its significance does not extend beyond *the form* of the Biblical covenant; *the substance* must be interpreted in terms of itself.

Chapter Nine

THE COVENANT WITH ISRAEL AND ITS BASIC THEOLOGY

E VEN THOUGH WE BELIEVE that the covenant with Israel is rooted in a previous covenant with Abraham, which is largely determinative of its content and purpose, we may agree with Millar Burrows that "the covenant with the nation at Sinai remains central" in the Old Testament.[1] It affects our understanding of both history and prophecy; it is essential to our interpretation of both religion and life. We may compare it to a mighty tree, whose far-flung branches can be traced in every book of the Old Testament library and extend into every nook of Israel's faith and life. The covenant with Abraham was the acorn out of which grew the covenant with Israel as the oak. The analogy, though imperfect, is helpful; especially if we bear in mind that here as in the area of physical life it is God who implants life in the seed and who also makes it grow. If we seem to think now more particularly of the covenant with Israel than of the covenant with Abraham, we are still aware of the living relationship between the two; a relationship which we believe is of God.

We want to consider briefly the contents of the covenant faith as we find it in the Old Testament, and the continuing religious implications of this covenant theology for us today. We shall center our study around six closely related aspects of this theology:

1. The covenant origin, or election.
2. The covenant experience, or fellowship.
3. The covenant requirements, or Torah.
4. The covenant purpose, or mission.
5. The covenant and prophecy.
6. The covenant and the gospel.

A common grouping is the threefold one of election, covenant, and mission. We believe, however, that the more detailed outline will make for greater clarity. We shall add a section on significant covenant-related words, or covenant vocabulary.

1

Covenant Origin, or Election

"For you are a people holy to the Lord your God; the Lord your God has chosen you to be a people for his own possession, out of all the peoples that are on the face of the earth" (Deut. 7:6).

It is a fundamental article of faith in the Old Testament that Israel was a chosen people, an elect nation. What is the religious significance of that faith?

Edmond Jacob defines election as "the initial act by which Yahweh comes into relation with His people and the permanent reality which assures the constancy of that bond."[2] Every intervention by God in history is an election, according to Jacob; whether He chooses a place in which to manifest His presence, a people to carry out His intentions, or a man to be His servant and messenger. To assert that God chose Abraham does not mean that He may not have chosen other men for some special purpose; nor does the election of Israel necessarily imply that God has nothing to do with the history of other nations. The prophet Amos made that emphatically clear, when he punctured the self-righteous pride of Israel with this word of the Lord:

"Are you not like the Ethiopians to me,
  O people of Israel?" says the Lord.
"Did I not bring up Israel from the land of Egypt,
  and the Philistines from Caphtor and the Syrians from Kir?"
                                             (Am. 9:7)

Nevertheless there was something unique about the election of Israel, as indeed there is in every divine election; for election, as we shall see, always implies a divine mission: and this in its very nature is selective and personal. For the moment, however, we are concerned only with the doctrine of election itself.

The religious implications of the doctrine of election are both many and significant.

It implies, for example, that there is a God who acts in history, not once but often, with sovereign free will and with gracious intent. There is no room in such a faith for a naturalistic determinism! God is, and God acts. To this the covenant faith of Israel bears constant witness; and it is relevant still, for God has not ceased to be nor to act—He chooses men still today to be His very own and to serve Him.

149

It implies also, as Jacob points out, the permanent reality of the covenant.[3] For election is more than an initial divine choice, which then leaves the one chosen to his own resources. God is faithful, not only to His word so as to keep His promise, but also to His purpose so as to achieve His goal with the covenant. There is a sense in which election is a continuing act of God, on which the faith of His people depends, and by which the outcome of His purpose is guaranteed.

For election implies that there is a divine goal to human history, towards which God is ever leading, and which will surely be reached in the end. What that goal is we shall see when we consider the covenant and prophecy. Regardless of how we define the goal, history is more than the irrelevant repetition of itself in cycles that it often seems to be: where men and nations repeat the same mistakes, and suffer the same consequences. This is one aspect of history, as we see even from the Book of Judges; and it is verified by secular history, where the events of today often have a monotonous similarity with those of yesterday. There is more of truth than of cynicism in the remark of Lin Yutang, "The great thing about the teaching of history is that we must teach history but must not let history teach us."[4] Certainly the history of man on this earth often seems to move in circles rather than in a straight line. The easy optimism of the first part of the twentieth century as to the progress of man has given way to an uneasy pessimism. In this change of attitude there is a measure of truth, a wholesome corrective for the naïve belief that man is slowly but surely getting better in himself, and that he is gradually achieving by his own unaided efforts a better world; but it is nevertheless not the whole truth. The eyes of faith see another aspect of history, which is one facet of the doctrine of election: that the living God has covenanted with men whom He has chosen to achieve His redemptive goal in the world that He has created. Our confidence is not in man but in God, whose call and election are sure.

In this broad sense election is related not only to Israel's history, but to her whole religious faith and life: to the place of worship, where God chooses to cause His name to be remembered (Ex. 20:24); to the raising up of prophets to preach His Word (see Am. 7:15); to the choice of her king, who should rule over her in the fear of the Lord (Deut. 17:15); to the "name of God" and "glory of God" theology, which in different ways stress the presence of God with His people whom He has chosen.

For concrete illustration of this doctrine of election in relation to the covenant with Israel we turn to a few selected Bible passages, chiefly in Deuteronomy and Deutero-Isaiah, where three verbs signifying election occur frequently: *bachar,* meaning choose; *qara,* meaning call; and *yadha,* meaning know.

We begin with Deut. 7:6-8, which may well be called *a key passage* to the doctrine of election in the Old Testament. The verb *bachar,* "has chosen," expresses the idea of "free unmotivated choice";[5] that is, it is not motivated from without, as if God were influenced by something He saw in Israel. The passage before us rules out *numbers* as such a motivation; for Israel was not at the beginning, nor at any time in her history, one of the great powers of the world. The principle of divine action stated in 1 Cor. 1:26-29 is a striking New Testament parallel to the election of Israel: "God chose what is weak in the world to shame the strong, God chose what is low and despised in the world, even things that are not, to bring to nothing things that are, so that no human being might boast in the presence of God." It is true that Is. 51:1-2 presents another slant on election and numbers: "For when he was but one I called him, and I blessed him and made him many." So also the promise to Abraham stressed that his seed should be as the stars of heaven and as the sand on the seashore in number; but the emphasis here is on result rather than cause, and the language is relative rather than absolute in meaning. In Deut. 9:4-6 any presumed *righteousness* on the part of Israel is emphatically ruled out as motivating the divine action in their behalf: "Know therefore, that the Lord your God is not giving you this good land to possess because of your righteousness; for you are a stubborn people" (v. 6). Nor did Israel initiate the covenant by choosing to be the people of Yahve and persuading Him to accept them; both election and covenant originated with God. We can speak of motivation for the choice of Israel *only from within,* that is, from the nature of God himself and from His revealed will.

From this point of view there is a double motivation. There is the motivation of *love.* The Hebrew word so translated in Deut. 7:7, 8 is first a noun and then a verb from the root *ahab.* Many scholars see a distinction between *hesed* (RSV, steadfast love) and *ahabah:* the former is said to be conditioned by the terms of the covenant, while the latter is unconditioned love. "It (ahabah) is not limited by the conditions of any covenant, but only by the will or the nature of the lover.

Actually God's *ahabah* (love) for Israel is the very basis and the only cause of the existence of the covenant between God and Israel."[6] For our present purpose we need not decide whether this distinction between God's election love and His covenant love is fully valid. It suffices to say that in either case it is *unmerited* love. God is love! Uniquely so. Love motivated the call of Abraham, and the election of Israel, as well as the sending of God's beloved Son to be the Savior of the world. There is also, however, in the case of the election of Israel the motivation of *faithfulness* to a previous promise, to the covenant with Abraham and with the fathers. "It is because the Lord loves you, and is keeping the oath which he swore to your fathers, that the Lord has brought you out with a mighty hand, and redeemed you from the house of bondage, from the hand of Pharaoh king of Egypt" (Deut. 7:8). God is the faithful God who keeps covenant: and in redeeming Israel He was keeping His covenant with Abraham. Kurt Galling stresses two "election traditions" in the Old Testament and says that the primary tradition is the one which connects election with the redemption of Israel.[7] In the passage before us the two traditions, if there are two, are joined together. Israel was chosen in Abraham as the seed of promise; and in the act of redemption which gave proof of their election, God manifested His *hesed,* or steadfast love, His faithful covenant love. They were selected "from among all peoples" (Ex. 19:5, ASV) because God was faithful and true to His purpose with the covenant of blessing, that through them blessing might come to others, even to all the peoples of the earth. Personal salvation is not the primary or immediate objective of this selection. A nation is selected for a special divine mission, whose ultimate objective is the salvation of all men of faith. Election and mission belong together. When we speak of the election of Israel the comparison should be with the church as a community of believers with a mission entrusted to them rather than with the Christian man as an individual and the problem of personal salvation. Israel was elected to continue, and in a measure to fulfill, the vocation of Abraham to be a blessing. Election cannot be understood apart from mission. The election of Israel is inseparable from the call of Abraham. They are united by a single divine purpose.

If election and mission belong together, so do election and covenant, in the sense of fellowship or relationship. That is clearly indicated in that God chose Israel to be "a people for his own possession" (Deut. 7:6; Ex. 19:5), or to be "his very own." We have noted earlier that the word *segullah* combines the thought of something *prized* and something *possessed* (see Moffat, "his prized possession"). Putting treasure and ownership together into a single religious concept, we get the combination of spiritual *privilege* and spiritual *responsibility,* or of receiving and being a blessing. This is supported by the parallelism in Is. 44:1-2 between "Jacob my servant" and "Israel whom I have chosen." God's servant is God's chosen one; a servant does not choose himself. Election is thus linked with the whole Servant concept as we find it in the Book of Isaiah and elsewhere, and therefore with a call to service, a covenant mission. But the same parallelism in Is. 41:8-10, between God's chosen and God's servant, links election with the spiritual privilege or blessing that is theirs as "the offspring of Abraham, my friend" (v. 8). The "fear not" that runs through these chapters in Isaiah is rooted in the gracious presence of the God of the covenant, to strengthen and help and to redeem His people. Therefore, election is also linked with God's saving acts, or with redemption. Election is expressed in redemption. By redeeming God elects those whom He redeems. That was the glorious significance for Israel's faith of the Exodus redemption. It is significant for Christian faith as well; for God's election in the past is an assurance of redemption in the present, even of "an eternal redemption" (Heb. 7:12). God's election is still "the permanent reality" which assures us of the constancy of God's covenant relationship with His people. "God is faithful, by whom you were called into the fellowship of his Son, Jesus Christ our Lord" (1 Cor. 1:9).

There are other passages which could profitably be examined in this connection; for example, where the verb *bachar,* choose, is used: as in Deut. 4:37ff., 10:14-15, and 14:2, and in Is. 49:7; or where the verb *qara,* call, is used: as in Is. 43:1 and 51:1-2, and in Hos. 11:1; or where the verb *yadha,* know, is used: as in Am. 3:1-2, Hos. 13:5, and Gen. 18:17-19. We could broaden the examination to include passages where Yahve is spoken of as the Creator and Maker of Israel, as well as their Redeemer and Savior; for election is certainly implied in the assertion that He "created" and "formed" Israel to be His people. (See Is. 43:1.) Let us, however, attempt a tentative summary of the Old Testament teaching concerning election:

1) The doctrine of election in the Old Testament is not directly concerned with the salvation of the individual but with the whole redemptive plan and activity of God in history. He chooses, calls, and

commissions men and nations to serve His purpose in various ways and at different times.

2) The doctrine of election in the Old Testament is as wide as the concept of, or the faith in, a personal God who acts in history to accomplish His own will and to reach His own predetermined goal of redemption.

3) The doctrine of election in the Old Testament is theologically the same as the Christian doctrine of vocation.

4) The relevant question arising from this doctrine of election is this: In what way am I, or my nation, or my church, chosen to serve the will of God in relation to this ongoing history of a sinful humanity, whose redemption God seeks because of His own unmotivated love and covenant faithfulness?

For unique as was the election of Israel, it was not so unique as to have no relevance for us who are also the sons of Abraham by faith in Jesus Christ. We, too, are "a chosen race" in the sense of the Old Testament doctrine of election (1 Peter 2:9).

2

Covenant Experience, or Fellowship

Johs. Pedersen has stressed the character of the covenant as *a relationship of belonging* between two contracting parties, with mutual rights and duties.[8] We may accept this characterization of the covenant in the case of Israel, if we do not make it a strictly bilateral contract between equals. This the divine covenant never was. Otto Baab, for instance, has pointed out that the Hebrew covenant is marked by the appearance of a new conception, "that God was not automatically obligated, upon request, to help his people."[9] God remains sovereign even after He has entered into covenant. He is bound by the covenant only in terms of His own *hesed,* or steadfast love, and His own "objectively righteous will"; and His people have a rightful claim upon Him under the covenant only as they themselves respond to His will in the spirit of obedient faith.

However, the covenant doctrine of the Old Testament does involve *relationship,* or a fellowship between God and man (as represented by the people of Israel). It involves a relationship of "belonging," in the sense of intimate communion; which on the human side becomes a vital spiritual experience. The covenant does involve a relationship of *mutuality,* not to be confused with *equality;* with mutual obligations voluntarily assumed and binding on each party. God is bound by His Word of promise, because He is by nature faithful and true, and cannot lie (see Heb. 6:17-18, and cf. 1 Jn. 1:9); and because of His covenant promise, Israel could look to Him for a unique experience of His presence in grace and blessing.

We turn again to the key passage in Ex. 19:5-6, and to the Hebrew word *segullah.* It is a significant though infrequent Old Testament word. It is used twice, in 1 Chron. 29:3 and Eccl. 2:8, in the sense of material treasure, or a treasure of gold and silver. It is used six times in the sense of Israel as a valued possession of God, a peculiar treasure which Yahve has chosen to be His very own. See Ex. 19:5; Deut. 7:6, 14:2, and 26:18; Mal. 3:17; and Ps. 135:4. A comparison of the different versions of the Old Testament will illumine the rich depth of meaning that lies in this word. One of the finest translations of Deut. 7:6 is the one by Ronald Knox, "Yours is a people set apart for its own God, chosen by its own God, out of all the nations on earth, as his own people."[10] Equally good is the translation by Smith-Goodspeed, "chosen . . . to be a people of his very own."[11] The word *segullah* is a key word in the Biblical doctrine of the covenant; and it clearly indicates a relationship of *belonging* to God: first, on the basis of the right of ownership and possession; and second, on the basis of a divine love which prizes this possession highly, and is ready to pour out the blessing of this love upon His chosen people within the relationship of the covenant The word points unmistakably an experience of intimate fellowship with God as His people; a religious or a spiritual fellowship experience as His "egendomsfolk," the fine Swedish equivalent for the phrase "his very own."

"The simplest resolution of the covenant relation," says Paul Heinisch, "is given in the words, 'you shall be to me a people and I will be God to you.'"[12] We have no difficulty in finding Biblical evidence for such a "your God" and "my people" relationship. The evidence is overwhelmingly convincing that this was the very heart of the covenant experience. It is not just a matter of using a Concordance to locate and list the passages where this terminology occurs; though there are several columns of such references in any good Concordance. More significant is the fact that, quite apart from the use of these characteristic phrases, the relationship that they represent completely controls the Old Testament message in its entirety: the history, the law or Torah, prophecy, worship, everything that relates to faith and life in the Old Testament religion. It is the greatest single unifying factor amidst all the diversity of viewpoint in the many Old Testament books. How it got there is not our question just now. The fact is that it is there. What does it signify? What is its theological significance?

Your God

"I am the Lord your God, who brought you out of the land of Egypt, out of the house of bondage" (Ex. 20:2).

The phrase "your God" belongs to the divine proclamation; the corollary phrase "our God" belongs to Israel's confession of faith. The religious significance of the phrase is the same, whether it be a part of the confession or of the proclamation.

It is a promise or an assurance of God's presence with His people, dwelling in their midst, near and accessible at all times, ready to defend and help in every time of need. It represents a faith that is the very opposite of deism. This is theism: implying that it is possible for man to have access to God in worship, to have fellowship with Him in faith, and to serve Him in willing obedience; expressing also that "I—Thou" relationship which is the very essence of Biblical religion.

It is also the very heart of the promise of blessing to Abraham; for we may put an equation sign between the word to Abraham in Gen. 12:2, "I will bless you," and the word to his seed in Gen. 17:7, 8, "I will be their God." The promise of Immanuel, "God with us," runs like a unifying thread through the gospel of the Old Testament and of the New alike, until we see it in its full glory in Jesus Christ, "who dwelt among us, full of grace and truth" (Jn. 1:14). For the final consummation we turn to Rev. 21:3-4, "Behold, the dwelling of God is with men. He will dwell with them, and they shall be his people, and God himself will be with them; he will wipe away every tear from their eyes, and death shall be no more, neither shall there be mourning nor crying nor pain any more, for the former things have passed away." The final fulfillment may be greater than the original promise to Abraham, or the beginning of the experience of its fulfillment on the part of Israel; but a "clear continuity of theological principle" can be seen running through them all.

It is closely linked theologically with the mercy seat (Hebrew "kapporeth," Greek "ilasterion"), where God promised to meet His people (Ex. 25:22): to instruct and guide them in the good and the right way; but also to reveal His forgiving grace and mercy, by providing a way of access for the sinner to a renewed experience of God's favor and fellowship. We think now of the whole sacrificial system in the Old Testament, reaching its experiential climax in the great Day of Atonement (Lev. 16), with the mercy seat as the focal center of it all. What was the basic religious significance of it all for Israel as God's chosen people? It has been well said that "the sacrifice is not intended to be a basis for entrance into the experience of grace, but for continuance in grace."[13] "The sacrifices and worship of Israel were not to procure grace," says Edersheim; "grace had been the originating cause of their worship. And so it ever is."[14] From the viewpoint of the covenant relationship, the mercy seat was simply a concrete projection of the promise to be "their God" into the actual experience of His beloved but sinful people.

It is also the assurance of the continuation of the saving acts of God in behalf of His people (Ex. 6:6-7; cf., Mic. 6:3-5). "Your God" is the God who constantly acts for "his people," but also through them as "his chosen ones," to accomplish His work which He has given them to do. The emphasis is on the *God who acts*. Gillis Gerleman, in his excellent little pamphlet, "Gamla Testamentet i Förkunnelsen," illustrates the importance of this divine acting in the Old Testament from the Book of Ruth; where he says we can hear "the wingstrokes of a great happening," or of God's election and redemption history.[15] If that be true of the story in the Book of Ruth, how much more so of the history of Israel as God's people, with Yahve as their God, their Maker, Creator, Redeemer, Savior, Shepherd, Lord, and King! The very history is a symbol of what God would be to all men, and a step towards the realization of this larger goal.

It is within the framework of this promise "to be God to you and to your descendants after you" that we can begin to understand the Old Testament doctrine of God. Let me cite just three examples: the proclamation of the name of Yahve in Ex. 34:5-7; the message of the incomparable greatness and goodness of God in Is. 40; the remarkable assertion of divine love for His wayward people in Hos. 11:8-9. There is in the latter passage no suggestion of automatic salvation just because His people ask for it; but there is the revelation of a depth in God's covenant love that will not permit Him to let them go, if love can persuade them to turn and to seek Him with all their hearts as their God. The God of the Old Testament is not "a philosopher's God," nor in a sense "a theologian's God," but the God of intimate personal covenant experience; but in that covenant promise and experience of the living God as "their God" and "your God," theology has some of its deepest roots.

My People

"And I will walk among you, and will be your God, and you shall be my people" (Lev. 26:12).

This is the other side of the covenant relationship; for the corollary of "your God" must ever be "my people." The Old Testament concept of Israel as the people of God is tremendously relevant for God's New Testament people today! The comparison is chiefly on the community level, or the relationship of *God's people* to their God, and vice versa. We can illustrate its significance from a threefold point of view:

1) What made them (and us) the people of God? The answer as far as Israel is concerned is clear: pure grace, or election love (Deut. 7: 6-8); an act of redemption (Ex. 19:3-6); an affirmation of covenant (Ex. 24:1-8). A careful reading of Eph. 1:3-14, to cite a single New Testament parallel, will reveal the same elements, grace and love and redemption and faithful promise, in *our* election to be His people, in the new dispensation of the fullness of the gospel in Christ.

2) What was God's concern for them (and for us today) as His people? Again the Old Testament answer is clear, and every item in it has its New Testament counterpart. They were to be holy to the Lord (Lev. 20:26), a holy nation (Ex. 19:6). They were to be a consecrated people, devoted both in inward attitude and in outward manner of life to the will of Him who had chosen them to be His prized possession. The positive injunction in Deut. 10:12-13 is aimed at such a wholehearted consecration to the Lord their God: "And now Israel, what does the Lord your God require of you, but to fear the Lord your God, to walk in all his ways, to love him, to serve the Lord your God with all your heart and with all your soul, and to keep the commandments and statutes of the Lord, which I command you this day for your good?" Such wholeheartedness in seeking the Lord is not to be confused with the actual achievement of a sinless life, nor with a

religion of righteousness by human works. This of which we speak is the response of the heart to the grace and mercy of God experienced within the covenant relationship. It is in terms of the covenant relationship that we understand the plea to remember past mercies and saving acts of the Lord (Mic. 6: 3-5); the warning that special privilege brings with it greater responsibility (Am. 3:1-2); the prophetic pleading with the wayward and stubborn and backsliding to return to the Lord God (Ezek. 18: 30-32); the encouragement to the penitent (Is. 40:1-2); and the portrayal of God's wonderful love for His oft-time wayward people (Hos. 11:8-9). It requires no list of matching "proof passages" to confirm that this is the spirit of the New Testament also; for the whole concept of "a chosen race, a royal priesthood, a holy nation, God's own people," is carried over into the New Testament and there applied to all who believe in Christ.

3) What was God's word of hope for them (and for us), when performance does not measure up to their privileged position as the people of God? Coupled with the stern preaching of repentance was the renewed invitation to "turn and live," and the assurance that "you will seek me and find me; when you seek me with all your heart, I will be found by you, says the Lord" (Jer. 29:13-14). The prophets held forth the hope of eventual restoration, after their unfaithfulness had brought them to the brink of ruin. The prophet Jeremiah spoke of a new covenant, which in a sense is simply a renewal of the old on the basis of what the epistle to the Hebrews boldly calls "better promises" (Heb. 8:6). Through it all shines the hope of a consummation of all that the covenant stood for; a reaching of the covenant goal, the goal of "an eternal redemption" (Heb. 9:12), "the period of the great Restoration" (Acts 3:21, Moffatt's translation). There begins to shine through even in the Old Testament the hope of perfect peace, and of perfect fellowship between God and His people, *one day,* "in the latter days." It is the sort of hope of which the final crystal-clear statement is first found in the last book of the Bible, in Rev. 21:3-4. We may ask, How clear was Christ to them in relation to this hope in the Old Testament? and we answer, that the God of the covenant of blessing was involved, the God of Abraham who is none other than the God and Father of our Lord Jesus Christ, the God who so loved the world that He gave His only Son, when the time had fully come, to be the Savior of the world. Their faith and hope was in God, the living God. It is significant that Peter, writing to us who believe in Jesus Christ,

says that "through him you have confidence in God, who raised him from the dead and gave him glory, so that your faith and hope are in God" (1 Peter 1:21). This is the heritage of God's people in every age. Christ has made more sure that which lay in the divine promise from the beginning, and has made more glorious this "I—Thou" relationship of the covenant, the relationship of "your God" and "my people," which is the heart of the covenant experience.

3

Covenant Requirements, or Torah

When we speak of the Torah, or the law, we must be very careful lest we give an unbiblical and misleading impression as to its meaning and function in Old Testament religion. The Hebrew word *torah* is usually translated as *law,* partly at least because of the influence of the Septuagint which translated it as *nomos,* or law; and the moment we hear the word *law* we think of *a legal relationship.* The original or etymological meaning of the Hebrew word, however, is *guidance* or *direction.* This is illustrated by the use of the related form of the verb from the same root, the Hiphil form of *yarah,* "Teach me," in several of the psalms. For example, in Ps. 86:11 we find a beautiful prayer for guidance:

> Teach me thy way, O Lord,
>   that I may walk in thy truth;
> unite my heart to fear thy name.

A classic example of the use of the noun Torah is in Is. 8:20, "To the teaching and to the testimony!" Almost as significant is the use of the participial form of the related verb in 2 Chron. 15:3, "For a long time Israel was without the true God, and without a teaching priest [kohen moreh], and without law [Torah]." W. A. Whitehouse has said, and rightly so, that the translation of the Hebrew *torah* by the Greek *nomos* and the English *law* has created "a misleading impression of the way God had dealt with Israel to make them His people. It obscures the wider and more personal communication which is partly suggested by 'teaching,' and implies that Israel is bound to God in a relation which is adequately expressed by strict obedience to a code of law."[16] It is true of the Torah, as John D. Davis says of the law, that it is "an authoritative rule of conduct";[17] but its primary frame of reference is not a code of law but *a covenant relationship*. "The law was given to the people in covenant," says A. B. Davidson. "It was a rule of life, not of justification; it was guide to the man who was already right in God's esteem in virtue of his general attitude towards the covenant."[18] Edersheim says much the same thing about the sacrifices, which are a part of the ritual law: "The sacrifices and worship of Israel were not to procure grace; grace had been the originating cause of their worship."[19] The frame of reference for the Torah is within the covenant relationship between God and His people Israel. To interpret the Torah as if it signified a pure legal relationship between God and Israel is to misinterpret it.

Let us take a look at what the Scripture says at this point.

1) The covenant originated in, and was a part of, an experience of redemption, the Exodus redemption. We need not belabor that point, already stressed. It is clear from the historical sequence (see Ex. 12 and 20); from the prophetic preaching (see Mic. 6:4-5); and especially from the key statement in Ex. 19:3-6, where the saving acts of God are set forth as the basis for establishing permanent relationship with Israel as His very own.

"For I brought you up from the land of Egypt,
    and redeemed you from the house of bondage" (Mic. 6:4).

2) The covenant relationship, which originates in an act of God, looks for a response from man. In the case of Abraham we have seen how God commended his faith by reckoning it to him as righteousness (Gen. 15:6), and his obedience by reaffirming in the most solemn way the covenant of blessing with him and his seed (Gen. 22:15-18). The natural, the to-be-expected, response to God's covenant is the obedience of faith. In the case of Israel faith was often conspicuously absent, but without it the blessings of the covenant relationship could not be theirs. The prophet Isaiah summed it up in these words to the king and people of his day:

"If you will not believe,
    surely you shall not be established" (Is. 7:9).

Inseparable from true faith in the covenant God is obedience to His good and gracious covenant will. "To obey is better than sacrifice" is a word which belongs to the very essence of a spiritual covenant relationship such as God sought with His people Israel. Without faith and obedience they could not serve Him effectively as His people in the mission of being a blessing. Without the heart attitude of faith and obedience on their part, it was mockery for them to call themselves the people of God. Without the obedience of faith the door was closed, not by God but by Israel, to the enjoyment of the blessings promised them as His chosen people. Don't think that this is a New Testament discovery, which we have no right to read into the Old Testament situation! It is a fundamental truth which inheres in the very nature of the covenant from the beginning. Israel did not always understand this spiritual character of God's covenant with her; but *some* did: and whether we call them a spiritual remnant, or think more narrowly in terms of those called of God to be prophets, they were what they were because they believed in Yahve; and it was because they believed and obeyed their God that the promise of blessing through Abraham's seed could begin to find fulfillment for the world. There is this mutuality about the covenant—mutuality, not equality—which must never be forgotten as we seek to interpret the covenant requirements in terms of the Torah.

3)   The Torah, or the law, and pre-eminently the Ten Commandments, which in Deut. 4:13 are called the covenant, was given by God as the Creator and Redeemer of Israel for the guidance of His people in the good and the right way (1 Sam. 12:23); the way of His will for them as a chosen, an elect, a redeemed, a covenanted people. When Paul says in Rom. 3:20, that "through the law comes knowledge of sin," we must not draw the conclusion that this is the only function of the law. In its Old Testament context the Torah must be seen first of all as the positive instruction of a loving God in a way that is good. It was given as "a rule of life" for a redeemed people. It was given "for our good always," says the Deuteronomist (Deut. 6:24; cf. 10:12-13). It is this aspect of the commandments that Luther stresses in his Small Catechism, when he begins the explanation of each commandment with the words, "We should fear and love God so that . . ." and when he concludes his discussion of all the commandments by saying, "God threatens to punish all who transgress these commandments. We should, therefore, fear his wrath, and in no wise disobey them. But he promises grace and every blessing to all who keep them. We should, therefore, love him, trust in him, and gladly keep his commandments."[20] Such interpretation is in complete harmony with the spirit of the Old Testament Torah. It reflects the same emphasis on *fear* and

love of God as does the book of Deuteronomy. It presupposes that any worthwhile obedience to the law must come as a willing response of faith to the saving acts of God. In more ways than one, the Old Testament anticipates the New Testament declaration that "we love because he first loved us"; and we cannot truly love Him without also loving the way of His commandments. It is only when we have such an understanding of the divine purpose with the law that we can say with the psalmist, "Oh, how I love thy law!" (Ps. 119:97)

4) For it is the redeeming love, the saving acts, of God which, according to the Old Testament, are the motivation for obedience in the keeping of the law. The covenant helps us to understand the Old Testament concept of ethics as a part of the Biblical religion. The most important single verse in Ex. 20 is the preamble to the commandments, "I am the Lord your God, who brought you out of the land of Egypt, out of the house of bondage" (v. 2). We would be perfectly justified in continuing with a "therefore" before each of the ten words that follow. The sequence of thought is exactly the same as in Rom. 12:1-2, where Paul says, "I appeal to you therefore, brethren, by the mercies of God, to present your bodies as a living sacrifice, holy and acceptable to God, which is your spiritual worship. Do not be conformed to this world but be transformed by the renewal of your mind, that you may prove what is the will of God, what is good and acceptable and perfect." Exodus 19:3-6, as we have seen, confirms the sequence from the viewpoint of the covenant relationship with Israel: "You have seen what I did. . . . Now therefore, if you will obey my voice and keep my covenant . . ." Israel was urged to "remember this day, in which you came out from Egypt" by keeping the feast of unleavened bread (Ex. 13:3-10); and Paul has correctly interpreted the spiritual symbolism of this Old Testament festival when he writes, "Let us, therefore, celebrate the festival, not with the old leaven, the leaven of malice and evil, but with the unleavened bread of sincerity and truth" (1 Cor. 5:8). The significance for the whole area of Christian ethics of this origin of the covenant relationship in an act of divine redemption is tremendous! Quoting Davidson again, "The law is not to Israel a law of morals on the bare ground of human duty, apart from God's exhibition of his grace."[21] The law ideally represents a grace-motivated, redemption-motivated, covenant-motivated obedience to the positive requirements with which God ever confronts, and must confront, His people; unless He abdicate from His own holiness, and

from that love which seeks not only the salvation of sinners, but also their sanctification of life, so as to be in truth "a holy nation" unto the Lord (see Ex. 19:6; 1 Peter 2:9).

5) What are then the requirements of God for His people as set forth in the law and the prophets of the Old Testament? Many answers could be given, which complement each other; we shall give only a few, by way of illustration. We find the divine requirements for the covenant people set forth:

First, in the Ten Commandments, which are called "his covenant" (Deut. 4:13). Voices are heard today saying that they are outmoded; but it will be a terrible day indeed when men generally come to think of them as morally irrelevant! For the Christian, however, they possess a deep spiritual relevance as well, for they belong to the covenant relationship between God and His redeemed people; they are an expression of His good and gracious, as well as His holy and righteous, will for His people. What kind of world would it be, if the Ten Commandments were obeyed by all? Think them through!

One true God, and He a living Spirit and a loving Redeemer, acknowledged, trusted, and worshiped.

The name of God used only for holy purposes, consonant with His holy character and gracious will.

The Lord's day respected, and used as a day of physical and spiritual rest and refreshing.

Parents honored and obeyed, and all rightful authority respected.

No murder, in thought or in deed; no anger or malice.

No impurity of heart or life in the realm of sex, and every marriage sanctified by love.

No theft of another's property, but each helping the other to improve his physical well-being.

No untrue or unkind talk about one another.

No envy of or coveting that which belongs to others, but godliness with contentment.

A new earth, wherein righteousness dwells! But now, all too often there is flagrant unrighteousness; so that the words of the prophet apply,

Justice is turned back,
    and righteousness stands afar off;
for truth has fallen in the public squares,
    and uprightness cannot enter.
Truth is lacking,
    and he who departs from evil makes himself a
       prey (Is. 59:14-15).

Second, in Jesus' summary of the commandments in Mt. 22:36-40, which reaches right down into the Old Testament text and teaching: "You shall love the Lord your God with all your heart, and with all your soul, and with all your might" (Deut. 6:5), and "You shall love your neighbor as yourself" (Lev. 19:18). Love is both the divine requirement and the human fulfillment of the law: a love which responds to, and also reflects, the love of God. "For I desire steadfast love" from my people, says the Lord by His prophet Hosea (6:6); even as the Lord himself is "a God merciful and gracious, slow to anger, and abounding in steadfast love and faithfulness" (Ex. 34:6). What a tragic contrast with the divine requirement when it must be said of His people, "Your love is like a morning cloud, like the dew that goes early away" (Hos. 6:4).

Third, in the Deuteronomic key words, "fear" and "love," as characterizing a right relation to God. It is this fear and love of God that motivates the keeping of the Torah and leads to a true covenant obedience. The first emphasis in the divine requirements is on a right spirit (see Deut. 10:12-13). If our attitude toward God is right, we will discover that His commandments are not burdensome (1 Jn. 5:3), but are given for our good always (Deut. 6:24).

Fourth, in the great prophetic summary of true religion, a summary of both the law and the prophets:

He has showed you, O man, what is good;
    and what does the Lord require of you
but to do justice, and to love kindness,
    and to walk humbly with your god (Mic. 6:8).

Fifth, in the simple words of the admonition of the psalmist, which might well be the motto of the people of God in every age: "Trust in the Lord, and do good" (Ps. 37:3). Faith and obedience: the two familiar key words from the life of Abraham!

6) But are not these requirements impossible; and does not the New Testament put an entirely different interpretation on the func-

tion of the law? (See e.g., Rom. 3:19-20, "through the law comes knowledge of sin.")

To this the answer is Yes and No! The Torah has a double function in relation to God's people. It guides them in the good and the right way; it also convicts them of sin, because even though they are the people of God they are not yet sinless. Franz Delitzsch has said that the very fact that so many of the commandments have a negative form, "Thou shalt not," is an acknowledgment of the reality of the situation: sin exists.[22] Therefore the Torah always exercises a double function, and it does so simultaneously, whenever it is read or preached: it always guides in the right way, and it always convicts of failure and shortcoming and missing the mark, even when we sincerely try to walk in the way of His commandments. The covenant sought wholehearted commitment but did not contemplate sinless perfection on the part of God's people. For sins committed inadvertently or through human weakness there was gracious provision for atonement and forgiveness *within the covenant.* The sin that threatened the very existence of the covenant was the sin so poignantly expressed in Hos. 2:13, "and forgot me, says the Lord." Might not this be said to be the cardinal sin of God's people still today? For there is something of willfulness about this kind of forgetfulness: it borders on rejection; and where sin expresses itself in rebellion (the Hebrew *pesha),* it is not so much a rebellion against the Torah, the transgression of a commandment, as it is rebellion against the covenant God. If we truly seek the Lord as "our God," we will not rebel against the guidance of His Torah as a rule of life. It is not impossible to let ourselves be so guided. It was never intended that the Torah should be a rule of justification.

4

Covenant Purpose, or Mission

The election of Israel and its vocation to be in a special sense the people of God is incomprehensible and indefensible apart from the covenant mission.

If we should suppose that God chose one nation from among the many for the sole purpose of pouring out on them alone all His material and spiritual blessings, it would give us an entirely different God from the One in whom we believe; it would create a cleavage and a contradiction between the Old Testament and the New impossible to bridge. The covenant of God can never be equated with narrow provincialism and selfish privilege. If there be such a thing as "Heilsgeschichte" or *holy history;* if there be such a thing as "en Guds utkorelse—och frälsningsgärning," or a divine act of election and redemption; if the God of covenant is also the God of creation, who in the same breath can call Israel "my own possession" and say that "all the earth is mine" (Ex. 19:5): if *these* things be true, as Scripture witnesses to them, there can be no thought of a covenant relationship without a missionary purpose. As Edmond Jacob says, "The election of Israel was to lead of necessity to a missionary duty."[23] The same, of course, is true of the church.

There are some rather clear indications of this missionary calling of Israel in the Old Testament.

1) There is a definite missionary implication in the call of Abraham (see Gen. 12:1-3).

The background for the Abraham story is seen in Genesis 10:32 and 11:9. The human family is divided into nations, separated by language barriers, and spread abroad on the earth. There is need of a chosen and consecrated human instrument through which God could work and manifest His will and purpose for all men. The call of Abraham in this situation was to be a blessing (Gen. 12:2). We have seen that the Hebrew imperative suggests that this was the intended result of God's blessing promised to him. Abraham was called to receive and to share with others the blessing of God; and sharing implies a mission: we receive in order to give.

What had Abraham to share, and how did he share it, in his own lifetime? The simplest, and yet perhaps the profoundest, answer is *his faith in God.* He was pre-eminently a man of faith, a remarkable faith, which was his response to God's covenant with him. This faith he shared, perhaps more by his manner of life than by his preaching. Though not a life of sinless perfection, it was a noble life of devotion to his God; a life which because it was blessed of God even in an outward way with material prosperity witnesses to Abimelech of Abraham's God (see Gen. 21). But he was also, as Ed. Böhl has said, one in the long line of men called to be "executors" of God's great promise that pointed forward to the Christ and to the gospel:[24] the promise that "in you [and in your seed] all the families of the earth will be blessed." His was a mission not only to his own generation but to us (see Gal. 3:14); for the whole soteriological plan of God is involved in the stewardship of this man, who was faithful to his part in the total mission, though he himself was given only a distant glimpse of the final blessing (see Heb. 11:13).

2) There is a still clearer indication of mission in the case of Israel.

It is involved in the call of Abraham, which included his seed (see Gen. 22:15-18). They were called as a people to the same faith and the same obedience so signally manifested by Abraham. By such an obedience of faith on the part of Israel the nations would be blessed. They would be blessed by the faithful witness of Israel in faith and life to their God, for it is wonderful to know God as Israel was privileged to know Him; but it was also the intent of the promise that by this obedient faith they with Abraham would become "executors" of the promise of blessing with its Messianic significance, the gospel preached beforehand to Abraham, as Paul calls it in Gal. 3:8. Theirs was to be a mission not only to their immediate environment but to future generations. As we said of Abraham, so we must say of Israel, that the whole soteriological purpose of God is involved in the stewardship of this nation, even though they themselves saw as yet only a faint glimpse of the final reality.

A divine mission for Israel is indicated also in Ex. 19:5-6. They were called to be "a kingdom of priests" unto God, in a divinely given and approved service which is motivated by the assertion, "for all the earth is mine." What was the nature of that service? The priestly service? The priestly service may be understood at least in part as that of a *teaching priest* (see 2 Chron. 15:3). The interpretation of Delitzsch is excellent. "As the priest is a mediator between God and man, so Israel was called to be the vehicle of the knowledge and salvation of God to the nations of the earth."[25] The kingly service may be understood as the resulting spiritual government of the world; "for spiritual and intellectual supremacy and rule must eventually ensure the government of the world, as certainly as spirit is the power that overcomes the world."[26] According to Rom. 3:2, "the Jews are entrusted with the oracles of God," implying a unique revelation of God to them and through them. Paul enlarges the picture in Rom. 9:4-5: "They are Israelites, and to them belong the sonship, the glory, the covenants, the giving of the law, the worship, and the promises; to them belong the patriarchs, and of their race, according to the flesh, is the Christ." With this agrees the Old Testament picture of Israel as a servant of the Lord. We meet the thought of this servant status as early as in Ex. 4:22-23, and it becomes especially prominent in Is. 40-55; but it is a fundamental Old Testament concept throughout. It is true that service in the Biblical sense of the word may sometimes be equated with *worship* (cf. e.g., the wording of Deut. 6:13 with the quotation in Mt. 4:10); but that does not necessarily exclude the service of *witness*. The parallelism in Is. 43:10 is significant:

> "You are my witnesses," says the Lord,
> "and my servant whom I have chosen,
> that you may know and believe me
> and understand that I am He."

As His servant, Israel was called to be a witness to the nations of the living God and of His salvation. She was the bearer in a unique sense of God's Word to mankind: Torah, prophecy, and above all, the Messianic hope based on the covenant promises of God.

3) There is definite indication of Israel's mission as divinely intended in her election to be God's own people; but was this mission also fulfilled? Again we must answer Yes and No.

The very evistence of the Old Testament as a body of sacred scripture says Yes. As these writings began to circulate outside of Israel, they became a witness to the world about the God of Abraham and of Israel. In evaluating Israel's mission we must keep in mind the enduring significance of what is often called the Judaeo-Christian tradition, which had its spiritual roots in the Old Testament Israel.

The very existence of Israel among the nations also says Yes; for as Jacob says, "The extraordinary vitality of Israel amid ever-increasing difficulties was in itself a missionary testimony to the pagans, the power and mercifulness of Israel's God was talked about abroad and people came to him to receive the benefit of it."[27] A good Biblical example is that of Naaman (see 2 Kings 5).

The presence always of a faithful remnant in Israel, however small, made it possible for them to continue as "executors" of God's redemptive purpose and to function as a covenant people of God in spite of widely prevalent unfaithfulness.

The winning of proselytes, of which we hear in both the New Testament and the Old, is further evidence of a sense of mission in Israel. An outstanding example is the story of the Ethiopian eunuch

(Acts 8). See also Acts 2:10, where "both Jews and proselytes" are said to have been included in the assembly on the day of Pentecost.

The acts of God in their history and the interpretation of those acts by the mouth of their prophets, give a strong impression of a sense of mission and of the hope of a goal which ultimately embraces the earth. There is a clear missionary implication in the growing universalism of the future hope in the prophetic preaching. A good example of this universalism is the familiar statement in Is. 56:7, "For my house shall be called a house of prayer for all people." An even more striking example is the Book of Jonah, which reveals God's compassionate concern even for the heathen city of Nineveh. The universalism of a passage like Mic. 4:1-4 (cf. Is. 2:2-4) is well known: it is not the nation, Israel, but the nations that say to one another,

> "Come, let us go up to the mountain of the Lord,
>   to the house of the God of Jacob;
> that he may teach us his ways
>   and that we may walk in his paths."

Of special interest is Is. 19:23-25, where the language is reminiscent of the covenant of blessing with Abraham: "In that day there will be a highway from Egypt to Assyria, and the Assyrian will come into Egypt, and the Egyptian into Assyria, and the Egyptians will worship with the Assyrians. In that day Israel will be the third with Egypt and Assyria, a blessing in the midst of the earth, whom the Lord of hosts has blessed, saying, 'Blessed be Egypt my people, and Assyria the work of my hands, and Israel my heritage.'" There is in the preaching of the prophets a preview, however faint, of the Pauline preaching of "the mystery of Christ": "that is, how the Gentiles are fellow heirs, members of the same body, and partakers of the promise in Christ Jesus through the gospel" (Eph. 3:4-6). It was a part of their mission as prophets of Israel to prepare the way for the clearer, fuller revelation in Christ.

It must be acknowledged, however, that the people as a whole missed the mark of their calling, if we think of that completely devoted faith and obedience which would have enabled them as a holy nation to glorify God before the nations. That is the burden of the prophets (see e.g., Ezek. 36:16-21). That is the shame all too often of the Christian church. Israel had no monopoly on unfaithfulness. The marvel of it is that even so *God acts* in judgment and salvation to vindicate His holy name, and to accomplish the covenant mission, so that it might eventually be fulfilled in Christ. The significant thing is not the faithlessness of Israel but the faithfulness of their God, which can be traced all the way from the blessing of Abraham through the history of Israel to the gospel of Christ.

4) For there is a mission motif in the whole of Israel's history when seen in the light of the gospel of Jesus Christ. It would be grossly unfair to try to interpret the history of Israel as the chosen people of God apart from some reference to the New Testament, which is itself a part and a product of that history. All history has significance beyond the present moment, be it ever so slight; how much more so sacred history, where God is seen to act! There is a typology about Biblical history that points forward to and reaches its fulfillment in Christ, and in His body, which is the Church; but it is *God's acting* in relation to Israel that is in a special sense a witness to us, and that gives to Israel this aspect of mission. It is not primarily what Israel does or is, but what God does and is in relation to Israel, that is significant; it is this that makes Israel's mission one of witness: a witness to the living God, a witness to the God of covenant, a witness to the God of redemption, a witness to the nature of the life relationship or fellowship between God and His people, a witness albeit in an indirect way to Christ; for in Him, and through Him, alone is the mission finally accomplished.

5

The Covenant and Prophecy

A prophet has been defined as "an authoritative and infallible teacher of God's will."[28] The definition is good; but it does not imply that the prophets came with a wholly new version of the will of God. They were not religious innovators; their ministry was a part of the covenant history of Israel, which included the Torah. When they applied the revealed will of God to the contemporaneous situation they were mindful of the lessons from the past; and it was in the light of the past and of the present that they foretold the future: they saw all of history in the light of the covenant.

In interpreting the message of the prophets, we must see it always in the light of three time-dimensions: past, present, and future. This is not strange when we consider that no moment in time can be understood by itself alone. *This* day in your life or mine, or in the history of a nation or of the world, is meaningless apart from yesterday or from tomorrow. It is what it is because of what happened in the past; and it is a part of the influence that will determine, and which therefore foreshadows, the future. Must not prophecy, which we believe to be an intervention of God *in history* at a given moment and with a divine purpose, have the same threefold time aspects? "Insight here implies foresight," says John Paterson, "for insight into the purposes and plan of God gives men knowledge of what God will do."[29] It was God's covenant with His people that provided the basis for the prophetic insight into His character and will and enabled them to understand the present and to foretell the future; for they believed in the basic principles and in the final consummation of the divine covenant. It follows that the vantage point from which to interpret any prophetic ·passage is the historical present, the prophet's own situation, as it is illumined by faith in the covenant from the past; and then to look for new flashes of insight as to what it may portend for the future.

Let us illustrate briefly from the four eighth-century prophets, Isaiah, Hosea, Amos, and Micah.

Isaiah

A passage like Is. 1: 2-4 is clearly indicative of the covenant background—the past. The reference is not to aliens but to sons, whom the Lord has lovingly reared and brought up (v. 2), but who rebel against love. Israel is called "my people" (v. 3), and God "the Holy One of Israel" (v. 4). Israel has *forsaken* YHWH, the Lord, whom it was their privilege to know and serve as their God. The covenant relationship of "your God" and "my people" is unmistakable. It is from within this frame of reference that we can understand the prophet's concern for the present: his indictment of the people for their rebellion (vv. 2-4); his plea that they might be sensible and cease a rebellion which leads only to suffering (vv. 5-6); his reference to the small remnant still left because the Lord is good (v. 9); his denunciation of false religion, which thinks it can combine "wickedness and worship" (vv. 10-15); his clear call to repentance in the ethical terms of the requirements of God (vv. 16-17). But from out of this situation and from within the covenant frame of reference he also looks forward (vv. 18-20). Under the covenant there can be forgiveness if sincerely sought. Under the covenant there can be renewed blessings

172

in the land of promise, a renewed experience of the blessing of God upon His people. There is, however, an "if" attached, just as there was in Ex. 19: 5; for the covenant calls always for a response in the obedience of faith. Therefore the prophet says, "If you are willing and obedient, you shall eat the good of the land" (v. 19). "But if you refuse and rebel, you shall be devoured by the sword; for the mouth of the Lord has spoken" (v. 20). From here on the preaching of present judgment and future hope (or redemption) alternate within the framework of the historical covenant relation with Israel. The relevance for us today who believe in Christ should be easy to see: a similar relationship; a part of the same divine plan; the same religious principles; the same God, who acts in the same way in similar life situations.

Hosea

The marriage relation, which is a symbol of the covenant between God and Israel completely dominates chapters 1-3 and much of the rest of the book. The sin of Israel, as Hosea presents it, is that of an unfaithful wife, or spiritual harlotry; she turns away from YHWH, the God of true covenant love, and goes after other lovers; she "forgot me, says the Lord" (2:13). By this unfaithfulness she has forfeited the right to be called a wife (2:2). The people of Israel have forfeited the right to be called the people of God (1:9). They have forfeited the right to be sons of God (11:1-7). The symbol changes, but that which is symbolized remains constant: the relationship of the covenant. The present sinful behavior of the people of Israel is seen from within that frame of reference. But coupled with the preaching of stern judgment on this covenant faithlessness are flashes of hope for the future because of the covenant faithfulness of God. (See e.g., 2: 14ff. and 11:8-9). "The Lord's Love for His People" is the heading for chapter 2 in RSV; and for chapter 11, "God Yearns for His Wayward People." As with Isaiah, the preaching of judgment and of redemption alternate within the framework of the historical covenant relation with Israel. The relevance for today is that of "a clear continuity of theological principle."[30] "The principles are eternal," says John Paterson, "but the setting is temporal"[31] (and transient). Israel's history had no permanent religious significance apart from the total unified redemptive plan of God which links the blessing of Abraham with the gospel of Christ. The prophets were messengers of a covenant which found its consummation in Christ and the church and the gospel, "the power of God for salvation to every one who has faith, to the Jew first and also to the Greek" (Rom. 1:16). That is why their message is as relevant now as it was in their day in interpreting the saving acts of God.

Amos

The covenant frame of reference is clearly indicated in Amos 3:1-2. The people of Israel were uniquely known or acknowledged by God as His very own; but just for this very reason they were uniquely responsible to Him in their manner of life. There is no God-given privilege without accompanying responsibility! The prophet's concern is with the present situation in Israel in relation to God's covenant purpose with them; and only within the covenant relationship can we understand what He says about sin, judgment, the possibility of repentance and of renewed divine favor, the seeking of God and of good, the ethical requirements of the Torah as the basic law of the covenant. But in spite of the threatening and deserved judgment on His delinquent people, God will not fail in the end to accomplish His covenant purpose with and through Israel (see chapter 9:7-15). "The last word of God can never be destruction."[32] The sinful kingdom will be destroyed, but there will be a careful divine sifting in order to save a remnant. "In that day," the day of future hope, the covenant with David, who also was called to be an "executor" of the covenant with Israel, shall be fulfilled in a new and marvelous way (vv. 11-12); and blessings shall be multiplied upon "my people Israel" in accordance with the original covenant promise. The "times-coloring"[33] is still largely national and material in character; but beneath the husk is the spiritual kernel, the heart of the covenant, which is fundamentally one with the New Testament "every spiritual blessing" in Christ.

Micah

The most significant passage in Micah is the Lord's controversy with his people in chapter 6:1-8. The covenant relationship is indicated by the twice-repeated "my people" (vv. 3, 5), whom God redeemed from the land of Egypt, and who had experienced the saving acts of the Lord in the past. They are urged to remember how the Lord had redeemed them, had raised up good leaders, had turned an intended curse into a blessing, and had brought them into the Promised Land. If they do not grow weary of their God and of His covenant, they may know such saving acts again (v. 5). The prophet is concerned, however, because the people give only a *ritual* response to the covenant and ignore the spiritual-ethical response, even pretending to be ignorant of the real requirements of God for His people always. They should have known what God required, for God had not left them without knowledge of His will.

> He has showed you, O man, what is good;
>   and what does the Lord require of you
> but to do justice, and to love kindness,
>   and to walk humbly with your God? (v. 8)

Their trouble was not a formal ignorance of the Torah so much as a willful ignoring of it. In such a basis the covenant relationship cannot function. Therefore judgment is predicted; but not the dissolution of the covenant. "It shall come to pass in the latter days" (chapter 4:1) that the covenant will be fulfilled in a marvelous way: many nations shall come and seek Israel's God, the God of the covenant; many nations shall be taught by the Torah as the Word of God, the God of the covenant; many nations shall walk in obedience to His will in the good and the right way, in response to the God of the covenant; and the result will be peace on earth in the final and fullest sense, the blessing of the God of the covenant.

God is faithful to His covenant and He will bring it to pass! Such is the faith of the prophets. This is the fundamental premise of prophecy. We must look for this central idea in the study of prophecy; and we bear in mind that it is *the covenant of blessing* which is the controlling factor in Old Testament religion, including prophecy.

6

The Covenant and the Gospel

Is it correct to speak of *a gospel* in the Old Testament?

We find ourselves confronted by a question of definition and of interpretation. What is the gospel? One answer, which the present writer used for many years as a parish pastor, is this: "The gospel is the glad tidings that God in his great love sent his Son Jesus Christ into the world to save sinners."[34] The definition is good, but it still requires interpretation. Where is the primary emphasis: on the great love of God which planned our salvation, or on the actual historical event of the sending and coming of Jesus Christ to be the Savior of the world? If the latter, there could naturally be no gospel in the Old Testament, for Christ had not yet come; and even the prediction of His coming would not change the situation greatly *unless* we should see *an actual sending and coming in the very preparation* for the event. If, however, the emphasis is on *the love of God*, then there certainly is gospel in the Old Testament, and not least in connection with God's covenant with Israel.

If we think just of the word *gospel*, which means good news, we find this concept of good tidings or glad news in the Old Testament on the basis of the Hebrew verb *basar*, translated by the Septuagint as *evangellizo*. Read, for example, Is. 40: 9-11 and 52: 7-10, where the word is used in connection with the redemption of Israel from Babylon. But is this the same as *the gospel* in the New Testament sense? The question persists even after reading Is. 61:1, where the word is used in a more personal Messianic context. In what way or form is the gospel present in the Old Testament?

It is not present in the sense of the completed historical redemptive act, which Martin Luther confessed as an article of faith: "I believe that Jesus Christ, . . . has redeemed me, . . . with His holy and precious blood, and with His innocent sufferings and death."[35] When the Old Testament was finished Christ had not yet come, nor had He suffered in the flesh and died on the cross for our redemption, nor had He risen from the dead to sit as the victorious Redeemer at the right hand of the Father. All this was in the future; it belonged to "the fulness of the time" (Gal. 4: 4, ASV). Therefore we should not expect to find in the Old Testament the same clear proclamation of the gospel as in John 3: 16, nor the same clear confession of faith as in 1 Tim. 1: 15-16.

But the gospel *is* present in the Old Testament if we think of it in terms of the love of God in action, which does not stop until it finds its full expression in Jesus Christ. The gospel is present in the form of the saving acts of God in behalf of His people and His covenant of blessing with them. The gospel is present in the experience of the forgiveness of sins by the grace and mercy of God, who is faithful to His covenant with a steadfast love. All of this is predicated on the fact that the covenant with Abraham and with Israel *from the moment of its inception* looked forward to the new covenant in Jesus Christ; foreshadowing and preparing the way for it, while at the same time mediating some of its blessings.

The gospel is present in the Old Testament, but it is not easy to articulate the sense in which it is present. It is certainly not present in the mechanical sense of a dogmatic textbook which outlines all the saving acts of God and their interpretation before they happen. Nevertheless we have Jesus' own word for it that the Scriptures (by which he meant the Old Testament writings) "bear witness to me" (see Jn. 5:39). Many attempts have been made to formulate precisely the exact nature of the relationship between the Old Testament and the New at this point of the Messiah and of the gospel. Ernst Sellin has said of the Old Testament that it is "a book written by imperfect or fallible men, children of their people and of their age, but out of which Jesus Christ our Lord has perceived the voice of His heavenly Father, in which He has found His word, whose 'fulfillment' He therefore regarded as His life mission, because according to Him it was the book which witnessed of the Christ, and indeed in all its three major divisions."[36] A. G. Hebert says that the Messianic Hope is the central theme of the Bible, which gives unity to the two Testaments. "Old Israel, believing in Yahweh and confessing that He has chosen her to be His people, looks forward to a time when He will have completed the Purpose which He has taken in hand; this will be the accomplishment of what He intended when He created man. The Christian Gospel is the announcement that the time is fulfilled and the promised Reign of God has arrived."[37] Speaking of preaching from the Old Testament Gillis Gerleman says that "it should actualize and make living the acts of God in Israel; it should make clear that the happening or event (Swedish, 'det skeende') of which the Old Testament tells is a divine history of salvation which moves forward toward a predetermined goal: the coming of Jesus Christ for judgment and for salvation."[38] Ed. Böhl uses a vivid illustration to explain the New Testament formula, "that it might be fulfilled": he compares the dewdrop and the ocean as a mirror of the same counsel of God for our salvation, saying, "In the dewdrop as in the ocean the same sun is reflected; only, there it is in a small mirror (on a small scale) and here in a large one. So also the life-history of each one of God's saints is a copy (or an impression: German *Abdruck*) of the divinely conceived counsel for our salvation; this is naturally true especially of Christ, but then also of all the saints before Him. Christ is the ocean, they are the dewdrops. But here as well as there the susceptible mirror is present which reflects the sun. In other words, there is a wonderful likeness between the life-way (Lebensweges) of Christ and that of His saints; they all go the same way, per aspera ad astra, and there is only this difference that Christ goes before and all the saints follow Him."[39]

The present author has used *this* approach in attempting to show how the Cross is present in psalm soteriology and in Old Testament worship: "The Cross is present in what we may call *a pregnant sense* in the covenant doctrine of the grace of God, in the gospel of *God's hesed* or goodness, His steadfast love, and of the means whereby man may come to the mercy seat. The covenant relationship with Israel implies the initial Exodus-redemption, including the shedding of the blood of the passover lamb. . . . The God who acted in that Exodus-redemption was the same as He who acted in the giving of His Son for the world's redemption, and the same redeeming love and purpose prompted both. God's 'hesed' is essentially one with His redeeming love in Jesus Christ. In that sense we dare to say that the Cross was present—present like the light of the sun at dawn, when it has not yet appeared over the horizon so that we can see the sun itself—present like the tree is present in the seed—present in the mind of God, and in His manner of dealing with men, and in His manifestation of His fundamental character or His essential Nature to men—before we see the historical event of the Cross on Calvary that is the climax and goal of what God purposed from the beginning and manifested in the fulness of time in Christ."[40]

Specific illustrations of the gospel in the Old Testament are not difficult to find. A select list would include at least seven: 1. the promise of blessing through Abraham and his seed, which Paul calls "the gospel preached beforehand" (Gal. 3:8); 2. the election love of God, which called Israel into a covenant and gave to them the mission of a servant, who should share the blessing of Abraham with the nations; 3. the mercy seat experience within the covenant, originating in grace and offering a way of access, a means of atonement, and the experience of forgiveness; 4. the steadfast love of God in relation to His covenant people, so beautifully illustrated by the very word *hesed* or steadfast love, by the wonderful proclamation of the name YHWH in Ex. 34:5-8, by the unrivalled description of God's love for His wayward people in Hos. 11:8-9, by the great passage in Is. 57:15, by all the saving acts of God in behalf of His people (Mic. 6:4-5): each promissory of greater things to come; 5. the institutions of Israel, "das Prophetentum" to speak God's Word and make known His will, the priesthood to mediate between God and men as "teaching priest" and as appointed to offer sacrifices in behalf of the people, the kingship to rule in the name of God and to establish His rule over men; 6. the specific Messianic promises, too numerous to mention and yet not as many as commonly believed; 7. the whole eschatological or forward-looking aspect of the covenant, the Messianic hope as the consummation of the covenant and the goal of history in "the period of the great Restoration" (Acts 3:21, Moffatt).

The Old Testament is rich in elements that belong to the New Testament gospel; but there is a distinction between the old and the new that must be kept clearly in mind always, even as we stress the likeness. Biblical religion gives evidence both of progression and growth, and of continuity and unity. It is unified by its faith in the living God, by His love, by His redemptive plan, by His saving acts, which all "beam in" on Christ. Without Christ the whole covenant plan of redemption and consummation falls. Christ is the keystone in the arch of God's *berith olam,* His everlasting covenant with man; but in reading the Bible, and preaching the gospel of Jesus Christ, the Old Testament may help us to remember that *God so loved* that He gave His only Son: it was not the work of Christ that first made Him love! What we see in Christ is the final and supreme expression of His love— and of His faithfulness to the covenant of blessing.

Covenant Vocabulary

There are a host of words in the religious vocabulary of the Hebrew Bible that are covenant related; whatever their etymology, their usage in Biblical religion reflects the covenant relationship between God and His people. Since one of the great hurdles to effective communication of thought is confusion as to the meaning of words, it is helpful to know something about this covenant vocabulary which we encounter in the reading of the Old Testament. A thorough exposition would take us far beyond the scope of our present purpose; but for the sake of illustration we list some of the more common and yet significant words, with a brief explanation of each.

1. The words *berith* and *Torah,* as well as the phrases "your God" and "my people," and the unique *segullah* which seems to de-

note God's *very own,* have been examined elsewhere and need no further comment. These are the most clearly covenant-related terms.

2.   The name of God which is most significant in terms of the covenant is the Hebrew tetragram YHWH. It is vocalized as *Jehovah* in ASV, rendered as the LORD in AV, AJV, and RSV, and as the *Eternal* by Moffatt. It is quite commonly assumed that the original pronunciation may have been *Yahve*. This is the personal name of the God of Israel; but like so many of the personal names in Hebrew, it seems also to be a descriptive or "telling" name. It is the name, according to John D. Davis, that represents "the God of revelation and grace, dwelling with His people, guiding and delivering them, and receiving their worship."[41] S. R. Driver says that its essential meaning is that of "self-manifesting existence";[42] and whatever we may say of the etymological argument for this meaning (based on Ex. 3), the religious argument from Old Testament history and religion in general supports it. YHWH is the God *who acts* in relation to His people and who makes known to them His will; He is the God of redemption and of revelation. According to Girdlestone the name occurs more than five thousand times in the Old Testament; more than twice as often as the general term for God, which is *Elohim*.[43] If we render it as *kyrios* or LORD (as in RSV), it should not be confused with the Hebrew *Adonai,* which in RSV is written as "Lord"; the latter stands for the lord-servant relationship and the former for the far wider covenant relationship, with its connotation of grace as well as of lordship.

3.   There is one very significant group of covenant-related words that describe God as to His character and His function in relation to men. They may be nouns or adjectives stemming from the same root. Thus God is a God of holiness (qodesh), of righteousness (tsedeq), of steadfast love (hesed), of truth (emeth), of faithfulness (emunah), of salvation (yesha), of mercy or compassion (rachamin), of grace or favor (chen), of glory (kavod), of justice (mishpat). He is holy (qadosh), righteous (tsaddiq), gracious (chanun), merciful (rachum), great (gadol), and good (tov). Six of these covenant rich words are found in a single passage in Ps. 40: 9-11. The psalmist says,

> "I have proclaimed glad tidings of righteousness in the great
>   assembly;
> Lo, I will not refrain my lips,
> O Jehovah, thou knowest.
> I have not hid thy righteousness within my heart;

I have declared thy faithfulness and thy salvation;
I have not concealed thy lovingkindness and thy truth from
the great assembly.
Withhold not thou thy tender mercies from me, O Jehovah;
Let thy lovingkindness and thy truth continually preserve
me."

The above quotation is from ASV. A comparison with RSV will show that each Hebrew word is richly flexible in meaning and therefore also in translation: thus tsedeq, righteousness, can in the context of this psalm be translated as "deliverance" (v. 9) and as "saving help" (v. 10), because the righteousness of God is a vindicating and saving righteousness; emeth from the same root as emunah, can be either *truth* or *faithfulness*, the emphasis being on that which is trustworthy; hesed, which in the older versions was translated as lovingkindness or mercy, can best be translated as *steadfast love* (RSV), for it has the connotation of faithfulness to the covenant, and the covenant is rooted in love; rachamim, sometimes rendered as *tender mercies* (ASV), means simply mercy or compassion; mishpat means first of all *judgment*, then *just judgment*, and finally the end of such judgment or *justice*. All of these words which are used to characterize God in relation to men are also related to man's expected response under the covenant. What God *is* man is called upon to reflect or to become. In the words of the New Testament, "We love because he first loved us" (1 Jn. 4:19). "You shall be holy; for I the Lord your God am holy" (Lev. 19:2). "Seek good, and not evil, that you may live" (Am. 5:14). "Seek righteousness, seek humility; perhaps you may be hidden on the day of the wrath of the Lord" (Zeph. 2:3). For righteousness and justice are of God, and if we truly seek the Lord, we will seek righteousness and justice also as the fruit of His Spirit. The faithfulness of God is a strong summons to faithfulness also on the part of man. The human response to the divine covenant in faith and obedience implies that we share His will and His spirit. The extent to which these covenant-related words dominate the religious faith and life of Israel can be seen from the fact that hesed, for example, is found 127 times in the Psalms alone; often in combination with berith, emeth, emunah, yesha, tsedeq, rachamim, tov (goodness), mishpat. We make no mistake in thinking of all of them as significant words in the covenant vocabulary of the Old Testament.

4. Thinking still of the God of the covenant, we must make note

of the significant descriptive names or titles ascribed to Him: such as, Maker, Redeemer, Savior, Rock, Shepherd, the Holy One of Israel, the Lord of hosts, the God of Amen, the Mighty One of Jacob, the Creator of the ends of the earth, the King of Israel and his Redeemer. Each expresses an activity of God in relation to Israel as His covenant people which has permanent relevance in relation to the people of God under the new covenant in Christ.

5.   There are significant terms also for the covenant people of God. We have noted the phrase "my people" and the word "segullah." Others are the adjective *hasid,* a godly one, or in the plural "saints"; tsaddiq, a righteous one, or in the plural "the righteous" (in the double sense of faith reckoned to them as righteousness, the experience of Abraham, and of earnest seeking after righteousness of life, the righteous requirements of God in all human relationships); geulim, or the redeemed; eved, or the servant of the Lord; beney Yisrael, or the children of Israel, who are also referred to as God's children or sons (see Is. 1:2); and of course, "my segullah," a people for my own possession. There is a nice blend of experienced grace with expected service, of divine election and human mission, in the whole covenant concept of a people of God.

6.   The Hebrew words for sin are many, and they are much more descriptive of what sin is than in other languages either ancient or modern. There is added vividness and concreteness when these words are seen within the covenant relationship between God and Israel. For example, *pesha,* usually translated as transgression, though its primary meaning is rebellion, is seen to be a rebellion not only against the authority of law but against the covenant love of God; *chataath,* the word usually translated as sin but with the etymological significance of missing the mark, or the way and the goal, is seen to be a falling short of the high calling of God under the covenant to be a holy nation, a people wholly dedicated to Him and willing to walk in His ways always; *awon,* or iniquity, which has in it the implication of perversion or distortion or corruption, can be seen as a corruption or a corrosion of the whole spiritual and moral fiber of the individual and of the covenanted community. Other words for sin, such as resha, wickedness; ra, evil; awen, futility or vanity, are often related by the context in which they are used to the covenant situation. The same is true of a longer list of less frequently used words which bear witness to the keen awareness of sin on the part of Israel's prophets, and

presumably also in some measure on the part of her people to whom they preached; for the nature of a people's vocabulary, whether it be in the direction of richness or poverty, reflects something of that with which they are most deeply concerned. For the people of the covenant one such area of deep concern was the faithfulness of the covenant God; another was their own breach of covenant with their God.

7. In the area of religious experience such words as peduth, redemption; yesha, salvation; the words for repentance, especially *shuv* meaning *to turn,* and for forgiveness (see Ps. 32:1-2); the oft-repeated plea for God to be gracious or merciful; the causative form of the verb Amen which means to believe (see Is. 7:9b, "If you will not believe, surely you shall not be established"); the words for hope and trust, for obedience, for service; the "fear" and "love" of the Book of Deuteronomy; the "fear not" of the Book of Isaiah—all are used within the framework of the covenant between God and His people. They are not the vocabulary of a general religious experience but of a specific form of religious experience—the covenant religion of Israel. Only as we keep this in mind shall we be able to understand their religious relevance for the New Testament people of God.

The basic theology of the covenant with Israel is like a river that runs deep and wide through all the shifting landscape of the Sacred Scriptures; but as with the mighty Mississippi, which starts with a little rivulet in Itasca Park, a stream so small that one can easily step across without wetting his feet, and then flows on with ever-increasing volume and power until it empties through the Gulf of Mexico into the mighty ocean, so this covenant theology, whose humble beginning can be seen in the covenant of blessing with Abraham, increases in width and depth, with accompanying freshness and power, as it moves on through the history of Israel to empty finally into the ocean depths of God's covenant revelation in Christ.

NOTES

1 Millar Burrows, *op. cit.,* p. 11.
2 Edmond Jacob, *op cit.,* p. 201.
3 *Ibid.*
4 Lin Yutang, *Between Tears and Laughter.* Copyright 1943 by Lin Yutang. New York: The John Day Company, Inc., Publishers. 1945. p. 9.
5 Edmond Jacob, *op. cit.,* p. 201.
6 Norman Snaith, *op. cit.,* p. 119.
7 Kurt Galling, *op. cit.*
8 Johs. Pedersen, *op. cit.*

[9] Otto Baab, *op. cit*, p. 136.
[10] Ronald Knox, *The Old Testament in English*. *op. cit.*
[11] Smith and Goodspeed, The Bible: an American Translation. *op. cit.*
[12] Paul Heinisch, *Theology of the Old Testament*. English edition by Rev. William Heidt. Copyright 1950 by The Order of St. Benedict, Inc. Collegeville, Minn.: The Liturgical Press. 1950. pp. 28-29.
[13] The author has not been able to trace this quotation to its source, but gratefully acknowledges its influence on his own thought.
[14] Alfred Edersheim, *Bible History*. New York and Chicago: Fleming H. Revell Co. 1876. Vol. II, pp. 115-116.
[15] Gillis Gerleman, *op. cit.*
[16] W. A. Whitehouse, art. "Law," *A Theological Word Book of the Bible*, edited by Alan Richardson. New York: The Macmillan Company. 1952. Used by permission. Pp. 122-125.
[17] John D. Davis, *op. cit.*
[18] A. B. Davidson, *op. cit.*, p. 280.
[19] Alfred Edersheim, *op. cit.*
[20] Martin Luther, *The Small Catechism*: Part I. *op. cit.*
[21] A. B. Davidson, *op. cit.*
[22] Franz Delitzsch, *op. cit.*
[23] Edmond Jacob, *op. cit.*, p. 217.
[24] Ed. Böhl, *op. cit.*
[25] C. F. Keil and Franz Delitzsch, *Commentary on the Pentateuch*. Edinburgh: T. and T. Clark. Vol. II, p. 98.
[26] *Ibid.*
[27] Edmond Jacob, *op. cit.*, p. 219.
[28] From *The Westminster Dictionary of the Bible*, *op. cit.*, p. 492.
[29] John Paterson, *The Goodly Fellowship of the Prophets*. New York: Charles Scribner's Sons. 1953. p. 7.
[30] A. G. Hebert, *The Throne of David*. London: Faber & Faber Limited. 1941. p. 130.
[31] John Paterson, *op. cit.*, p. 7.
[32] J. E. McFadyen, *A Cry for Justice*. New York: Charles Scribner's Sons. 1912. p. 136.
[33] Ed. Riehm, *Messianic Phophecy*. Edinburgh: T. and T. Clark. 2nd ed. 1891, p. 133. The revised edition of 1900 has "this historical dye" instead of "this times-coloring."
[34] *Dr. Martin Luther's Small Catechism with Explanation*. Rock Island: Augustana Book Concern. 1939. p. 25.
[35] Martin Luther, *The Small Catechism*: Second Article. *op. cit.*
[36] Ernst Sellin, *Das Alte Testament im Christlichen Gottesdienst und Unterricht.* 1936.
[37] A. G. Hebert, *op. cit.*, p. 39.
[38] Gillis Gerleman, *op. cit.*
[39] Ed. Böhl, *op. cit.*, p. 9.
[40] J. P. Milton, *The Psalms*. Rock Island: Augustana Book Concern. 1954. pp. 71-72.
[41] John D. Davis, *op. cit.*
[42] S. R. Driver, *Commentary on Genesis*. *op. cit.*
[43] R. B. Girdlestone, *op. cit.*

Chapter Ten

THE NEW COVENANT IN JEREMIAH

THE PROPHETIC ANNOUNCEMENT in Jer. 31:31-34 of "a new covenant" which the Lord will make with the house of Israel and with the house of Judah has received glowing words of praise as "the most important single teaching of Jeremiah"[1] and "one of the salient disclosures of Old Testament prophecy";[2] and such praise is well deserved. It is necessary, however, to enter a word of caution lest we be carried away by the fulsomeness of our praise and forget the true relationship between the new covenant and the old.

Let us be clear, first of all, as to our use of the terms "old" and "new" at this point in our study. What we have tried to show is that the covenant of blessing with Abraham and the covenant relationship between God and Israel as formulated at Sinai, and as interpreted in the history of Israel, are essentially one and the same covenant. We have seen the covenant with Israel as the first stage in the historical fulfillment of the covenant with Abraham. To this first stage in the fulfillment of the covenant of blessing belong the Torah literature, the interpretation of Israel's history, and the prophecy and psalmody which were a part of that history and an expression of the covenant faith. It is this covenant, which is so closely connected with the history of Israel in Old Testament times, and which includes the totality of God's dealings with them as His people, that we will from here on refer to as the "old" covenant. The "new" covenant we shall try to define, first, on the basis of the prophecy of Jeremiah, and second, in the light of the second stage in the historical fulfillment of the Abrahamic covenant as seen in the New Testament.

When we are told that "Moses was the means of an external covenant; Jeremiah the proclaimer of an internal covenant; Jesus, the Messiah, was to be the Creator of the eternal covenant, of which Jeremiah was a fit forerunner,"[3] how literally shall the words be taken? Was the Mosaic covenant wholly external in intent and emphasis; was it a complete failure in achieving "inwardness" in religion? Is that what the prophet means to say? We will agree that "religion is a matter of the heart, and not of the cultus";[4] this truth Jeremiah stressed, but was he the first to discover it? The question sharpens for us, if we believe that the covenant involved an actual divine initiative and not only a deepening religious insight on the part of man. If God acted at all in the making of the covenant, must we not assume that He acted "in character"? And "God is spirit" (Jn. 4:24). *He* did not require the experiences of the Exile to teach Him the need of a spiritual covenant or the futility of external discipline. If, as we have said before, there is such a thing as *holy history* (and the answer of Scripture is an emphatic Yes), the words of Jeremiah must be understood within this frame of reference, within the ongoing purpose of the saving acts of God. The new covenant of which he speaks must be related to the covenant of blessing with Abraham as well as to the covenant with Israel which we label Sinaitic or Mosaic; and all three must be seen in the light of the New Testament interpretation of the covenant: and when we try to do that, we discover that an adequate interpretation must look beyond the seemingly absolute contrast between "old" and "new" in the Jeremiah passage to "newness" in a different sense.

Jer. 31:31-34 should be read in the light of Jer. 7:21-23. "Thus says the Lord of hosts, the God of Israel: 'Add your burnt offerings to your sacrifices, and eat the flesh. For in the day that I brought them out of the land of Egypt, I did not speak to your fathers or command them concerning burnt offerings and sacrifices. But this command I gave them, Obey my voice, and I will be your God, and you shall be my people; and walk in all the way that I command you, that it may be well with you.'" Here is reflected the primary emphasis on the inner attitude of obedience (as in Ex. 19:3-6) as over against the secondary emphasis on external ordinances, be they ritual or social in nature. This is Jeremiah's interpretation of the fundamental character of the Sinai covenant. Who shall say that it is false? If Scripture is allowed to bring its witness in its own way, we must admit that God sought the obedience of faith from the very beginning; it was not an afterthought with Him. We see this pre-eminently in the Abraham story in the Book of Genesis. It is equally true, however, of the covenant with Israel, which included the giving of the Torah, or the law.

It was the Septuagint translation of Torah as nomos or law that gave rise to "a misleading impression of the way God had dealt with

Israel to make them his people"; the implication being that "Israel is bound to God in a relation which is adequately expressed by strict obedience to a code of law."[5] According to etymology and in Biblical usage the word Torah would rather suggest instruction or guidance in the good and the right way. "It is a line marked out along which the life of the people or the person in covenant with God, and already right with God on that ground, is to unfold itself."[6] As an indication of the divine will the Torah possessed both spirituality and inwardness even when clothed in external forms. Through the Torah God laid claim to man's heart as well as to his life; to his faith as well as to his obedience. As a part of the Deuteronomic Code stands the *Shema:* "Hear, O Israel: The Lord our God is one Lord; and you shall love the Lord your God with all your heart, and with all your soul, and with all your might" (Deut. 6:4-5). Imbedded in the Levitical legislation is the command, "You shall love your neighbor as yourself" (Lev. 19: 18). These are but two outstanding examples of the spirit of inwardness in the Torah of the old covenant. In all strata of the Torah literature we find the motivation from the covenant relationship of "your God" and "my people"; it is not so much through the cracking of a whip by a God of law that obedience is sought as it is through the loving appeal of a God of covenant grace. Even the New Testament gives this interpretation of the commandments as given for our good: "For this is the love of God, that we keep his commandments. And his commandments are not burdensome" (1 Jn. 5:3). The preceding context makes clear which commandments are meant: "And this commandment we have from him, that he who loves God should love his brother also" (1 Jn. 4:21). This is a summary of the law; this was the purpose of the law from the moment God gave it to Israel within the covenant relationship. We do not deny its other function, which the New Testament rightly stresses: to convict of sin; but we must insist, if we are to be true to the Old Testament, that the law was given with gracious intent, and that God sought through it the willing obedience of His people to His good and gracious as well as righteous will. We shall miss the point of Jeremiah's prophecy if we see in it an absolute contrast between the two covenants of which he speaks. The same is true if we make too strict an equation between the new covenant in Jeremiah and in the New Testament. The analysis will illustrate the reason for saying so.

187

The Time Element

The prophecy is introduced by the words, "Behold, the days are coming, says the Lord, when I will make a new covenant with the house of Israel and the house of Judah" (v. 31). The time reference is future, but indefinite. The context, however, supplies a frame of reference which makes the situation a bit more concrete. The theme of the chapter is the promise of a return from exile and of restoration as the people of God, supported by the assurance of God's everlasting love and abiding faithfulness to them even in the day of their affliction for their sins. In verse 17 we are told:

> "There is hope for your future, says the Lord,
>   and your children shall come back to their own country."

The language of v. 28 reflects the key verse of the book of Jeremiah (1:10): "And it shall come to pass that as I have watched over them to pluck up and break down, to overthrow, destroy, and bring evil, so I will watch over them to build and to plant, says the Lord." The future restoration is seen in vivid contrast with the present judgment. The prophet predicts the captivity as a result of the broken covenant; but after the captivity will come a spiritual renewal and a return home, a time of restoration for Israel as the people of God. It will be a restoration religious in character, yet intertwined with Israel's history as a nation. It might be well to compare the three passages introduced by the prophet with identical words:

"Behold, the days are coming, says the Lord, when I will sow the house of Israel and the house of Judah with the seed of man and the seed of beast" (v. 27).

"Behold, the days are coming, says the Lord, when I will make a new covenant with the house of Israel and the house of Judah" (v. 31).

"Behold, the days are coming, says the Lord, when the city shall be rebuilt for the Lord from the tower of Hananel to the Corner Gate" (v. 38).

What the prophet envisions is a national experience with profound spiritual implications. If we look at the "times-coloring" of the whole chapter, the prophecy of the new covenant would seem to have more of the character of renewal than of replacement of the old. The covenant purpose of God will be fully realized with his people, so that "my people shall be satisfied with my goodness, says the Lord" (v. 14).

The New Covenant

We note that the direction of the covenant, as is always the case where the Bible writers speak of a divine covenant with man, is from God to man: "*I* will make a new covenant." The Lord will take the initiative again. The new covenant originates in an act of God's grace. There is the usual hint, however, that it is intended to become a mutual covenant; for it is a covenant *with* the house of Israel and the house of Judah. The historical "times-coloring" is evident; the reference is to the nation of Israel in its present divided state, yet in such a way as to reveal a significant awareness of the original unity. Jeremiah, like Hosea and Ezekiel, has before him the vision of a reunited Israel, in conformity with the original election of Israel to be a people for God's own possession. If the scope of the prophecy is wider than Israel, the language does not suggest it; though it permits of a universal application along the lines of "a clear continuity of theological principle," in harmony with the covenant of blessing with Abraham.

The specific reference to Israel is borne out by the contrast with the covenant "which I made with their fathers when I took them by the hand to bring them out of the land of Egypt" (v. 32). The backward look is to the covenant at Sinai; but whether to the basic provisions of the covenant in Ex. 19:3-6, which reflect something of the spirituality of the covenant with Abraham, or to the addition of the law of commandments and ordinances (Eph. 2:15), is not made clear. It makes very little difference as far as our interpretation of the last part of v. 32 is concerned, "my covenant which they broke"; for in reality Israel had violated both the spirit and the letter of God's covenant with them. In the words of the prophet Isaiah a century and more before Jeremiah,

> "Sons have I reared and brought up,
> but they have rebelled against me" (Is. 1:2).

Or as Hosea, the contemporary of Isaiah, put it in a few poignant words,

> "and forgot me, says the Lord" (Hos. 2:13).

We shall never understand Jeremiah if we think simply in terms of a protest against ritual religion, and then dismiss the ritual as if it were wholly a device of man and in no sense an ordinance of God: as if the prophecy of the new covenant were simply one more expression of a fundamental conflict between prophetic and ritual religion. He did indeed make such a protest (see chapter 7); but his protest went beyond ritual to something more fundamental, of which ritualistic formalism may have been one of the symbols: he protested against a basic unfaithfulness on the part of Israel to their God and to His covenant with them, unfaithfulness as of a wife to a loving and faithful husband. The picture is the same as that which dominates the book of Hosea; they broke the covenant of Him who says, "though I was their husband." Does that indicate a relationship devoid of inwardness, a wholly external covenant based on law rather than on love? Certainly not from God's side! The translation in RSV, "I was their husband," can be defended, even though the Hebrew permits another, "I was their rightful lord or master." The frequent affinity between Jeremiah and Hosea, as well as the whole context of chapter 31, supports the tenderer note, "their husband." To make the "old" covenant out to be a stern master-servant relationship based on a strict code of law means that we misinterpret the old and prejudice our interpretation of the new. True, Israel broke the covenant; but in so doing they rejected God's love: they rebelled not only against authority but against grace. What was needed was not a new covenant on God's part so much as a new response on the part of His people. "The new covenant is to transcend the old, not to annul it."[7] "The covenant is to be new in the sense that it will confer a new, inward motivation and power for fulfilling the already known."[8] God would make a new—in the sense of a supreme and successful—effort to persuade and empower His people to respond to His love in the joyous obedience of faith. For without faith which is obedient, how can there be a true "your God"—"my people" relationship, such as the covenant called for from the beginning? Such, at least, would seem to be the viewpoint from which the prophet Jeremiah speaks of "a new covenant." Our analysis of the covenant as he describes it will confirm the interpretation.

This Is the Covenant Which I Will Make

There are four distinctive marks of the new covenant as Jeremiah describes it. They overlap and intertwine, for they are simply so many aspects of a single covenant; but for the sake of convenience we may keep them separate for purposes of analysis.

1. The first mark relates to the law: "I will put my law within

them, and I will write it upon their hearts" (v. 33). The Torah or law was not to be set aside under the new covenant; at least not in the deeper spiritual sense of the Moral Law, which is a declaration of the good and gracious will of God. God would continue to look for the response of faith-obedience to His will for the life of His people. The twin commandments in Deut. 6:4-5 and in Lev. 19:18 would continue to bear witness to the requirements of God for any people that is to be called "a holy nation" unto the Lord. Jesus' summary of the law in Mt. 22:37-40 makes clear that the law of love for God and neighbor has not been abrogated. So does the great prophetic word in Mic. 6:8. It is absurd to suppose that Jeremiah was ignorant of this significant emphasis in the old covenant, or that he understood the old covenant wholly in terms of ritual religion. He does not even speak of the abolition of the law; the point at issue is not so much a new law as a new power. God will write his law in the hearts of His people. This need not imply, as is often assumed, either criticism or rejection of the written law, or of the law of Moses in whatever form it existed at the time the prophet wrote. To say with Pfeiffer, "To the Deuteronomic covenant based on a book, Jeremiah opposed a 'new covenant' based on a law written not in a book but in the hearts of the people,"[9] is an ingenious but wholly conjectural interpretation of the position of Jeremiah in relation to the development of Israel's religion. Jeremiah does not deny that God's appeal under the old covenant had always been for the obedience that comes from the heart, the obedience of a faith like Abraham's; nor does he say that this appeal will now be changed, or that God will now seek for another kind of response to the covenant. What the prophet declares is rather that God will try a new and stronger method of persuasion. He will make a new and successful attempt to write His law in the hearts of men, so that He may receive from them the willing obedience that befits a people of God. The thought of Jeremiah moves along the same track as that of Paul in Rom. 8:3-4, when he says that God sent His Son not only to save from the condemnation of the law of sin and death but "in order that the just requirement of the law might be fulfilled in us, who walk not according to the flesh but according to the Spirit."

There is, however, one important difference between Jeremiah and Paul; and the difference is significant for our understanding of the new covenant.

What was the new power that would finally succeed in writing

191

God's law "upon their hearts"? Jeremiah does not say; he is content to leave it as an undefined act of God. The likelihood is that he did not know. The Old Testament generally is no more specific. Therein lay the weakness of the old covenant throughout, even of the covenant of blessing with Abraham, and of a redemption experience like that of the Exodus or of the return from Babylonian Captivity. There were indeed mighty saving acts of God, which revealed Him to His people as a God of mercy and of might, "in love and pity infinite";[10] but what the Old Testament lacked throughout was the final outpouring of the power of persuasive love, first, through the redeeming act of God in Christ on Calvary's cross, and second, through the ministry of the Holy Spirit *after* Good Friday, Easter, and Pentecost, when He could take of the things of Jesus and declare them to us as the greatest imaginable evidence of the depths of God's love. Towards this goal the prophecy of Jeremiah points, but in language borrowed still from the old covenant; assured only of the promise of God, and of His power to perform what He has promised, in spite of the seeming failure of the moment. "I will put my law within them, and I will write it upon their hearts." This is God's promise. It indicates the need of inwardness in religion and of a divine power to achieve this inwardness. The promise is that He will do it; He will not only renew His covenant which has been broken, but He will fulfill it. How will He do it? The inspired commentary on this new saving act of God is given in the New Testament, in passages such as Jn. 3:16, Jn. 12:32, 2 Cor. 5:14-15, Rom. 8:3-4 (in the context of the whole chapter), and Gal. 2:20, to mention only a few. There is an essential unity of purpose between the covenants; but it makes a difference that Christ has come, a difference in the power of God's persuasion and in the human response: "for the love of Christ controls us." At this crucial point the covenant of Jeremiah belongs more to the old covenant than to the new, of which it is a prediction.

2. The second mark relates to the covenant fellowship: "I will be their God, and they shall be my people" (v. 33). Certainly this was not a new promise, a new idea, a new relationship! Since the time of Abraham God had spoken of his seed in a manner that implied a special relationship to him as His people. In terms of the covenant with Israel we recall the "segullah" promise in Ex. 19:5; Israel was called to be *his very own*. We remember also the remarkable picture of God's yearning love for His wayward people in Hos. 11:8-9, a cen-

tury and a half before Jeremiah's day; to which we could add Is. 1:2-4, and Mic. 6:1-8, and even Amos 5: all of them moving prophetic utterances within the framework of the old covenant. They had been called from the beginning into this relationship of "your God" and "my people"; but they had proved to be rebellious children (Is. 1:2-4). Therefore the message of the prophets is largely a plea to return to the Lord in the spirit of penitence and faith. "Turn to him from whom you have deeply revolted, O people of Israel" (Is. 31:6). "Seek the Lord and live" (Am. 5:6). "Take with you words and return to the Lord; say to him,

> 'Take away all iniquity;
> accept that which is good
> and we will render
> the fruit of our lips'" (Hos. 14:2).

"Repent and turn from all your transgressions, lest iniquity be your ruin. Cast away from you all the transgressions which you have committed against me, and get yourselves a new heart and a new spirit! Why will you die, O house of Israel? For I have no pleasure in the death of anyone, says the Lord God; so turn, and live" (Ezek. 18: 30b-32). "For I know the plans I have for you, says the Lord, plans for welfare and not for evil, to give you a future and a hope. Then you will call upon me and come and pray to me, and I will hear you. You will seek me and find me; when you seek me with all your heart, I will be found by you, says the Lord, and I will restore your fortunes and gather you from all the nations and all the places where I have driven you, says the Lord, and I will bring you back to the place from which I sent you into exile" (Jer. 29:11-14).

The theme of repentance and restoration represents a fundamental prophetic viewpoint. May we then interpret the new covenant of Jeremiah within the same prophetic framework? Is it fundamentally only a return to, and a renewed experience of, the previous covenant relationship, with a revitalized response in the obedience of faith? Is it primarily in the human response to the covenant that we look for the newness; as if the Lord were saying that *now at last* there will be the genuine response sought from the very start of God's dealing with Israel? Certainly this is involved, in conformity with the teaching of Hosea (see e.g., the contrast between present and future in Hos. 1: 8-10); but if we bear in mind the direction of the covenant, from God to man, and then the response, from man to God, we must look for something more. What is indicated is a new saving act of God which will bring about a deepening of the whole experience of fellowship with Him as His people. If we look backward from Jeremiah, we must admit that there was a real faith-fellowship with God under the old covenant. If we look forward from Jeremiah, we discover a new experience of fellowship with God through Jesus Christ our Lord which is more intimate and personal, or if we may say so, *more real,* as befits a covenant enacted "on better promises" (Heb. 8:6). "God is faithful, by whom you were called into the fellowship of his Son, Jesus Christ our Lord" (1 Cor. 1:9). It is this sort of fellowship that is foreshadowed in the Jeremiah prophecy, though he speaks of it in characteristic Old Testament fashion as a God-Israel and not as a Christ-man relationship. We can only say with assurance that he anticipated a deeper spiritual fellowship between God and His people in days to come than in time past; but it was with the coming of Christ in the fullness of time that the promised act of God became effective. The former "your God"—"my people" relationship was a genuine experience of fellowship with God by faith; yet, in comparison with the fellowship experience in Christ it was but a shadow of the real thing. Through Him the covenant experience of blessed fellowship as children of God is brought to full fruition. There can be no greater motivation to covenant faithfulness or faith on the part of the people of God than the cross of Christ. Without it, the prophecy of Jeremiah concerning a new covenant would have remained so many empty and futile words. What he saw as an act of God took on concrete form with the coming of Jesus Christ as the living incarnation of the love of God, which is the only effective power unto a right relationship between God and us.

3. The third mark relates to a true knowledge of God: "And no longer shall each man teach his neighbor and each his brother, saying, 'Know the Lord,' for they shall all know me, from the least of them to the greatest, says the Lord" (v. 34). To know the Lord was not an altogether new experience. The Exodus narrative declares repeatedly that the purpose with the mighty acts of God was that Pharaoh, the Egyptians, and also Israel, should know "that I am the Lord." This is knowledge in the sense of acknowledgment; but if the acknowledgment be sincere it shades over into the knowledge of experience. The Old Testament does not represent this knowledge as something impos-

sible to attain, though often absent even in the people of God's covenant. It is pictured rather as the norm of a true covenant relationship:

"For I desire steadfast love and not sacrifice,
   the knowledge of God, rather than burnt offerings"
                                                 (Hos. 6:6).

This knowledge of God was Israel's heritage; and it was their tragedy when the Lord their God must level against them the indictment that "there is no faithfulness or kindness, and no knowledge of God in the land" (Hos. 4:2).

My people are destroyed for lack of knowledge;
   because you have rejected knowledge,
   I reject you from being a priest to me.
And since you have forgotten the law of your God,
   I also will forget your children (Hos. 4;6).

The Hebrew concept of knowledge is intensely pragmatic. We do not know God in the Biblical sense unless it leads to right action. It is Jeremiah who illustrates this pragmatic quality of true knowledge most strikingly (see e.g., chapter 9:23-24 and 22:15-16); but Jeremiah did not originate it. "To know God" in Old Testament speech means to know Him with the heart as well as with the head, experientially and not only intellectually; and such a knowledge even the old covenant mediated to many.

What then does it mean when the prophet uses "the knowledge of God" as one of the significant marks of the new covenant? It must mean that under the new covenant there will be *a growth* in the knowledge of God so great as to make the knowledge of Him under the old covenant seem insignificant to the point of non-existence. It might be a growth in knowledge about God: a clearer, fuller revelation of God such as we have actually received in Jesus Christ. See by way of illustration Jn. 1:14, 18, Heb. 1:1-3, and 2 Cor. 4:6. It might be growth in the sense of a wider dissemination of the true knowledge of God, until it becomes universal; this is the theme of prophecy in many places, such as Is. 11:9 and Hab. 2:14. We might well call this the ultimate goal of the covenant of blessing with Abraham, for only so does the promise to him make sense: "In you [and in your seed] will all the nations of the earth be blessed." It might be in the sense of a wider and deeper participation in the experiential knowledge of God by those who are called his people; so wide and so deep that there is no longer need for one to admonish another to know the Lord, since *all* now give evidence in their manner of life that they know and acknowledge him as Lord. We might call this the immediate goal of the prophecy, for it is directed in the first instance to God's covenant people Israel. A comparable prophecy is found in Joel 2:28-29:

> "And it shall come to pass afterward,
>   that I will pour out my spirit on all flesh;
>   your sons and your daughters shall prophesy,
>   your old men shall dream dreams,
>   and your young men shall see visions.
>   Even upon the menservants and maidservants
>   in those days, I will pour out my spirit."

It is only as the New Testament makes clear to us the wider relevance of this and every other reference to God's covenant purpose with His people Israel that we see the relation between the prediction of a new covenant in Jeremiah and its fulfillment in the new covenant in Jesus' blood. From the viewpoint of its terminology, the Jeremiah prophecy may seem to point to *a renewal* of the old covenant, coupled with a hint of a new invigorating power that shall transform the old into something so much greater and more wonderful as to warrant calling it a *new* covenant. Jeremiah seems to speak of a newness of knowledge akin to that of which we read in 2 Peter 3:18, "But grow in the grace and knowledge of our Lord and Savior Jesus Christ"; this is the experiential aspect of "newness" in relation to the covenant. From another aspect the words of Jesus with reference to the law and the prophets are true also of the covenant to which they belonged: "I have not come to abolish them but to fulfill them" (Mt. 5:17). This is the historical aspect of "newness" in relation to the covenant. The new covenant is new because, whether we see it from one aspect of "newness" or the other, it is the final consummation of the old.

4. The fourth mark relates to the forgiveness of sins: "for I will forgive their iniquity, and I will remember their sin no more" (v. 34). Though in form an explanatory clause and therefore closely connected with the knowledge of God in the preceding context, it merits special attention; for the forgiveness of sins is the choicest fruit of the new covenant as we know it in Jesus Christ. Was it otherwise under the old covenant? It was certainly not an unknown experience. We think of God's revelation of himself to Moses: "And the Lord descended in

the cloud and stood with him there, and proclaimed the name of the Lord. The Lord passed before him, and proclaimed, "The Lord, the Lord, a God merciful and gracious, slow to anger, and abounding in steadfast love and faithfulness, keeping steadfast love for thousands, forgiving iniquity and transgression and sin" (Ex. 34:5-7). We recall that Moses was so moved by the vision that he prostrated himself before the Lord, and worshiped, and prayed, "If now I have found favor in thy sight, O Lord, let the Lord, I pray thee, go in the midst of us, although it is a stiff-necked people; and pardon our iniquity and our sin, and take us for thy inheritance" (Ex. 34:9). We remember also the beautiful confession of David in Ps. 32:5,

> I acknowledged my sin to thee,
> and I did not hide my iniquity;
> I said, "I will confess my transgressions to the Lord";
> then thou didst forgive the guilt of my sin.

We are reminded of the absolution pronounced on Isaiah in the Temple at the time of his call: "Then flew one of the seraphim to me, having in his hand a burning coal which he had taken with tongs from the altar. And he touched my mouth and said: 'Behold, this has touched your lips; your guilt is taken away, and your sin forgiven" (Is. 6:6-7). The excellent statement by A. B. Davidson comes to mind, "The institutions of atonement provided for the taking away of sins done through infirmity, and the law was a direction to the believer how to bear himself practically within the covenant relation."[11] We must not minimize the significance of the mercy seat (Hebrew *kapporeth,* Greek *ilasterion)* and of the provisions for atonement by sacrifice in Old Testament religion; but as George Adam Smith has pointed out, the religious significance of Isaiah's experience is unique in that "the only sacrifice he offers is the purely spiritual one of confession." He adds: "It is most notable. Look at it from a human point of view, and we can estimate Isaiah's immense spiritual originality; look at it from a Divine and we cannot help perceiving a distinct foreshadow of what was to take place by the blood of Jesus under the new covenant. To this man, as to some others of his dispensation, whose experience our Christian sympathy recognizes so readily in the Psalms, there was granted aforetime boldness to enter into the holiest."[12] We may agree with Smith that this direct forgiveness of sins on the basis of confession alone, with the institutions of atonement fading away into the background, was a unique experience, shared by relatively few in Israel; and yet, we must not limit it too narrowly. It was the experience of David as well as of Isaiah. The words of the psalmist express the faith of the devout Israelite under the old covenant:

> If thou, O Lord, shouldst mark iniquities,
>   Lord, who could stand?
> But there is forgiveness with thee,
>   that thou mayest be feared (Ps. 130:3-4).

Another psalmist could speak with calm certainty of the blessedness of forgiveness in words which even Christian faith could not improve:

> Blessed is he whose transgression is forgiven,
>   whose sin is covered.
> Blessed is the man to whom the Lord imputes no iniquity,
>   and in whose spirit there is no deceit (Ps. 32:1-2).

The hymn book of the old covenant contains not only penitential prayers but jubilant songs of praise because the Lord is gracious and merciful and forgiving. The classic example is Ps. 103.

> Bless the Lord, O my soul;
>   and all that is within me, bless his holy name!
> Bless the Lord, O my soul,
>   and forget not all his benefits,
> who forgives all your iniquity (1-3).

There was forgiveness under the old covenant: a real, valid experience of forgiveness. There could be forgiveness even under the old covenant because the whole redemptive work of God is *one*—and whether a man stood in the far distant shadows cast by the cross of Christ before itself, or in the bright noonday sun when the love of God was revealed in its final fullness through that cross of Jesus, *he was in the fellowship of the forgiven* if he had faith in the saving acts and promises of God. Yet, how much greater the assurance of forgiveness after Calvary than before! There can be growth even in the assurance of the forgiveness of sins. The Jeremiah prophecy does not speak of Christ's redemption in relation to forgiveness; but when seen in the light of the New Testament, *it is redemption through the blood of Christ that makes the covenant new* with respect to forgiveness. Here is the greatest guarantee that God could give of the love that forgives each penitent sinner who seeks mercy and forgiveness from a God who is "good and forgiving" (Ps. 86:5).

The point that we would make is that the new covenant of Jeremiah is a continuation of the old covenant with Israel at the same time as it is an anticipation of the "better" covenant mediated by Christ (Heb. 8:6). It stands midway between the two, and it partakes of the nature of both. It is in a sense a connecting link between the old and the new; it helps us to see that the transition from the one to the other is not a matter of radical rejection of the old but of glorious consummation in the new.

For when we sum up our thinking after this study of the "covenants" in the Old Testament we reach these conclusions:

First, that God's covenant with man is fundamentally one covenant, which culminates in Jesus Christ who came "in the fulness of time" to secure "an eternal redemption."

Second, that the various "covenants" are simply historical phases of the unfolding of this one eternal covenant purpose.

Third, that some elements of the covenant had a temporary, and others a permanent, significance; for the covenant is adapted to God's manner of working out His redemptive purpose *in history*.

Fourth, that the contrast between "old" and "new" is a relative contrast rather than a sharp antithesis of basic character and purpose; after the analogy of the new commandment of love in Jn. 13:34 (cf. Lev. 19:18). With Christ came a new covenant *based on fulfillment* of everything that was permanent and abiding in the old.

Fifth, that the "old" covenant is lacking in just one thing: the full revelation of redemptive love as realized in history in the cross of Christ, and the full power of such love to constrain men to that response in the obedience of faith which completes the experience of blessing and permits the fellowship with God that He has ever sought with men.

Sixth, that the covenant in Jesus' blood is "new," if by *new* we mean the final, crowning act of grace in God's covenant with men; but that it is one with the others, the covenant with Abraham and with Israel and with the house of David, in ultimate aim and purpose. For it is "the blessing of Abraham" that in Christ Jesus comes even upon the Gentiles; the same blessing, but with all its glorious content now fully revealed.

NOTES

[1] James Philip Hyatt, "Jeremiah," *The Interpreter's Bible.* New York and Nashville: Abingdon Press. 1956. Vol. 5. p. 1037.

[2] J. M. Myers, "Jeremiah," *Old Testament Commentary,* edited by Herbert C. Alleman and Elmer E. Flack. Philadelphia: Muhlenberg Press. 1948. p. 723.

[3] F. Cawley, *"Jeremiah,"* *The New Bible Commentary,* edited by F. Davidson, A. M. Stibbs, and E. F. Kevan. Grand Rapids: Wm. B. Eerdmans Publishing Co. 1953. p. 627.

[4] J. M. Myers, *op. cit.*

[5] W A. Whitehouse, *op. cit.*

[6] A. B. Davidson, *op. cit.,* pp. 280-281.

[7] From *The Westminster Study Edition of the Holy Bible.* Copyright 1948, W. L. Jenkins. Philadelphia: The Westminster Press. P. 1111.

[8] James Philip Hyatt, *op. cit.* p. 1038.

[9] Robert H. Pfeiffer, *Introduction to the Old Testament.* New York: Harper & Brothers. 1941. p. 55.

[10] Godfrey Thring, *op. cit.*

[11] A. B. Davidson, *op. cit.,* p. 281.

[12] G. A. Smith, *The Book of Isaiah, The Expositor's Bible.* New York: Geo. H. Doran Co. Vol. I. p. 73.

Chapter Eleven

ABRAHAM IN NEW TESTAMENT TEACHING

THE SIGNIFICANCE OF THE STORY OF ABRAHAM is borne out by the frequent mention of his name in the New Testament. The name occurs some seventy times, more than that of Moses or any other Old Testament man. It is true that many of these are repeated references within a single context; but they nevertheless play a very important part in the New Testament message. Let us look briefly at this New Testament use of the Abraham story to see how it is interpreted and how it is applied to the New Testament situation.

Mt. 1:1

The First Gospel opens with a genealogy, in which three names stand out: Jesus Christ, David, and Abraham. The genealogy in Lk. 3 adds a fourth: Adam. What is the significance of relating Jesus in this special way to these three men, as the son of David, the son of Abraham, and the son of Adam? We say that it is genealogical; but why should these men be singled out for special emphasis? Why in particular should the Christ be called "the son of Abraham"? Why should the genealogy in Matthew have as its two termini Abraham and Jesus Christ?

There is a religious significance that seems to be intended by the reference to each of these three men.

"The son of Adam" identifies Jesus as *true man,* who shares our "flesh and blood" (Heb. 2:14), and who stands in a relationship to humanity comparable to that of Adam: "For as by one man's disobedience many were made sinners, so by one man's obedience many will be made righteous" (Rom. 5:19).

"The son of David" identifies Him as the anointed King, the Messiah of prophecy as well as of popular expectation, who came to usher in that final glorious kingly rule of God of which the covenant with David was a feeble foreshadowing type.

201

"The son of Abraham" may seem at first to do no more than to identify him as a Jew "according to the flesh" (Rom. 9:5), a true descendant of Abraham, and therefore a member of the Chosen People; but here too there is a religious significance akin to that suggested by the reference to David: an implied claim that this Jesus who is called Christ is the fulfillment of the covenant with Abraham, and that in Christ we discover the full meaning of the promise of blessing made first to Abraham.

The religious significance becomes clear when we examine other references in the New Testament to "sons of Abraham."

1. In Mt. 3:8-9 we have the words of John the Baptist to the Jews, or more specifically the Pharisees and Sadducees, who came to him for baptism. "Bear fruit that befits repentance, and do not presume to say to yourselves, 'We have Abraham as our father'; for I tell you, God is able from these stones to raise up children to Abraham." To the Pharisees and Sadducees "sons of Abraham" implied a national or a racial connection with the patriarch, with perhaps a slight religious tinge of "special privilege" as being "the people of God." To John the phrase had a pure religious relevance. It denoted a relationship that was marked by "fruit worthy of repentance" (v. 8, ASV). It stood for a God-fearing or righteous life, as the fruit of a God-pleasing faith.

2. In Jn. 8:31-44 Jesus challenges the right of the Jews to say "Abraham is our father" (v. 39), while refusing to do "the works of Abraham" (ASV): "If you were Abraham's children, you would do what Abraham did." With the Jews, to be a son of Abraham meant simply a blood relationship, or the relationship of national origin; plus a mistaken sense of spiritual privilege without a genuine spiritual response on their part for the privilege. For Jesus it meant a completely spiritual relationship: it meant doing what Abraham did; it meant leading "his kind of life." What that kind of life was we shall see from other passages in the New Testament that make mention of Abraham. Here we are told what it was not: "If you were Abraham's children, you would do what Abraham did, but now you seek to kill me, a man who has told you the truth which I heard from God; this is not what Abraham did" (v. 39, 40). It was by their attitude toward the word of truth which Jesus spoke to them from God that they gave convincing proof that they were not "true descendants of Abraham"; by inference, Abraham was a man of faith who loved the truth and re-

sponded to it. If Abraham had been in their midst that day, he would have welcomed the word of Jesus as he did the word of God in his lifetime. He was receptive to the truth as it was revealed to him by God.

3. In the light of these two passages it becomes easier to interpret a cluster of other passages which refer to the children of Abraham. For example:

In Lk. 13:16 Jesus refers to the woman who was healed of a spirit of infirmity on the sabbath as "a daughter of Abraham whom Satan bound for eighteen years." Doubtless she was a daughter of Abraham by birth; her thankful praise to God for healing would indicate that she was also a daughter of Abraham by faith.

In Lk. 19:9 Jesus says of Zacchaeus, "Today salvation has come to this house, since he also is a son of Abraham." In the light of the context, who would say that this means simply that he was born a Jew? It is the seeking of Zacchaeus, and his response to the seeking of Jesus, that marks him as a spiritual son of Abraham.

In Acts 13:26 there seems to be a parallelism between "sons of the family of Abraham" and "those among you that fear God"; as if to say that he who fears God is also a true son of Abraham, or that a son of Abraham is one who fears God. For a similar construction see v. 16, "Men of Israel, and you that fear God." It is possible, of course, on the basis of v. 43, to distinguish between "Jews" and "proselytes," or "devout converts to Judaism," and to read this differentiation back into Paul's words in verses 16 and 26. It would still be true that the primary emphasis is religious rather than racial; for it was the fear of God, the God of Abraham, the God of the covenant with Israel, that united the believing Jew and the devout proselyte in one spiritual fellowship.

In Rom. 9:6-8 Paul makes a clearcut distinction between the Israelites who are merely the "descendants" of Abraham and those who are the "children" of Abraham, or between those who are indeed "children of Abraham" and those who are not: a distinction based in part on the quotation of Gen. 21:12, "Through Isaac shall your descendants be named." The emphasis on a spiritual seed of Abraham is unmistakable: "This means that it is not the children of the flesh who are the children of God, but the children of the promise are reckoned as descendants" (v. 8). In order to be a child of Abraham, something more than blood relationship is needed; there must be a religious relationship that is in some way connected with God's original promise of blessing to this man.

The same distinction, or one very similar to it, is stressed in the allegory of the two covenants, the one represented by Hagar the slave and the other by Sarah the free woman, in Gal. 4:21-31. The true son of Abraham, like Isaac, is a child of promise (v. 28), and "born according to the Spirit" (v. 29); such was the case with Isaac, and "so it is now." Though the allegory seems to contrast the covenant with Abraham, as a covenant of promise, with the Mosaic covenant, as a covenant of law, it does not follow that one living under the covenant with Israel could not at the same time be a son of Abraham and a child of promise; for Paul has already said emphatically in Gal. 3 that the law, which was added, did not annul the promise, which was given earlier to Abraham: the two function together in God's redemptive economy; but it is by faith in the promise and not by obedience to the law that we recognize the true child of Abraham.

Even more specific are the statements in Gal. 3:6-7 and 3:28-29. In the first passage Paul quotes Gen. 15:6, "Thus Abraham 'believed God, and it was reckoned to him as righteousness,'" and then draws this conclusion, "So you see that it is men of faith who are the sons of Abraham." In the passage at the end of the chapter he says, "There is neither Jew nor Greek, there is neither slave nor free, there is neither male nor female; for you are all one in Christ Jesus. And if you are Christ's, then you are Abraham's offspring, heirs according to promise." Here "the son of Abraham" is given its final spiritual interpretation: a true son of Abraham is one who shares Abraham's faith, his manner of life, his relationship to God.

The definition given leads naturally to another question, partially answered in the definition itself but calling for further clarification: What kind of life was Abraham's? We have seen the answer given in the Old Testament; what now says the New?

James 2:21-24

According to James it was a life of faith and works. "Was not Abraham our father justified by works, when he offered his son Isaac upon the altar? You see that faith was active along with his works, and faith was completed by works, and the scripture was fulfilled which says, 'Abraham believed God, and it was reckoned to him as righteousness'; and he was called the friend of God." This corresponds with the Old Testament emphasis on faith (Gen. 15:6) and obedience (Gen. 22:15-18). Another way to express it is in terms of "faith and life." When James says that Abraham was called "the friend of God" he is not only echoing the Old Testament (see Is. 41:8; 2 Chron. 20:7), but he is interpreting it: he is saying in effect what Jesus said about the nature and test of friendship, "You are my friends if you do what I command you" (Jn. 15:14). Abraham's life is an illustration of the obedience of faith, which qualifies a man to be called a friend of God. Jesus himself was "the son of Abraham" because He too, and in a still greater measure than we, exemplified the life of obedient faith in God. No one can be a true son of Abraham in any other way.

Heb. 11:8-12, 17-19

In Heb. 11 Abraham occupies what we may well call *the place of honor* among those who are examples of faith. It is not his faith alone, however, that comes in for emphatic attention. The very first thing said about him is that "by faith Abraham obeyed" (v. 8). Four experiences from his life are singled out for mention, and in each his faith is combined with obedience: 1, his response to the call to set out for an unknown destination on the strength of the divine promise; 2, his patient lifelong waiting, as a sojourner in a foreign land, for the fulfillment of the promise of a land of his own; 3, his faith experience of the power and faithfulness of God in the birth of the son of promise in his old age; and 4, his readiness to offer up this child of promise as a sacrifice in obedience to the command of God. By faith, faith in the living God, he obeyed; and because he obeyed God blessed him. The Old Testament version of the Moriah experience says, "Because you have done this, and have not withheld your son, your only son, I will indeed bless you, . . . and by your descendants shall all the nations of the earth bless themselves [or be blessed], because you have obeyed my voice" (Gen. 22:15-18). The New Testament interpretation of this remarkable faith obedience says, "He considered that God was able to raise men even from the dead; hence, figuratively speaking, he did receive him back" (Heb. 11:19). The two agree that the life of Abraham was the life of a man of unusual faith and of unique obedience, a man who trusted God and whom God found faithful.

Romans 4

We find another significant reference to Abraham's faith in the fourth chapter of Paul's letter to the Romans. This is a key chapter in New Testament theology, and Abraham is the key figure in the teaching of the chapter. It concerns the question of justification, or how to become righteous before God. The Apostle cites the experience of Abraham to illustrate the truth that righteousness comes by faith: "Abraham believed God, and it was reckoned to him as righteousness" (Rom. 4:3; Gen. 15:6). In vv. 9-12 he points out that this experience came to Abraham *before* he was circumcised (cf. the sequence in the Abraham story in Genesis), and that he received circumcision "as a sign or seal of the righteousness which he had *by faith* while he was still uncircumcised" (v. 11). So also the promise to Abraham and his seed "that they should inherit the world," the promise of an inheritance far greater than the land of Canaan, "did not come through the law but through the righteousness of faith" (v. 13). Paul seems to be thinking here of *the gospel* within the original promise of blessing, whose fulfillment is in Christ. Through Him all men of faith of every nation become a part of the spiritual inheritance of Abraham. The vision of the psalmist is fulfilled:

> The princes of the people gather
> as the people of the God of Abraham (Ps. 47:9).

It was *by faith* also that Abraham received the fulfillment of the promise of a son. "No distrust made him waver concerning the promise of God, but he grew strong in his faith as he gave glory to God, fully convinced that God was able to do what he had promised" (vv. 20-21). Throughout the chapter Abraham is the living symbol of what it means to live in a firm faith fellowship with God and to have this faith reckoned to him as righteousness. "By faith Abraham" could be written over Rom. 4 as well as over Heb. 11:8ff. It does not say that "by faith Abraham obeyed"; and yet, there is an implicit obedience involved in his faith. He believed God and acted accordingly. This is "the example of the faith which our father Abraham had [even] before he was circumcised" (v. 12). The example is for us, and the experience can be ours; and as "men of faith" we become "the sons of Abraham" (Gal. 3:7) and "blessed with Abraham who had faith" (Gal. 3:9).

Galatians 3

But in Gal. 3 Paul takes us back *beyond the experience* of right-eousness by faith *to the divine promise* on which it was based, the covenant of blessing. This was the promise, as we recall, that Abraham should both *receive* and *be* a blessing. Significantly, Paul calls it a preaching of the gospel beforehand to Abraham (v. 8): the Scripture anticipating the truth that God would justify the Gentiles by faith. Significantly also, Paul sees the final fulfillment of the promise of a seed through whom the blessing should come *in Christ* (v. 16). Significantly too, he stresses the fact that the covenant promise of blessing and inheritance given to Abraham was not annulled by the law which came later (v. 17). The word of promise to Abraham, according to Paul, was one of those prophetic words which a man could lay hold of and believe even while he waited for God who gave the promise to interpret the full depth of its meaning. Choose what words you will to describe the relationship between the promise and the fulfillment: the important thing is that *they are related* as promise to fulfillment. It is "the blessing of Abraham" that has come also upon the Gentiles "in Christ Jesus" (v. 14). It is the promise of inheritance given to Abraham that we claim also for ourselves "in Christ Jesus"; for "if you are Christ's, then you are Abraham's offspring, heirs according to promise" (v. 29). How strangely, how wonderfully, the story of this man is related to the gospel of Christ—as an illustration, as a preparation, as a living prefiguration! "So you see that it is men of faith who are sons of Abraham."

Acts 3:25-26

It is in Acts 3 that we have the clearest statement of New Testament interpretation of the covenant with Abraham. It marks the conclusion of Peter's address to the people crowded around him in Solomon's portico in the Temple. We ought to read his sermon from start to finish; noting especially the opening words which identify the audience, "Men of Israel" (v. 12); the acknowledgment that it was "the God of Abraham and of Isaac and of Jacob, the God of our fathers," who glorified "his servant Jesus" (v. 13); the reference to the word of God by the prophets "that his Christ should suffer" (v. 18); the preaching of repentance for the remission of sins in the name of this Jesus whom God appointed to be the Christ (vv. 19-20); and the sweeping assertion that "all the prophets who have spoken, from Samuel and those who came afterwards, also proclaimed those days" (v. 24). The speaker concludes with these words of direct application and personal appeal to his audience: "You are the sons of the prophets and of the covenant which God gave to your fathers, saying to Abraham, 'And in your posterity shall all the families of the earth be blessed.' God, having raised up his servant, sent him to you first, to bless you in turning every one of you from your wickedness."

The point of the sermon is unmistakable. Jesus is the fulfillment of the covenant with Abraham. The blessing of the covenant is a spiritual one, which involves not only repentance but also faith. The faith experience of Abraham and the example of his obedience must be seen in its relation to the covenant of blessing with him, which in Christ can be seen to be a covenant also with us. Jesus Christ as the Servant of the Lord brings to final fruition the calling first given to Abraham to be a blessing. What an unfolding glory as God interprets what the blessing of Abraham really meant through its complete realization in Jesus Christ, in whom is "every spiritual blessing" that man can seek or God can give! (Eph. 1:3) The backward look of the New Testament makes it clear that there is an essential unity between the covenant with Abraham and the new covenant in Jesus Christ. The one looked forward to the other. The new covenant is not the annulment but the fulfillment of the old; and the "old" began with the covenant of promise, the covenant of blessing, the covenant with Abraham. Such is the consistent New Testament viewpoint, on which the Christian interpretation is based.

There are other significant references to Abraham in the New Testament: the proud claim by Paul that "I myself am an Israelite, a descendant of Abraham" (Rom. 11:1, cf. 2 Cor. 11:22); the historical résumé by Stephen in Acts 7; the interpretation of Christ's redemptive work in terms of God's concern for "the descendants of Abraham" (Heb. 2:14-16); the oath of God in confirmation of the promise to Abraham (see Heb. 6:13-20); the interpretation of the Abraham-Melchizedek story in Heb. 7; the parallelism between "his covenant" and "the oath which he swore to our father Abraham" (Lk 1:72-73), which is a key to the understanding of the prophecy of Zechariah; Jesus' use of the words from Ex. 3:6, "I am the God of Abraham, and the God of Isaac, and the God of Jacob," in "proof" of the doctrine of the resurrection of the dead: "He is not God of the dead, but of the living" (see Mt. 22:31-32 and Lk. 20:37-38); the eschatological implications in the use of the phrase "Abraham's bosom" (Lk. 16:19-31), as well as in Jesus' teaching that "many will come from east and west and sit at table with Abraham, Isaac, and Jacob in the kingdom of heaven" (Mt. 8:11; cf. Lk. 13:28); and last, but not least, the assertion of Jesus, "Truly, truly, I say to you, before Abraham was, I am" (Jn. 8:58).

Perhaps we should have included an appendix containing the total list of New Testament references to Abraham: an impressive list, 71 in all. Perhaps we should have added some of the passages where the name does not occur but where the content is clearly reminiscent of the story of Abraham and of the promise to him. For this we ought to look as we read our New Testament. There is truth in the thesis of Willis J. Beecher, that a single promise runs through all prophecy, and that in the thinking of the New Testament writers this promise was the promise of blessing through Abraham and his seed.[1] There is truth in the statement that the covenant with Abraham is essentially one with the new covenant mediated by Jesus Christ. To this covenant, as to the goal of the saving acts of God that we see in the life of his servant Abraham, we shall now turn our attention in the final chapter.

NOTES

[1] W. J. Beecher, *op. cit.*

Chapter Twelve

THE NEW COVENANT IN JESUS' BLOOD

IN SETTING FORTH WHAT WE BELIEVE to be the religious significance of the Old Testament teaching concerning the divine covenant we have reached two main conclusions.

The first conclusion is that God's covenant is essentially *one* covenant: a covenant of grace and blessing, whose ultimate fulfillment includes Christ and the Christian gospel; a spiritual covenant that has never been changed as to its fundamental character and purpose, though it has been clarified from time to time, and has even received differing emphases at various stages in this ongoing process that we call sacred history. The addition of the law is a significant addition in terms of the covenant with Israel; but it did not annul the original character of the covenant with Abraham as a covenant of promise and of blessing. The covenant remained essentially the same.

The second conclusion is that the religious concept of a covenant between God and men constitutes the fundamental framework within which to understand the teaching not only of the Old Testament, but of the Bible in its unified wholeness; for it expresses better than any other concept the redemptive purpose and the saving acts of God, which are the unifying theme of Scripture: it *gives unity* to the Scriptures, which otherwise may seem to the reader to be quite disjointed in character and content. It was not by accident that the church came to think and to speak of the two covenants as comprising the whole of Scripture: one Bible with two parts, the Old Testament and the New Testament, the old diatheke and the new diatheke, the old berith and the new berith. This is an accurate way of speaking of the Sacred Scriptures, if we allow always for the unity that inheres in the whole because God is One, and acts with singleness of purpose in relation to man whom He has created. In Christ we see the unity. Paul speaks of it in terms of a bridging of the old separation between the Jews and the Gentiles: "For he is our peace, who has made us both one, and has broken down the dividing wall of hostility, by abolishing in his flesh the law of commandments and ordinances, that he might create in himself one new man in place of the two, so making peace, and might reconcile us both to God in one body through the cross, thereby bringing the hostility to an end" (Eph. 2: 14-16). It is Jesus, however, who provides us with the real key to the unity of the Scriptures of the Old and the New Testaments when He says concerning himself: "Think not that I have come to abolish the law and the prophets; I have not come to abolish them but to fulfil them" (Mt. 5:17). The unity of Scripture is a unity of fulfillment.

It is this unity of fulfillment that is so important when we try to think through the relation of the old covenant to the new. The actual references to *diatheke* or covenant in the New Testament are comparatively few. The word occurs only 33 times, as compared with the 278 references to *berith* in the Old Testament; but as in the Old Testament, the direct covenant references are found in significant contexts, and the covenant concept controls the whole New Testament message.

1

The shifting viewpoint

We note almost immediately that the viewpoint in these references to the covenant seems to be a shifting one, even as in the Old Testament; and therefore each passage must be carefully exegeted in its context.

For example, in Acts 7: 8 the covenant of blessing with Abraham is called "the covenant of circumcision." There is no hint of interpretation of the meaning of the phrase as Stephen uses it. It could be an unreflective backward reference to the story in Gen. 17, where circumcision is seen to be a part of the covenant experience of Abraham, though not its beginning. Stephen does not *think through* on the relation between circumcision and Abraham's faith, or the promise of God that inspired that faith. He has another purpose in this review of covenant history than does Paul in Rom. 4, where Paul is concerned with covenant theology. It would be unfair to Stephen to say that he rules out the promise in favor of the commandment concerning circumcision as being the most significant factor in the covenant with Abraham. He does use a part for the whole, as Paul also does on occasion. It is certainly possible to read Acts 7 in the light of Rom. 4 and to understand by "the covenant of circumcision" its function as a confirming sign or seal of the righteousness which Abraham already had by faith; or, since Acts 7 is primarily a historical résumé, to read Acts 7 in the light of Gen. 17, where it is a sign rather than the substance of the covenant of God with Abraham. Nevertheless, the manner of reference in Acts 7:8 is an interesting variation from that in Gal. 3, where the covenant with Abraham is constantly and emphatically referred to as a covenant of promise and of blessing (Gal. 3:8, 14, 15-18). In the Epistle to the Galatians generally it is the Mosaic law given at Sinai that seems to be identified in Paul's thought with circumcision, being in effect a "covenant of circumcision." (See Gal. 3:17; 5:2-4, 11; 6:12-15.) It is evident from the comparison of Acts 7:8 with Rom. 4 and Gal. 3 that "the covenant of circumcision" might mean one of two things, depending on the speaker's viewpoint and purpose. This shifting viewpoint is precisely the same as the situation that we have indicated in the Old Testament: the one reflects the role of circumcision in the life of Abraham, the other its function in the later history and religion of Israel; the one relates it to the covenant with Abraham, as the external sign of the faith of Abraham in God's promise to him, the other relates it to the Sinaitic covenant with Israel as the symbol of the law that was added to the covenant of promise in which Israel's vocation had its real historical and religious roots.

2

The Covenant with Abraham

We note several direct references to the covenant with Abraham, which seem to justify the importance that we have attached to it in our study of the Old Testament.

In the Benedictus, the song of Zechariah in Lk. 1:68-79, the redemption that is about to take place is seen to have its roots in the covenant with Abraham rather than in the Sinaitic covenant. The emphasis is on the divine promise: "the oath which he swore to our father Abraham" (v. 73). It is true that the nature of the promised redemption is set forth in terminology that is reminiscent also of God's covenant relationship with Israel as His people. The significant starting point, nevertheless, is the promise to Abraham. The fulfillment also is in harmony with the promise of blessing. The blessings of redemption are "spelled out" in such a way as to make explicit what was implicit in the blessing of Abraham: a service of God in holiness and righteousness; a knowledge of salvation through the forgiveness of sins; and gracious guidance by God "into the way of peace." Some of these blessings were realized in part within the covenant history of Israel. The full realization was now at hand. It is in this triumphant faith that Zechariah exclaims,

> "Blessed be the Lord God of Israel,
> for he has visited and redeemed his people,
> and has raised up a horn of salvation for us
> in the house of his servant David,
> as he spoke by the mouth of his holy prophets from of old,
> that we should be saved from our enemies,
> and from the hand of all who hate us;
> to perform the mercy promised to our fathers,
> and to remember his holy covenant,
> the oath which he swore to our father Abraham, to grant us
> that we, being delivered from the hand of our enemies,
> might serve him without fear,
> in holiness and righteousness before him all the days of
>   our life."

There is another reference to the oath of God, in confirmation of "a promise to Abraham," in Heb. 6:13ff. The promise quoted is that of a blessing upon Abraham, rather than through him to others: "Surely I will bless you and multiply you" (v. 14). Nevertheless the blessing through Abraham is not excluded; for the purpose of the writer is not to define the content of the blessing so much as to make clear the significance of the oath as "final for confirmation." In the Abraham story in Genesis we find this oath of God in chapter 22:15-18, of which the quotation in Heb. 6 is a part. On the principle that the part may stand for the whole we are quite justified in understanding the promise in Heb. 6 as the whole promise to Abraham in Gen. 22. The word covenant is not used in Heb. 6; but in the context it is obvious that both "promise" and "oath" imply the "covenant," and are indeed synonyms for covenant. It is the covenant of promise with Abraham in its inclusive sense that is confirmed by God with an oath. And what was the purpose of the oath in relation to the promise, in the Genesis story, and according to the writer of the New Testament epistle? "So when God desired to show more convincingly to the heirs of the promise the unchangeable character of his purpose, he interposed with an oath, so that through two unchangeable things, in which it is impossible that God should prove false, we who have fled for refuge might have strong encouragement to seize the hope set before us" (Heb. 6:17-18). There is no fictitious falsity about the promise to Abraham! Its truth was confirmed by the oath of God and attested by the saving acts of God which culminated in Jesus Christ.

We have noted earlier the reference to the covenant with Abraham in Peter's temple sermon in Acts 3. This would seem to represent the faith of the early Christians that Jesus as the Messiah is the mediator of the blessing of Abraham, to the Jew first, but also (impliedly) to the Gentile. As a preacher Peter finds in the words of promise to Abraham the very heart or kernel of God's covenant purpose with His people, "And in your posterity shall all the families of the earth be blessed"; and he sees in Jesus as the servant of God the fulfillment of the divine purpose of blessing, in a truly spiritual ministry issuing in repentance and faith. "God, having raised up his servant, sent him to you first, to bless you in turning every one of you from your wickedness" (v. 26).

In Eph. 2:11-12 we have a rather unusual reference to "covenants" instead of "covenant," as if there were a plurality of covenants. Speaking to the Gentile Christians Paul says, "Remember that you were at that time separated from Christ, alienated from the commonwealth of Israel, and strangers to the covenants of promise, having no hope and without God in the world." He uses the plural also in Rom. 9:4-5: "They are Israelites, and to them belong the sonship, the glory, the covenants, the giving of the law, the worship, and the promises; to them belong the patriarchs, and of their race, according to the flesh, is the Christ." This reflects, of course, the Old Testament manner of speaking, where there seems to be a number of covenants: with Noah, with Abraham, with Israel at Sinai, with Israel in the plains of Moab, with David, with the Levitical priests, as well as the new covenant foretold by the prophets. It does not rule out, however, the right to speak of all of them together as essentially one covenant. The important thing is to note the emphasis in Eph. 2:12 on the "promise," which according to Gal. 3:17 was the fundamental element in the covenant with Abraham; for by his choice of words Paul implies in Eph. 2:12 that the "promise" was also the fundamental element in all the so-called "covenants." Just as the thought of the Apostle moves freely back and forth between "covenant" (Gal. 3:17) and "covenants" (Rom. 9:4; Eph. 2:12), so also it shifts easily from "the promise" (Gal.

3:17; Eph. 2:12) to "the promises" (Gal. 3:16; Rom. 9:4). By repetition and reaffirmation, by the clarifying process of prophetic interpretation and application to new situations, the *one* promise, within which is the seed of the gospel, becomes *many* promises; even as *the one man* Abraham, to whom this promise was first given, becomes *a great nation*, numberless as the stars of heaven and the sand of the seashore. The analogy can be carried a step further, moving in the other direction; for just as the vocation of Abraham *and his seed* to be a blessing is concentrated finally in *the one offspring*, which is Jesus Christ (Gal. 3:16), so the promise to Abraham, which unfolds in many promises to Israel as the people of God, is concentrated finally in the gospel of God's redeeming love in Jesus Christ our Lord.

3

The New Covenant

There are three significant groups of passages in the New Testament, however, that do more than imply a "new" covenant: they speak of it directly. It is with these that we are chiefly concerned right now. What was "the new covenant" according to Jesus, and Paul, and the unknown writer of the Epistle to the Hebrews? We change the tense and ask, What *is* "the new covenant" as seen from the viewpoint of the New Testament understanding of it?

1. In the first group of passages are the words of Jesus in connection with the institution of the Lord's Supper. All three of the Synoptics as well as Paul in 1 Cor. 11 record the event (Mt. 26:26-29; Mk. 14:22-25; Lk. 22:14ff; 1 Cor. 11:23-26). They differ slightly in their record of the actual words of Jesus. For example, Matthew and Mark agree in saying, "This is my blood of the covenant, which is poured out for many"; with Matthew adding, "for the forgiveness of sins." As pointed out in marginal notes in both ASV and RSV, some ancient authorities insert the word "new" before "covenant." In the case of Luke the uncertainty as to the original text seems to be greater, for RSV puts all of v. 20 and part of v. 19 in a footnote instead of in the body of the text. The translation of v. 20 includes the word "new" before "covenant": "This cup which is poured out for you is the new covenant in my blood." Only in 1 Cor. 11, where Paul records what he claims to have received from the Lord and to have taught the Cor-

inthians when he was among them, is the text undisputed: "This cup is the new covenant in my blood" (v. 25).

Despite the textual problem, we are not on shaky ground when we speak of "the new covenant in Jesus' blood." The whole situation implies it, whether Jesus actually used the word "new" or not. The words of Paul make quite clear what he believed that Jesus said, and what Jesus meant by linking so significantly together *the covenant* and *his blood.* There is a new covenant, a covenant of blood; the covenant of which we as Christians love to sing:

> "God is faithful; God will never
> Break his covenant of blood,
> Signed when our Redeemer died,
> Sealed when he was glorified."[1]

But what was then the "old" covenant, according to Jesus, and what happened to it at this time? Was it abrogated or annulled, "set aside because of its weakness and uselessness," as we read in Heb. 7:18 about the "former commandment"? Or is the intended contrast in saying "a new covenant" not with the law at all, but with the covenant of promise; a covenant which was not annulled, says Paul, "so as to make the promise void" (Gal. 3:17)? Even if we think of "the old covenant" as "a covenant of law," we must bear in mind that Jesus said that He had not come to abolish but to fulfill "the law and the prophets" (Mt. 5:17). What is the exact relationship between these two covenants that we call the "old" and the "new"; and what happened to the "old"?

Jesus does not say in the passages that we are considering just what the relationship is; but two possible lines of interpretation are open and must be considered.

In Heb. 9, which also speaks of "a new covenant" ratified with blood, the reference to "the blood of the covenant" with which "the first covenant" was ratified reflects the solemn ratification ceremony in Ex. 24:1-8. The sentence in Heb. 9:20 is a free quotation from Ex. 24:8, "This is the blood of the covenant which God commanded you." In this chapter, then, the "first" covenant (v. 18), which is another way of saying the "old" covenant, is seemingly equivalent to the covenant at Sinai, the covenant with Israel "upon all these conditions" which were set forth in the book of the covenant (see Ex. 24:18, ASV mg). The language of Jesus when He speaks of a new covenant may imply that He was thinking along the same lines. If this be the antithesis intended, the covenant in Jesus' blood was "new" in that it fulfilled the divine purpose with the law; so that from one point of view the believer is set free from the law and its condemnation on anyone who does not perfectly keep it, and from another point of view the law is written by the empowering Spirit of God in his heart and in his life, as something that he loves to do because it is the will of God, and God's will is good, and guides him in a good and a right way.

On the other hand, the occasion for Jesus' words was the feast of the Passover, with its paschal lamb which celebrated the redemption of God's people under the old covenant from their bondage in Egypt, and which prefigured Christ as "our paschal lamb" (1 Cor. 5:7) and as the "lamb without blemish or spot" (1 Peter 1:19), by which *we* were ransomed from our inherited "futile ways" or "vain manner of life." This suggests that the antithesis in Jesus' thinking may have been between the blood of the passover lamb, which effected a typical or symbolical redemption, and His own blood, which has secured for us "an eternal redemption" (Heb. 9:12). If this be the antithesis intended, the covenant in Jesus' blood was "new" in the sense that it *realized* completely what the "old" *anticipated* dimly; it fulfilled what the old prefigured; it was the goal toward which the old looked forward in faith. The newness would then consist, not in the rejection of the old but, as it were, in its transfiguration; so that all that is valid and true in the faith and hope and spiritual experience under the old covenant is caught up into the new, and there transformed into something so gloriously great as to seem "altogether other" when compared with the old. That is what happened to the promise of blessing to Abraham. That is what happened with the servant status of Israel, and with the "your God" and "my people" relationship in the Old Testament. That is what happened with such religiously relevant elements in Israel's faith and life as atonement, redemption, and salvation. That is what happened with her religiously significant institutions of priest and sacrifice, of prophet and divine word, of king and saving acts of the Lord. That is what happened with the Messianic hope, so naturally expressed in terms of the covenant expectations of Israel as a people, and so wonderfully fulfilled in a universal hope. That is what happened with the prediction of a return from the Babylonian Captivity as ushering in what the New Testament calls the great Restoration (Acts 3:21, in Moffatt's translation).[2] That is what happened with the "old" covenant, first made with Abraham, and reaffirmed with his descendants, the people of Israel.

The "new" covenant did not contradict the "old." It did not alter the "gospel" contained in the blessing of Abraham, nor did it change the basic provisions of the Sinai covenant as they are stated in Ex. 19: 3-6. It did not introduce a "different" way of salvation; for in both the old and the new the emphasis is on God's grace, which is experienced by faith and expressed in an obedient walk with God. And yet, in another sense there is a difference; and Jn. 1:14 puts, as it were, the finger upon that difference when it says, "The Word became flesh and dwelt among us, *full of* grace and truth." The antithesis is not between a covenant of law and a covenant of gospel, as if there were no gospel in the "old" and no law in the "new"; the antithesis is between "the fullness" and that which is only "in part." In Christ we see *the fullness* of all that which the saving acts of God prefigured from the beginning. In the new covenant in His blood we see the consummation of the central truth of all the prophetic promises of God spoken under the old covenant. For from the point of view of the Biblical self-interpretation it is true as the old saying goes:

> The New is in the Old contained.
> The Old is by the New explained.

2. In the second group of passages are the statements of Paul in 2 Cor. 3:4-18 and in Gal. 4:21-31.

Paul says in the former passage that "our sufficiency is from God, who has qualified us to be ministers of a new covenant, not in a written code but in the Spirit; for the written code kills, but the Spirit gives life" (vv. 5-6). It is not until v. 14 that he makes direct mention of "the old covenant"; but it is obvious that this "old covenant" is identical with "the dispensation of death carved in letters on stone" (v. 7) and with "the dispensation of condemnation" (v. 9). Quite evidently Paul is here equating "the old covenant" with *the law,* which in Gal. 3:17 he differentiates from the covenant of *promise* that came earlier. The law was added, he says in Gal. 3:19, "because of transgressions"; it did not annul the promises made earlier to Abraham, which he refers to as "a covenant previously ratified by God." The shifting viewpoint may confuse us at first; but it is characteristic of Paul, and it corresponds to the Old Testament witness. There is *one covenant only* in the Old Testament, of which the several "covenants" are so many different facets: and by letting a part stand for the whole, it is possible to stress it either as a covenant of law or as a covenant of promise; it functions in both ways: but the promise came first, and it was not made void by the addition of the law. Each reference to the "old" covenant must be understood in the light of the total context, which in this case means the context of the over-all Pauline teaching. There was a definite insufficiency about the old covenant; yet, as Paul says in this very chapter, it had a splendor and a glory of its own. He speaks in relative terms in v. 10: "Indeed, in this case, what once had splendor has come to have no splendor at all, because of the splendor that surpasses it." The glory that surpasses would seem to be fully as much the glory of the consummation as that of mere contrast. Moses and Jesus may have different functions, but they are not at loggerheads with each other. The sufficiency of the new covenant is not due to a change of direction, but to an increase of power. "The Spirit of the living God" is now able to take of the things of Jesus and declare them to us as accomplished fact—and that makes the difference. The gracious purpose of God to call into covenant relationship with himself a people that shall be "his very own" remains the same.

The allegory of the two covenants in Gal. 4:21-31 is keynoted by the question, "Tell me, you who desire to be under law, do you not hear the law?" The man who is led by the Spirit is "not under the law," says the apostle in Gal. 5:18; but he also points out that there is *no law against* "the fruit of the Spirit" (Gal. 5:22-23): and in that list of spiritual fruit there is more than one of which we see beautiful evidence under the old covenant. And why not, if God is One, and His will for sinful humanity is eternally the same: that they might be saved? The difference between the old and the new lies not in the purpose but in the persuasion: in Christ is the persuasion of divine love at its greatest "breadth and length and height and depth" (Eph. 3:18). "For the love of Christ controls us [ASV, constrains us], because we are convinced that one has died for all; therefore all have died. And he died for all, that those who live might live no longer for themselves but for him who for their sake died and was raised" (2 Cor. 5:14-15). This is "love divine, all love excelling."[3] "For God so loved the world that he gave his only Son, that whoever believes in him should not perish but have eternal life" (Jn. 3:16). Here is the supreme saving act of divine love; but He who so loved the world is the same as He who proclaimed His name to Moses, "The Lord, the

Lord, a God merciful and gracious, and abounding in steadfast love and faithfulness, keeping steadfast love for thousands, forgiving iniquity and transgression and sin" (Ex. 34:6-7). God did not first begin to love, or to act in grace and mercy, in Bethlehem or on Calvary! That marked the climax of His love, the fulfillment of the old covenant in the new! And of this Paul, as well as Jesus, was well aware.

3. The third major group of references to "covenant" in the New Testament is in the Epistle to the Hebrews. We have considered some of these already in other connections. It was a study of this epistle under the late Geerhardus Vos at Princeton Seminary many years ago that first awakened the present author's interest in the Biblical concept of a divine covenant with man.[4] We could spend many hours in a similar study here, for it actually involves the teaching of the whole epistle; but for our present purpose it may not be necessary to make such an extensive, and at the same time intensive, study. For if we looked up every reference to the word *diatheke* or covenant in the epistle, and if we examined in detail the teaching of the epistle concerning the *first* covenant and the *second,* and concerning Christ as the mediator of a new and better covenant, the conclusion would be substantially the same as the one that we have reached on the basis of Jesus and of Paul. The first, or the old, covenant, which by contrast with the new and better covenant may be regarded as in one sense inferior, is the covenant at Sinai as seen from the facet of the law *which was added.* The former commandment is set aside because of its "weakness and uselessness'" (chapter, 7:18); for in itself the law lacked the power to make perfect those who draw near (10:1). The epistle quotes approvingly the words of the prophet Jeremiah concerning a new covenant with the house of Israel, with its emphasis on the *inwardness* of the covenant, but with its basic terms essentially the same as in the covenant with the fathers. Nowhere does the epistle say anything that would rule out the covenant of promise, the blessing of Abraham, as the fundamental aspect of the covenant also with Israel. Nowhere does it deny that the old covenant, even as the new, called for the response of faith and for the true obedience of the heart. The difference between the old and the new is not one of *aim* but of *achievement.* It is the difference, in one sense, between *shadow* and *reality* (10:1), beween anticipation and fulfillment; and yet, if pressed, the writer of the epistle would have been quick to acknowledge that there was a real experience of spiritual blessing even under the old

covenant: for how otherwise account for the glorious examples of faith in chapter 11? These men and these women, those mentioned by name and many more of whom he does not have time to tell, were indeed "well attested by their faith" (11:39); they lived and died in faith, the faith which according to the writer is "the assurance of things hoped for, the conviction of things not seen" (11:1). If from one point of view it must be admitted that they "did not receive what was promised" (11:13, 39), but the thing promised hovered before them as a future hope, the same must be said of us who are under the new covenant; for Paul says, "We know that the whole creation has been groaning in travail together until now; and not only the creation, but we ourselves, who have the first fruits of the Spirit, groan inwardly as we wait for adoption as sons, the redemption of our bodies. For in this hope we were saved. Now hope that is seen is not hope. For who hopes for what he sees? But if we hope for what we do not see, we wait for it with patience" (Rom. 8:22-25). There was for them who lived under the old covenant, and there is now for us who live under the new covenant, a large segment of hope as yet unfulfilled; but we even as they have faith in the promises of God, whether they have been fulfilled or still await fulfillment. For one thing we need not wait: in Christ and through the preaching of the gospel *the blessing of Abraham has been fulfilled*. This is the heart of the matter. This fulfillment of the central idea of the covenant gives us confidence to say with Paul, "For all the promises of God find their Yes in him. That is why we utter the Amen through him, to the glory of God" (2 Cor. 1:20).

We return to the question as to the real difference between the "old" covenant and the "new." If under the old covenant there were men of faith, even heroes of faith and examples for us—if it can honestly be said of them, or even of a few among them, that by faith "they obeyed" and by faith "they received divine approval" (Heb. 11:2)— if the story of Abraham can rightly be used to illustrate the truth that faith is reckoned as righteousness, and a psalm of David to illustrate the blessing of forgiveness, and the life of Moses to illustrate what it means to be a faithful servant "in all God's house," and the history of Israel to illustrate what God had in mind in choosing a people to be "his very own": if the New Testament is correct in its interpretation that these things were actually so, *what was lacking?* What was the need of a new covenant? What does the new covenant have that the old did not?

The answer rushes to meet us in vivid staccato fashion from the pages of the New Testament! The full consummation of the promised blessing which they experienced only in part! *The fullness* of grace and truth! *The supreme sacrifice for sin* in the obedience of Christ unto death "to put away sin" (Heb. 9:26). An eternal redemption! The opening of a new and living way to fellowship with God! The outpouring of the floodtide of God's love for sinners in the giving of himself in the gift of His Son! The love of God in Christ Jesus, "who loved me and gave himself for me" (Gal. 2:20)! The saving act of God that transcends all others! The gospel that openly embraces all! The living Christ himself as the very incarnation of the blessing which was the promise and is the gift of God to mankind!

A *new* covenant in Jesus' blood? Yes indeed! New with the newness of final fruition of the old—the last word in God's covenant with men—the complete realization of the blessing of Abraham in that God has now blessed us in Christ "with every spiritual blessing in the heavenly places" (Eph. 1:3).

NOTES

[1] James Montgomery, "Come to Calvary's Holy Mountain." Service Book and Hymnal of the Lutheran Church in America. 1958.

[2] James Moffatt, *op. cit.*

[3] Charles Wesley, "Love Divine, All Loves Excelling." Service Book and Hymnal of the Lutheran Church in America. 1958.

[4] Geerhardus Vos, *The Teaching of the Epistle to the Hebrews.* Grand Rapids: Wm. B. Eerdmans Publishing Co. 1956.

CONCLUSION

IN THE WRITING OF ANY BOOK there is revealed something of the personal faith of the man who writes it. It matters not if the writer tries to hide his "subjective" faith behind a facade of "objective" or "factual" judgment: the faith, the personal convictions, of the man who writes will nevertheless shine through; and that is as it should be, for a "value judgment" devoid of personal conviction is valueless.

In the present instance the author has made no serious attempt to conceal his personal involvement in the story that he has tried to tell. He happens to believe that the Biblical faith as we have outlined it in terms of the covenant is fundamentally true. It is only fitting, therefore, that ere we write Finis to this little volume on "The Covenant of Blessing with Abraham" we face squarely the question of *Christian faith in relation to the Biblical witness* as to "the saving acts of the Lord."

That the Old Testament does bear witness to such saving acts in relation to Israel as the people of His covenant is undeniable. "You have seen what I did to the Egyptians, and how I bore you on eagles' wings and brought you to myself" (Ex. 19:4).

"For I brought you up from the land of Egypt,
 and redeemed you from the house of bondage;
and I sent before you Moses,
 Aaron, and Miriam.
O my people, remember what Balak king of Moab devised,
 and what Balaam the son of Beor answered him,
and what happened from Shittim to Gilgal,
 that you may know the saving acts of the Lord" (Mic. 6:4-5).

"For you are a people holy to the Lord your God; the Lord your God has chosen you to be a people for his own possession, out of all the peoples that are on the face of the earth. It was not because you were more in number than any other people that the Lord set his love upon you and chose you, for you were the fewest of all peoples; but it is because the Lord loves you, and is keeping the oath which he swore to your fathers, that the Lord has brought you out with a mighty hand,

and redeemed you from the house of bondage, from the hand of Pharaoh king of Egypt" (Deut. 7:6-8).

> In all their affliction he was afflicted,
>   and the angel of his presence saved them;
> in his love and in his pity he redeemed them;
>   he lifted them up and carried them all the days of old.

> Like cattle that go down into the valley,
>   the Spirit of the Lord gave them rest.
> So thou didst lead thy people,
>   to make for thyself a glorious name (Is. 63:9, 14).

> O give thanks to the Lord, call on his name,
>   make known his deeds among the peoples!

> Remember the wonderful works that he has done,
>   his miracles, and the judgments he uttered,
> O offspring of Abraham his servant,
>   sons of Jacob, his chosen ones! (Ps. 105:1, 5, 6)

Again and again, in history, in prophecy, and in psalmody, in direct reference and indirect, we hear as in a jubilant refrain of the Exodus redemption, and of the making of the covenant, and of the giving of the Torah, and of the gracious leading through the wilderness, and of the conquest and possession of the Promised Land—and then, after Israel has been dispossessed of her land and sent into exile, we hear "a new song" of a new redemptive act of God, effecting a return and a restoration. It is not too much to say with Wright that the whole faith of Israel seems to center around five "events" from their history, interpreted as "saving acts of God": the call of Abraham, the Exodus redemption, the Sinai covenant, the conquest of Canaan, and the Davidic kingship.[1] Were they correct in their interpretation? Did God really have anything to do with these events? Did these events have anything to do with a divine plan or purpose of redemption which leads ultimately to the eternal redemption secured by Jesus Christ? How is the Biblical witness related to the Christian faith that God is a God who acts?

Let us think specifically of the call of Abraham. That the Bible witnesses to God's call of a man named Abraham to be a blessing, and a medium of blessing, to all the nations of the earth cannot be denied. According to the record, an act of God is involved in the story of

224

Abraham: God called him, and Abraham responded to His call, and his life was made to serve a specific purpose within God's redemptive plan for mankind. *God acted* in relation to Abraham: such was Israel's faith; such is the Biblical witness. What says Christian faith? Does it assert a theological principle only, that God is a God who acts; or does it dare to confess that God acted, with purpose and design, in the concrete situation of the call of Abraham?

Let us carry the question a step further. That the Old Testament witnesses to a fulfillment of the covenant with Abraham in the history and mission of Israel as the Old Testament people of God is also undeniable. We have called it the first of two major stages in the fulfillment of the covenant of blessing; we shall consider the second after we have considered the first. According to the record a series of acts of God are involved in the history of Israel: by His blessing they became "a great nation," whom He redeemed "with a mighty hand" from the slavery of Egypt, and with whom He made a covenant that they should be "a people for his own possession," and to whom He gave a law designed to guide them in "the good and the right way," and whom He brought victoriously into the land that had been promised to their fathers, and among whom He raised up good leaders, Moses and Aaron and Miriam in the days of the exodus, kings and priests and prophets, men like Samuel and David and Isaiah; and whom He disciplined in the Babylonian Exile, in order that through them as His servant His covenant purpose of blessing might be fully accomplished. *God acted* in relation to Israel: such is the Biblical witness; such was Israel's faith. What says Christian faith? Does it pay homage to the theological proposition that God acts, while refusing to acknowledge that God has acted in the election of Israel to be His people, with a mission related to His own covenant will and purpose?

Let us take still a third step in our questioning. That the New Testament witnesses to a fulfillment of the covenant with Abraham *in Christ* and in the Christian church is undeniable. We have called this the second of two major stages in the fulfillment of the covenant of blessing, which is also a fulfillment of the covenant religion of Israel. According to the record, there is an act of God with many facets involved in this supreme event of all history: God loved the world, and sent His Son, and spoke to men by Him, and raised Him from the dead, and through Him redeemed a fallen world. *God acted* in relation to humanity in its need of redemption: such is the Biblical witness;

such was the faith of the early Christian church. And what says Christian faith today? Can it be satisfied to reduce the gospel to a theological formula about a God who acts, while it hedges at the confident confession *that God did act,* and that on this "saving act" of God rests man's hope of salvation?

Our question is not concerned with peripheral details of the Biblical story, which might vary in the telling without discrediting the central events which constitute the core of the tradition; nor is it concerned with mere verification of the factual character of the central events, though we believe that they can be given a rather convincing verification *as events.* Our question is concerned with *the interpretation that faith has given* of these key events of which we have been speaking: the call of Abraham, the redemption of Israel out of bondage in Egypt, the making of a covenant with Israel at Sinai which involved a "your God"—"my people" relationship, the giving of the Torah, the conquest of Canaan and the possession of it as an inheritance from the Lord, the covenant with the house of David, in the Old Testament; the birth of Jesus, His death and burial, and His resurrection, in the New Testament. Is it wholly immaterial whether we believe in a God who acts, but whose acts must remain forever undefined in the concrete terms of an actual divine-human relationship; or whether we believe in a God *who has acted* according to a redemptive plan in which one "saving act" confirms another that preceded it by fulfilling it?

We would plead for the Christian faith today something of the concreteness that characterizes the Biblical faith throughout, whether in the Old Testament or the New. "The saving acts of the Lord" represent an objective reality: events that really took place, and in which God really acted with redemptive purpose and power. To be sure, it requires theological reflection, or prophetic insight, to see in the event the hand of the Lord; but the theological reflection, or the prophetic insight, corresponds to the reality of the situation. God did act! The Bible is not a theological theorizing about, but a prophetic testimony to, "saving acts of God" which actually occurred. Not as something that can be historically proved, but as a confession of faith that can be shared, we venture the assertion that the saving acts of God from Abraham to Christ represent *an objective reality;* and that God has acted *not just once* in the sending of His Son to be the Savior of the world, but in that redemptive plan which included an Abraham, and a

Moses, and an Isaiah, and a David, and the people of Israel, and countless other "forerunners" of the Christ, through whom God began to reveal His saving acts in relation to mankind; for without these acts of God the world would have been totally unprepared for "the redemption which is in Christ Jesus our Lord." They are part and parcel of one saving purpose and plan. They witness to a living God, who acted in the creation of man, and who continues to act for man's redemption. "When the time had fully come, God sent forth his Son, born of woman, born under the law, to redeem those who were under the law, so that we might receive adoption as sons" (Gal. 4:4-5). "For it is the God who said, 'Let light shine out of darkness,' who has shone in our hearts to give the light of the knowledge of the glory of God in the face of Christ" (2 Cor. 4:6).

A former president of Luther Seminary was wont to speak often of the human need to see "the face," the face of Jesus Christ, in order to know God as He really is.[2] May we not say that in like manner we need to see "the plan," God's redemptive plan of blessing, that unfolds step by step from Abraham to Jesus, in order to understand why the Scriptures of the Old and the New Testaments are truly "Holy Scripture." They do bear witness to a God who acts, by interpreting for us where and when and how and why God has acted. To these saving acts of God *faith says Amen.* "For all the promises of God find their Yes in him. That is why we utter the Amen through him, to the glory of God."

NOTES

[1] From *The Book of the Acts of God* by G. Ernest Wright and Reginald H. Fuller. Copyright 1957 by G. Ernest Wright. Reprinted by permission of Doubleday & Company, Inc., pp. 19-21.
[2] With grateful acknowledgment to my friend and former colleague, Dr. T. F. Gullixson.

BIBLIOGRAPHICAL INDEX

Albright, W. F., *The Archaeology of Palestine and the Bible*, 1922. 26*
   The Bible after Twenty Years of Archaeology, reprint from "Religion in Life," 1952. 26, 28
Alleman, Herbert C., and Flack, Elmer E., *O. T. Commentary*, 1948. 46, 51, 57, 60, 62, 86, 185, 186
Asch, Sholem, *The Prophet*, 1955. 37, 56
Augustana Explanation to *Luther's Catechism*, 1939. 175
Baab, Otto, *The Theology of the Old Testament*, 1949. 16, 18, 154
Beecher, Willis J., *The Prophets and the Promise*. 1905. 20, 52, 118, 209
Begrich J., art. "Berit," *Zeitschrift für die Alttestamentliche Wissenschaft*, 1944. 2, 3, 85
Bibeln, eller den Heliga Skrift, 1917. 53
Book of Concord, The, ed. by Henry Eyster Jacobs, 1916. 89
Boyer, Merle William, *Everyman's Adventure*, 1947. 19
Bright, John, *A History of Israel*, 1959. 28, 147
Browning, Robert, "Rabbi Ben Ezra." 137
Burrows, Millar, *An Outline of Biblical Theology*, 1946. 19, 136, 148
Böhl, Ed., *Christologie des Alten Testaments*, 1882. 52, 59, 61, 62, 167, 177
Böhl, Franz, *Das Zeitalter Abrahams*, 1930. 25, 38, 45, 58, 99, 112, 131
Cawley, F., *Jeremiah, New Bible Commentary*, 1953. 185
Coppens, J., *The Old Testament and the Critics*, 1942. 34
Davidson, A. B., *The Theology of the Old Testament*, 1904. 94, 161, 163, 187, 197
Davis, John D., *A Dictionary of the Bible*, 4th ed., 1925. 7, 11, 25, 160
Deissmann, Adolf, *Light from the Ancient East*, Eng. tr. 4th ed., 1927.
Delitzsch, Franz, *A New Commentary on Genesis*, 1889. 84, 86
   Commentary on the Psalms, Eng. tr. 1871. 108
   Messianic Prophecies, 1890, Eng. tr. 1891. 19, 60, 70
Dodd, C. H., *The Bible To-day*, 1952. 20, 28, 99
Douay Version of the Holy Vible, The, 83
Driver, S. R., *Hebrew Tenses*, 1892. 51
   The Book of Genesis, 1905. 57, 124, 180
Dummelow, J. R., *A Commentary on the Holy Bible*, reprint 1944. 13
Eissfeldt, Otto, *Die Genesis der Genesis*, 1958. 49, 50, 58
Edersheim, Alfred, *Bible History*. 157, 161
Galling, Kurt, *Die Erwählungstraditionen Israels*, 1928. 24, 29, 152
Gerleman, Gillis, *Gamla Testamentet i Förkunnelsen*, 1956. 31, 35, 50, 157, 177
Gesenius, William, *Hebrew Lexicon*, tr. by Edward Robinson, ed. by Francis Brown, S. R. Driver, and Charles A. Briggs, 1907. 7, 94, 140
Girdlestone, R. F., *Synonyms of the Old Testament*, reprint 1948. 8, 180

---

* Numbers indicate pages where work is quoted in the book.

God's Covenant of Blessing

Procksch, Otto, "Genesis," *Sellin's Kommentar zum A. T.,* 1913. 54, 55, 57, 79

Richardson, Alan, *Genesis I-XI,* 1953. 20

Riehm, Ed., *Messianic Prophecy,* tr. 2nd ed. 1891. 174

Ryle, Herbert E., *The Book of Genesis,* Cambridge Bible for Schools and Colleges, 1921. 11, 57, 60

Sellin, Ernst, *Die Bedeutung des A. T. als Heilige Schrift fur die Christliche Kirche,* 1936. 177

Smith, G. A., *Commentary on Isaiah,* 1902-1903. 197

Smith, J. M. P., and Goodspeed, Edgar, *The Bible, An American Translation,* 1939. 141, 155

Smith, Wilbur, in *Christianity Today,* Dec. 24, 1956. 47

Snaith, Norman H., *The Distinctive Ideas of the Old Testament,* 1946. 17, 151, 152

Stade, Bernard, *Biblische Theologie des Alten Testaments,* 1905. 23

Stirling, John, *The Bible for Today,* 1941. 50, 56, 58

Thring, Godfrey, *O God of Mercy, God of Might.* 127, 192

Trumbull, H. Clay, *The Blood Covenant,* 1893. 4

United Testimony on Faith and Life, 1952. The American Lutheran Church. 99

Vischer, Wilhelm, *The Witness of the Old Testament to Christ,* 1949. 33, 103

Vos, Geerhardus, *Lecture Notes on the Epistle to the Hebrews,* 1926-27. 7, 11
  Art. "Covenant," *Dictionary of Christ and the Gospels.* 15
  Biblical Theology, 1948. 53
  The Teaching of the Epistle to the Hebrews, 1956. 220

Webster's *New Intenrational Dictionary,* 2nd ed., 1948. 2, 11

Weiser, A., art. "Abraham," *Die Religion in Geschichte und Gegenwart,* 3rd ed., 1957. 26, 49, 56

Wellhausen, J., *Prolegomena to the History of Israel,* Eng. tr. 1885. 24, 25

Wesley, Charles, *Love Divine, All Loves Excelling.* 219

Westminster *Dictionary of the Bible,* 1944. 16, 57, 94, 124, 126, 171, 180

Westminster *Historical Atlas to the Bible,* rev. ed., 1956, ed. by G. E. Wright and Floyd Filson. 15, 26, 46, 147

Westminster *Study Edition of the Bible,* 1948. 190

Weymouth, Francis, *The New Testament in Modern Speech,* 4th ed., 1924. 103

Whitehouse, W. A., art. "Law," *A Theological Word Book of the Bible,* ed. by Richardson, 1950. 160, 187

Wilson, Robert Dick, *Lecture Notes,* 1927. 141

Wiren, Edv., *När Han Öppnade Boken,* 1946. 41

Woolley, Leonard, *Abraham,* 1935. 28, 34, 39, 40

Wright, G. Ernest, *Biblical Archaeology,* 1957. 27

Wright, G. Ernest, and Fuller, Reginald H., *The Book of the Acts of God,* 1957. 224

TOPICAL INDEX

Ahab, ahaba, election love, 151-152

Amen, 18, 183, 227

Archaeology, 25-28, 29-30, 34

Atonement, 116-117, 157, 197, 217

Anthropomorphic language, 122, 125

Awen, vanity, futility, 182

Awon, iniquity, 182

Bachar, choose, 151, 153

Barak, bless, 51, 53-55

Basar, evangellizo, preach good tidings, 176

Basic provisions, Mosaic covenant, 137-143

Berakah, blessing, 51

Berith, covenant, XI, 1-8, 10-11, 179, 210, 211

Berith olam, everlasting covenant, 90, 113-114

Blessing of Abraham, the, 54, 74, 78, 85, 199, 207, 212, 220-222

Blessing, promise of, XII, 17, 41, 44, 49-63, 73-76, 77-80, 88, 92-93, 96-97, 106-108, 133-134

Blood-covenanting, 4

Burnt offering, 92, 94, 96

Chate'ah, chataath, sin XII, 182

Chanun, gracious, 180

Chen, grace, favor, 180

Children of Abraham, 22-23

Child sacrifice, 96

Circumcision, 86, 89-91, 110-112, 206, 211-212

Classical Wellhausenism, 24

Command, 38-41, 76

Contract, 2, 11, 154

Covenant, Abrahamic, 6, 11, 19, 20, 80-98, 133, 214

Covenant, Davidic, 132-133

Covenant, Mosaic, Sinaitic, 2-3, 6, 17, 133, 136, 148-183, 185, 186, 214, 220

Covenant, Noachian, 5-6, 133, 214

Covenant of blessing, 76, 100, 104-105, 125-126, 130, 133, 136, 138, 139, 146, 185-186, 189, 207-208, 210, 212-215, 223

Covenant of revelation and redemption, 16

Covenant-keeping God, 14

Diatheke, testament, covenant, XI, 1, 8-10, 210, 211, 220

Disobedience, 8

Divine goal to history, 150, 159

Divine initiative, the, 11, 186

Ecumenicity of covenant, 112-113

Eingeweihte, 45

Election, 15, 17, 43, 70, 81, 141, 149-154, 158, 166-167, 182

Election love, 151-152, 178, 189

Emeth, truth, XII, 18, 138, 180, 181

Emunah, faithfulness, 180

Essential historicity, 23, 28, 31, 34, 50, 98-100

Essential objectivity, 25, 29-30, 50

Eved, servant, of the Lord, 182

Every spiritual blessing, 123, 174, 222

Exodus-redemption, 120-129, 138, 161, 178, 192, 226

Faith, 8, 29-34, 39-41, 79, 81-84, 87, 88, 90, 92-94, 100, 108-109, 125, 131-132, 163, 167, 221

Faithfulness, of God, 17-19, 85, 126, 127, 130, 138, 175, 182

Faithfulness, unfaithfulness, of Israel, 18-19, 182, 190

Fellowship, religious, 15, 57-58, 88, 106, 108, 130, 132, 138, 152, 154-160, 171, 192-194, 198

Forgiveness of sin, 196-199, 212, 221

Gadol, great, 180

Geulim, redeemed, 181

232

NOTES

NOTES

NOTES

NOTES

NOTES

NOTES

NOTES

NOTES

NOTES